A

POPULAR ACCOUNT

OF

DISCOVERIES AT NINEVEH.

BY AUSTEN HENRY LAYARD, ESQ. D.C.L.

ABRIDGED BY HIM FROM HIS LARGER WORK.

WITH NUMEROUS WOODCUTS.

NEW YORK:
HARPER & BROTHERS, PUBLISHERS,
No. 82 CLIFF ST.

1852.

PREFACE TO THE ABRIDGMENT.

THE interest felt in the discoveries on the site of Nineveh having been so general, it was suggested to me that an abridgment of my work on "Nineveh and its Remains," published in a cheap and popular form, would be acceptable to the public. I had already commenced such an abridgment, when I was called away on a second expedition into Assyria, which left me no leisure for literary occupations.

On my return to England, I found that several inaccurate and incomplete accounts of my first researches had already been published. I determined, therefore, to complete without delay the abridged work which is now presented to the public.

In this abridgment I have omitted the second part of the original work, introducing the principal Biblical and historical illustrations into the narrative, which has thus, I hope, been rendered more useful and complete.

As recent discoveries, and the contents of the inscriptions, as far as they have been satisfactorily deciphered, have confirmed nearly all the opinions expressed in the original work, no changes on any material points have been introduced into this abridgment. I am still inclined to believe that all the ruins explored represent the site of ancient Nineveh, and while still assigning the later monuments to the kings mentioned in Scripture, Shalmanezer, Sennacherib, and Essarhadon, I am convinced that a considerable period elapsed between their foundation and the erection of the older palaces of Nimroud. The results of the attempts to decipher the inscriptions are still too uncertain to authorize the use of any actual names for the earlier kings mentioned in them.

September, 1851.

INTRODUCTION.

BEFORE submitting the following narrative of my labors in Assyria to the reader, it may not be uninteresting to give a slight sketch of what had been done in the field of Assyrian antiquities, previous to the recent discoveries on the site of Nineveh.

A few fragments scattered among ancient authors, and a list of kings of more than doubtful authenticity, is all that remains of a history of Assyria by Ctesias; while of that attributed to Herodotus not a trace has been preserved. Of later writers who have touched upon Assyrian history, Diodorus Siculus, a mere compiler, is the principal. In Eusebius, and the Armenian historians, such as Moses of Chorene, may be found a few valuable details and hints, derived, in some instances, from original sources not altogether devoid of authenticity.

It is remarkable that in profane history we meet with only three Assyrian monarchs of whose deeds we have any account,—Ninus, Semiramis, and Sardanapalus. Ninus and his queen, like all the heroes of primitive nations, appear to have become mythic characters, to whom all great deeds and national achievements were assigned. Although originally historic personages, they were subsequently invested to some extent with divine attributes, and were interwoven with the theology of the race of which they were the first, or among the earliest, chiefs. Above thirty generations elapsed between Semiramis and Sardanapalus, during which more than one dynasty of kings occupied the Assyrian throne, and maintained the power of the empire. Yet of these kings nothing has been preserved but doubtful names.

The Assyrians are not particularly alluded to in Holy Writ, until the period when their warlike expeditions to the west of the Euphrates brought them into contact with the Jews. Pul, the first king whose name is recorded in Scripture, having reigned between eight and nine hundred years before the Christian era, and about two hundred previous to the fall of the empire, must have been nearly the last of a long succession of kings who had ruled over the greater part of Asia. The later monarchs are more frequently mentioned in the Bible on account of their wars with the Jews, whom they led captive into Assyria. Very little is related of even their deeds unless they particularly concern the Jewish people.

Of modern historians who have attempted to reconcile the discrepancies of Assyrian chronology, and to restore to some extent, from the fragments to which I have alluded, a history of the Assyrian empire, I scarcely know whom to point out. From such contradictory materials, it is not surprising that each writer should have formed a system of his own; and we may, without incurring the charge of skepticism, treat all their efforts as little better than ingenious speculations. In the date alone to be assigned to the commencement of the Assyrian empire, they differ nearly a thousand years; and even when they treat of events which approach the epoch of authentic history,—such as the death of Sardanapalus, the invasion of the Medes, and the fall of the empire,—there is nearly the same comparative discrepancy. The Bactrian and Indian expeditions of Ninus, the wonderful works of Semiramis, and the effeminacy of Sardanapalus, have been described over and over again, and form the standard ingredients of the Assyrian history of modern authors. The narratives framed upon them convey useful lessons, and are, moreover, full of romantic events to excite the imagination. As such they have been repeated, with a warning that their authenticity rests upon a slender basis, and that it is doubtful whether they are to be regarded as history, or to be classed among fables. Although the names of Nineveh and Assyria have been familiar to us from childhood, and are connected with the earliest impressions we derive from the Inspired Writings, it is only when we ask ourselves what we really know concerning them, that we discover our ignorance of all that relates to their history, and even to their geographical position.

It is indeed one of the most remarkable facts in history, that the records of an empire, so renowned for its power and civilization, should have been entirely lost; and that the site of a city as eminent for its extent as its splendor, should for ages have been a matter of doubt: it is not perhaps less curious that an accidental discovery should suddenly lead us to hope that these records may be recovered, and this site satisfactorily identified.

The ruins in Assyria and Babylonia, chiefly huge mounds, apparently of mere earth and rubbish, had long excited curiosity from their size and evident antiquity. They were the only remains of an unknown period,—of a period antecedent to the Macedonian conquest. Consequently they alone could be identified with Nineveh and

Babylon, and could afford a clew to the site and nature of those cities. There is, at the same time, a vague mystery attaching to remains like these, which induces travelers to examine them with more than ordinary interest, and even with some degree of awe. A great vitrified mass of brick-work, surrounded by the accumulated rubbish of ages, was believed to represent the identical tower, which called down the divine vengeance, and was overthrown, according to an universal tradition, by the fires of heaven. The mystery and dread, which attached to the place, were kept up by exaggerated accounts of wild beasts, who haunted the subterraneous passages, and of the no less savage tribes who wandered among the ruins. Other mounds in the vicinity were identified with the hanging gardens, and those marvelous structures which tradition has attributed to two queens, Semiramis and Nitocris. The difficulty of reaching these remains, increased the curiosity and interest with which they were regarded; and a fragment from Babylon was esteemed a precious relic, not altogether devoid of a sacred character. The ruins which might be presumed to occupy the site of the Assyrian capital, were even less known, and less visited, than those in Babylonia. Several travelers had noticed the great mounds of earth opposite the modern city of Mosul, and when the inhabitants of the neighborhood pointed out the tomb of Jonah upon the summit of one of them, it was natural to conclude, at once, that it marked the site of Nineveh.*

---

* It need scarcely be observed, that the tomb of Jonah could not stand on the ruins of a palace, and that the tradition placing it there is not authenticated by any passage in the Scriptures. It is, however, received by Christians and Mussulmans, and probably originated in the spot having been once occupied by a Christian church or convent, dedicated to the pro-

The first to engage in a serious examination of the ruins within the limits of ancient Assyria was Mr. Rich, many years the political resident of the East India Company at Baghdad,—a man whom enterprise, industry, extensive and varied learning, and rare influence over the inhabitants of the country, acquired as much by character as position, eminently qualified for such a task. The remains near Hillah, being in the immediate vicinity of Baghdad, first attracted his attention; and he commenced his labors by carefully examining their position, and by opening trenches into the various mounds. It is unnecessary to enter into a detailed account of his discoveries. They were of considerable interest, consisting chiefly of fragments of inscriptions, bricks, engraved stones, and a coffin of wood; but the careful account which he drew up of the site of the ruins was of greater value, and has formed the ground-work of all subsequent inquiries into the topography of Babylon.

In the year 1820, Mr. Rich, having been induced to visit Kurdistan for the benefit of his health, returned to Baghdad by way of Mosul. Remaining some days in this city, his curiosity was naturally excited by the great mounds on the opposite bank of the river, and he entered upon an examination of them. He learned from the inhabitants of Mosul that, some time previous to his visit, a sculpture, representing various forms of men and animals, had been dug up in a mound forming part of the great inclosure. This strange object had been the cause of general wonder, and the whole population had issued

phet. The building, which is supposed to cover the tomb, is very much venerated, and few Christians have been allowed to enter it. The Jews, in the time of St. Jerome, pointed out the sepulcher of Jonah at Gath-hepher, in the tribe of Zabulon.

1*

from the walls to gaze upon it. The ulema having at
length pronounced that these figures were the idols of the
infidels, the Mohammedans, like obedient disciples, so
completely destroyed them, that Mr. Rich was unable to
obtain even a fragment.

His first step was to visit the village containing the
tomb of Jonah. In the houses he met with a few stones
bearing inscriptions, which had probably been discovered
in digging the foundations; and under the mosque containing the tomb, he was shown three very narrow and
apparently ancient passages, one within the other, with
several doors or apertures.

He next examined the largest mound of 'the group,
called Kouyunjik by the Turks, and Armousheeah by
the Arabs; the circumference of which he ascertained to
be 7690 feet. Among the rubbish he found a few fragments of pottery, bricks with cuneiform characters, and
some remains of building in the ravines. On a subsequent occasion he made a general survey of the ruins,
which is published in the collection of his journals, edited
by his widow.

With the exception of a small stone chair, and a few
remains of inscriptions, Mr. Rich obtained no other Assyrian relics from the site of Nineveh; and he left Mosul,
little suspecting that in the mounds were buried the
palaces of the Assyrian kings. As he floated down the
Tigris to Baghdad, he visited Nimroud, and was struck
by its evident antiquity. The tales of the inhabitants of
the neighboring villages connected the ruins with Nimrod's own city, and better authenticated traditions with
those of Al Athur, or Ashur, from which the whole
country anciently received its name. He collected a few

bricks bearing cuneiform characters, and proceeded with his journey.

The fragments obtained by Mr. Rich were subsequently placed in the British Museum, and formed the principal, and indeed almost only, collection of Assyrian antiquities in Europe. A case scarcely three feet square inclosed all that remained, not only of the great city, Nineveh, but of Babylon itself!

Other museums in Europe contained a few cylinders and gems, which came from Assyria and Babylonia; but they were not classified, nor could it be determined to what exact epoch they belonged. Of Assyrian art nothing was known. The architecture of Nineveh and Babylon was a matter of speculation, and the poet or painter restored their palaces and temples, as best suited his theme or his subject. A description of the temple of Belus by Herodotus, led to an imaginary representation of the tower of Babel. Its spiral ascent, its galleries gradually decreasing in circumference, and supported by innumerable columns, are familiar to us from the illustrations, adorning almost the opening page of that Book, which is associated with our earliest recollections.

Such was our acquaintance four years ago with Nineveh —its history, its site, and its arts. The reader will judge from the following pages, how far recent discoveries are likely to extend our knowledge.

As inscriptions in the *cuneiform* character will be so frequently mentioned in the following pages, a few words on the nature of this very ancient mode of writing may not be unacceptable to the reader. The epithets of cuneiform, cuneatic, arrow-headed, and wedge-shaped—*tête-à-clou* in French, and *keilförmig* in German—have been assigned to it according as the fancy of the describer saw in its component parts a resemblance to a wedge, the barb of an arrow, or a nail. The term "cuneiform" is now most generally used in England, and probably best expresses the peculiar form of the character, each letter being composed of several distinct wedges combined together. The following may be given as an example:—

This inscription contains the names of an Assyrian king, and his title of king of Assyria. It is not improbable that these letters were originally formed by mere lines, for which the wedge was afterward substituted as an embellishment; and that the character itself may once have resembled the picture writing of Egypt, though all traces of its ideographic properties have been lost. The Assyrians, like the Egyptians, possessed at a later period a cursive writing, resembling the rounded character of the Phœnicians, Palmyrenes, Babylonians, and Jews, which was probably used for written documents, while the cuneiform was reserved for monumental purposes. There is this great difference between the two forms of writing, which appears to point to a distinct origin,—the cuneiform runs always from left to right, the cursive from right to left.

The cuneiform under various modifications, the letters being differently formed in different countries, prevailed over the greater part of western Asia to the time of the overthrow of the Persian empire by Alexander the Great. It is to this circumstance that we mainly owe the progress which has been made in deciphering the Assyrian inscriptions, and the hope that we shall ultimately be able to ascertain, with some degree of certainty, their contents. The Persian kings ruled over all the nations using this peculiar form of writing. These nations consisted of three principal races, the Babylonian (including the Assyrian) speaking a language allied to the Hebrew and Arabic, the Persian, and the Tatar, the last two using dialects nearly approaching those still found among their descendants. When recording their victories, as was their custom, on rocks and pillars, these monarchs used the three languages spoken by their subjects. Such was the origin of what are called the trilingual inscriptions of Persia, which afford the principal clew to the Assyrian writing. The tablets containing these inscriptions are divided into three columns, each column being occupied by a version of the same inscription in one of the three national languages, and each language being written in the modification of the cuneiform character peculiar to it. Fortunately, the contents of the Persian incriptions have long been accurately ascertained, and the alphabet and grammar reduced to a system. Owing, however, to the very large number of distinct characters in the Assyrian inscriptions, there being nearly 400 different signs, while in the Persian there are but thirty-nine or forty, and the great apparent laxity in the use of letters and the grammar, the process of deciphering is one of considerable difficulty, notwithstanding the aid which a version of the same inscription in a known tongue naturally supplies.

The most important trilingual inscriptions hitherto discovered are those on the palaces of Darius and Xerxes at Persepolis, over the tomb of Darius, and in the rock tab-

lets of Behistun. The latter are by far the most extensive and valuable. They contain a history of the principal events of the reign of Darius, and giving a long list
of countries and tribes subdued by that monarch, and
the names of conquered kings and rebels, afford the best
materials for deciphering the Assyrian character, proper
names being the real clew to the value of letters. The
inscriptions of Behistun are upon the face of a lofty pre-
cipice, so difficult of access that Colonel Rawlinson has
alone succeeded in copying them. He has printed the
Persian column with a translation, but the corresponding
Babylonian or Assyrian column is still in his possession,
and the scientific world is anxiously awaiting the pub-
lication of an inscription which can afford the only trust-
worthy materials for deciphering the Assyrian records.

In the meanwhile, Colonel Rawlinson has communicated
to the public, through the journals of the Royal Asiatic
Society, some of the results of his own inquiries, which
are of great interest and importance; and other scholars,
among whom may be mentioned Dr. Hincks, have made
such progress in deciphering the Assyrian character as
the means at their disposal would permit. It is to Dr.
Hincks we owe the determination of the numerals, the
name of Sennacherib on the monuments of Kouyunjik
and of Nebuchadnezzar on the bricks of Babylon—three
very important and valuable discoveries. The actual
state of our knowledge of the cuneiform character will
enable us to ascertain the general contents of an inscription, although probably no one can yet give a literal
translation of any one record, or the definite sound of
many words.

The custom of engraving inscriptions on stone, as well

as on baked clay, the two methods of perpetuating their annals adopted by the Assyrians, is of the very highest antiquity. The divine commands were first given to man on stone tables; Job is made to exclaim, "Oh that my words were now written! . . . *that they were graven with an iron pen and lead in the rock forever;"* * and Ezekiel, when prophesying on the river Chebar, was directed "to take a tile and portray upon it the city of Jerusalem." † There could have been no more durable method of preserving the national records; and the inscribed walls of palaces and rock tablets have handed down to us the only authentic history of ancient Assyria.

* Ch. xix. 23, 24.   † Ch. iv. 1.

CONTENTS.

CHAPTER I.

CHAPTER II.

CHAPTER III.

CHAPTER IV.

CHAPTER V.

CHAPTER VI.

CHAPTER VII.

CHAPTER VIII.

CHAPTER IX.

CHAPTER X.

CHAPTER XI.

CHAPTER XII.

CHAPTER XIII.

LIST OF WOODCUTS AND PLANS.

————— ◆•◆ —————

NINEVEH

AND ITS REMAINS.

CHAPTER I.

DURING the autumn of 1839 and winter of 1840, I had been wandering through Asia Minor and Syria, scarcely leaving untrod one spot hallowed by tradition, or unvisited one ruin consecrated by history. I was accompanied by one no less curious and enthusiastic than myself.* We were both equally careless of comfort and unmindful of danger. We rode alone; our arms were our only protection; a valise behind our saddles was our wardrobe, and we tended our own horses, except when relieved from the duty by the hospitable inhabitants of a Turcoman village or an Arab tent. Thus unembarrassed by needless luxuries, and uninfluenced by the opinions and prejudices of others, we mixed among the people, acquired without effort their manners, and enjoyed without alloy those emotions which

---

* My traveling companion, during a long journey from England to Hamadan, was Edward Ledwich Mitford, Esq., now of her Majesty's civil service in the island of Ceylon.

A

scenes so novel, and spots so rich in varied association, can not fail to produce.

I look back with feelings of grateful delight to those happy days when, free and unheeded, we left at dawn the humble cottage or cheerful tent, and lingering as we listed, unconscious of distance and of the hour, found ourselves, as the sun went down, under some hoary ruin tenanted by the wandering Arab, or in some crumbling village still bearing a well-known name. No experienced dragoman measured our distances, and appointed our stations. We were honored with no conversations by pashaws, nor did we seek any civilities from governors. We neither drew tears nor curses from villagers by seizing their horses, or searching their houses for provisions: their welcome was sincere; their scanty fare was placed before us; we ate, and came, and went in peace.

I had traversed Asia Minor and Syria, visiting the ancient seats of civilization, and the spots which religion has made holy. I now felt an irresistible desire to penetrate to the regions beyond the Euphrates, to which history and tradition point as the birth-place of the wisdom of the West. Most travelers, after a journey through the usually frequented parts of the East, have the same longing to cross the great river, and to explore those lands which are separated on the map from the confines of Syria by a vast blank stretching from Aleppo to the banks of the Tigris. A deep mystery hangs over Assyria, Babylonia, and Chaldea. With these names are linked great nations and great cities dimly shadowed forth in history; mighty ruins, in the midst of deserts, defying, by their very desolation and lack of definite form, the description of the traveler; the remnants of mighty races still roving over the land; the fulfilling and fulfillment of prophecies; the plains to which the Jew and the Gentile alike look as the cradle of their race. After a journey in Syria, the thoughts naturally turn eastward; and without treading on the remains of Nineveh and Babylon our pilgrimage is incomplete.

I left Aleppo, with my companion, on the 18th of March.

We still traveled as we had been accustomed—without guide or servants. The road across the desert is at all times impracticable, except to a numerous and well-armed caravan, and offers no object of interest. We preferred that through Bir and Orfa. From the latter city we traversed the low country at the foot of the Kurdish hills, a country little known, and abounding in curious remains. The Egyptian frontier, at that time, extended to the east of Orfa, and the war between the sultan and Mohammed Ali Pasha being still unfinished, the tribes took advantage of the confusion, and were plundering on all sides. With our usual good fortune, we succeeded in reaching Nisibin unmolested, although we ran daily risks, and more than once found ourselves in the midst of foraging parties, and of tents, which, an hour before, had been pillaged by the wandering bands of Arabs. We entered Mosul on the 10th of April.

During a short stay in this town, we visited the great ruins on the east bank of the river, which have been generally believed to be the remains of Nineveh.* We rode also into the desert, and explored the mound of Kalah Sherghat, a vast ruin on the Tigris, about fifty miles below its junction with the Zab. As we journeyed thither, we rested for the night at the small Arab village of Hammum Ali, around which are still the vestiges of an ancient city. From the summit of an artificial eminence we looked down upon a broad plain, separated from us by the river. A line of lofty mounds bounded it to the east, and one of a pyramidical form rose high above the rest. Beyond it could be faintly traced the waters of the Zab. Its position rendered its identification easy. This was the pyramid which Xenophon had described, and near which the ten thousand had encamped: the ruins around it were those which the Greek general saw twenty-two centuries before, and which were even then the remains of an *ancient* city. Although Xenophon had confounded a name, spoken by a strange race, with one

* These ruins include the mounds of Kouyunjik and Nebbi Yunus.

familiar to a Greek ear, and had called the place Larissa, tradition still points to the origin of the city, and, by attributing its
foundation to Nimrod, whose name the ruins now bear, connect
it with one of the first settlements of the human race.*

Kalah Sherghat, like Nimroud, was an Assyrian ruin: a
vast, shapeless mass, now covered with grass, and showing
scaroely any traces of the work of man except where the winter
rains had formed ravines down its almost perpendicular sides,
and had thus laid open its contents. A few fragments of pottery and inscribed bricks, discovered after a careful search
among the rubbish which had accumulated around the base of
the great mound, served to prove that it owed its construction
to the people who had founded the city of which Nimroud is the
remains. There was a tradition current among the Arabs, that
strange figures, carved in black stone, still existed among the
ruins; but we searched for them in vain, during the greater
part of a day in which we were engaged in exploring the heaps
of earth and bricks, covering a considerable extent of country
on the right bank of the Tigris. At the time of our visit, the
country had been abandoned by the Bedouins, and was only
occasionally visited by a few plunderers from the Shammar or
Aneyza tents. We passed the night in the jungle which clothes
the banks of the river, and wandered during the day undisturbed
by the tribes of the desert. A cawass, who had been sent with
us by the Pashaw of Mosul, alarmed at the solitude, and dread-
ing the hostile Arabs, left us in the wilderness, and turned homeward. But he fell into the danger he sought to avoid. Less
fortunate than ourselves, at a short distance from Kalah Sherghat, he was met by a party of horsemen, and fell a victim to
his timidity.

Were the traveler to cross the Euphrates to seek for such
ruins in Mesopotamia and Chaldea as he had left behind him
in Asia Minor or Syria, his search would be vain. The

---

* "He (Nimrod) went out into Assyria and builded Nineveh, the city
Rehoboth and Calah, and Resen, between Nineveh and Calah; the same
is a great city." (Gen. x. 11, 12.)

graceful column rising above the thick foliage of the myrtle, ilex, and oleander; the gradines of the amphitheater covering a gentle slope, and overlooking the dark blue waters of a lake-like bay; the richly-carved cornice or capital half hidden by luxuriant herbage,—are replaced by the stern, shapeless mound rising like a hill from the scorched plain, the fragments of pottery, and the stupendous mass of brick-work occasionally laid bare by the winter rains. He has left the land where nature is still lovely, where, in his mind's eye, he can rebuild the temple or the theater, half doubting whether they would have made a more grateful impression upon the senses than the ruin before him. He is now at a loss to give any form to the rude heaps upon which he is gazing. Those of whose works they are the remains, unlike the Roman and the Greek, have left no visible traces of their civilization, or of their arts: their influence has long since passed away. The more he conjectures, the more vague the results appear. The scene around is worthy of the ruin he is contemplating; desolation meets desolation: a feeling of awe succeeds to wonder; for there is nothing to relieve the mind, to lead to hope, or to tell of what has gone by. These huge mounds of Assyria made a deeper impression upon me, gave rise to more serious thoughts, and more earnest reflection, than the temples of Balbec, and the theaters of Ionia.

In the middle of April I left Mosul for Baghdad. As I descended the Tigris on a raft, I again saw the ruins of Nimroud, and had a better opportunity of examining them. It was evening as we approached the spot. The spring rains had clothed the mound with the richest verdure, and the fertile meadows, which stretched around it, were covered with flowers of every hue. Amid this luxuriant vegetation were partly concealed a few fragments of bricks, pottery, and alabaster, upon which might be traced the well-defined wedges of the cuneiform character. Did not these remains mark the nature of the ruin, it might have been confounded with a natural eminence. A long line of consecutive narrow mounds, still

retaining the appearance of walls or ramparts, stretched from
its base, and formed a vast quadrangle. The river flowed at
some distance from them: its waters, swollen by the melting
of the snows on the Armenian hills, were broken into a thousand foaming whirlpools by an artificial barrier, built across
the stream. On the eastern bank, the soil had been washed
away by the current; but a solid mass of masonry still with-
stood its impetuosity. The Arab, who guided my small raft,
gave himself up to religious ejaculations as we approached this
formidable cataract, over which we were carried with some
violence. Once safely through the danger, he explained to me
that this unusual change in the quiet face of the river was
caused by a great dam which had been built by Nimrod,* and
that in the autumn, before the winter rains, the huge stones of
which it was constructed, squared, and united by cramps of
iron, were frequently visible above the surface of the stream.†
It was, in fact, one of those monuments of a great people, to be
found in all the rivers of Mesopotamia, which were undertaken
to insure a constant supply of water to the innumerable canals,
spreading like net-work over the surrounding country, and
which, even in the days of Alexander, were looked upon as the
works of an ancient nation.‡ No wonder that the traditions
of the present inhabitants of the land should assign them to
one of the founders of the human race! The Arab explained
the connection between the dam and the city, built by Athur,

* This dam is called by the Arabs, either Sukr el Nimroud, from the
tradition, or El Awayee, from the noise caused by the breaking of the water over the stones. Large rafts are obliged to unload before crossing it,
and accidents frequently happen to those who neglect this precaution.

† Diodorus Siculus, it will be remembered, states that the stones of the
bridge built by Semiramis across the Euphrates were united by similar
iron cramps, while the interstices were filled up with molten lead.

‡ These dams greatly impeded the fleets of the conqueror in their navigation of the rivers of Susiana and Mesopotamia, and he caused many of
them to be removed. (Strabo, p. 1051. ed. Ox. 1807.) By Strabo they were
believed to have been constructed to prevent the ascent of the rivers by
hostile fleets; but their use is evident. Tavernier mentions, in his Travels
(vol. i. p. 226), this very dam. He says that his raft went over a cascade
twenty-six feet high; but he must have greatly exaggerated.

the lieutenant of Nimrod, the vast ruins of which were then before us, and its purpose as a causeway for the mighty hunter to cross to the opposite palace, now represented by the mound of Hammum Ali.   He was telling me of the histories and fate of the kings of a primitive race, still the favorite theme of the inhabitants of the plains of Shinar, when the last glow of twilight faded away, and I fell asleep as we glided onward to Baghdad.

My curiosity had been greatly excited, and from that time I formed the design of thoroughly examining, whenever it might be in my power, these singular remains.

It was not until the summer of 1842 that I again passed through Mosul on my way to Constantinople. I was then anxious to reach the Turkish capital, and had no time to explore ruins. I had not, however, forgotten Nimroud. I had frequently spoken to others on the subject of excavations in this and another mound, to which a peculiar interest also attached; and at one time had reason to hope that some persons in England might have been induced to aid in the undertaking. I had even proposed an examination of the ruins to M. Coste, an architect who had been sent by the French government, with its embassy to Persia, to draw and describe the monuments of that country.

I found that M. Botta had, since my first visit, been named French consul at Mosul; and had already commenced excavations on the opposite side of the river in the large mound of Kouyunjik. These excavations were on a very small scale, and, at the time of my passage, only fragments of brick and alabaster, upon which were engraved a few letters in the cuneiform character, had been discovered.

While detained by unexpected circumstances at Constantinople, I entered into correspondence with a gentleman in England on the subject of excavations; but with this exception, no one seemed inclined to assist or take any interest in such an undertaking. I also wrote to M. Botta, encouraging him to proceed, notwithstanding the apparent paucity of results, and particularly calling his attention to the mound of Nimroud, which, however, he declined to explore on account of its distance from Mosul and its inconvenient position. I was soon called away from the Turkish capital to the provinces ; and for some months numerous occupations prevented me turning my attention to the ruins and antiquities of Assyria.

In the meanwhile M. Botta, not discouraged by the want of success which had attended his first essay, continued his excavations in the mound of Kouyunjik ; and to him is due the honor of having found the first Assyrian monument. This remarkable discovery owed its origin to the following circumstances. The small party employed by M. Botta were at work on Kouyunjik, when a peasant from a distant village chanced to visit the spot. Seeing that every fragment of brick and alabaster uncovered by the workmen was carefully preserved, he asked the reason of this, to him, strange proceeding. On being informed that they were in search of sculptured stones, he advised them to try the mound on which his village was built, and in which, he declared, many such things as they wanted had been exposed on digging the foundations of new houses. M. Botta, having been frequently deceived by similar stories, was not at first inclined to follow the peasant's advice, but subsequently sent an agent and one or two workmen to the place. After a little opposition from the inhabitants, they were permitted to sink a well in the mound ; and at a small distance from the surface they came to the top of a wall which, on digging deeper, they found to be lined with sculptured slabs of gypsum. M. Botta, on receiving information of this discovery, went at once to the village, which was called Khorsabad. Directing a wider trench to be formed, and to be carried in the direction of the wall, he soon found that he had entered a chamber, connected with others, and surrounded by slabs of gypsum covered with sculptured representations of battles, sieges, and similar events. His wonder may easily be imagined. A new history had been suddenly opened to him— the records of an unknown people were before him. He was equally at a loss to account for the age and the nature of the monument. The style of art of the sculptures, the dresses of the figures, the mythic forms on the walls, were all new to him, and afforded no clew to the epoch of the erection of the edifice, or to the people who were its founders. Numerous inscriptions, accompanying the bas-reliefs, evidently contained the explanation of the events thus recorded in sculpture, and being in the cuneiform, or arrow-headed, character, proved that the building belonged to an age preceding the conquests of Alexander; for it is generally admitted that after the subjugation of the west of Asia by the Macedonians, the cuneiform writing ceased to be employed. It was evident that the monument appertained to a very ancient and very civilized people; and it was natural from its position to refer it to the inhabitants of Nineveh, a city, which, although it could not have occupied a site so distant from the Tigris, must have been in the vicinity of these ruins. M. Botta had discovered an Assyrian edifice, the first, probably, which had been exposed to the view of man since the fall of the Assyrian empire.

M. Botta was not long in perceiving that the building which had been thus partly excavated, unfortunately owed its destruction to fire; and that the gypsum slabs, reduced to lime, were rapidly falling to pieces on exposure to the air. No precaution could arrest this rapid decay; and it was to be feared that this wonderful monument had only been uncovered to complete its ruin. The records of victories and triumphs, which had long attested the power and swelled the pride of the Assyrian kings, and had resisted the ravages of ages, were now passing away forever. They could scarcely be held together until an inexperienced pencil could secure an imperfect evidence of their former existence. Almost all that was first discovered thus speedily disappeared; and the same fate has befallen nearly every thing subsequently found at Khorsabad. A regret is almost felt that so precious a memorial of a great nation should have been exposed to destruction; but as far as the object of the monument is concerned, the intention of its founders will

A*

be amply fulfilled, and the records of their might will be more widely spread, and more effectually preserved, by modern art, than the most exalted ambition could have contemplated.

This remarkable discovery having been communicated by M. Botta, through M. Mohl, to the French Academy of Fine Arts, that body lost no time in applying to the Minister of Public Instruction for means to carry on the researches. The recommendation was attended to with that readiness and munificence which almost invariably distinguish the French government in undertakings of this nature. Ample funds for excavations were at once assigned to M. Botta, and an artist of acknowledged skill was placed under his orders to draw such objects as could not be removed. The work was carried on with activity and success, and by the beginning of 1845, the monument had been completely uncovered. M. Botta did not extend his researches beyond Khorsabad; but, having secured many fine specimens of Assyrian sculpture for his country, he returned to Europe with a rich collection of inscriptions, the most important result of his discovery.

The success of M. Botta had increased my anxiety to explore the ruins of Assyria. It was evident that Khorsabad could not stand alone. It did not represent ancient Nineveh, nor did it afford us any additional evidence as to the site of that city. If the edifice discovered had been one of its palaces, surely other buildings of a vaster and more magnificent character must exist nearer the seat of government, on the banks of the river Tigris. It was true that M. Botta had labored unsuccessfully for above three months in the great mound opposite Mosul, which was usually identified with the Assyrian capital; but that mound much exceeded in extent any other known ruin; and it was possible that in the part hitherto explored the traces of the buildings which it once contained were as completely lost as they were in many parts of the mound of Khorsabad. My thoughts still went back to Nimroud, and to the traditions which attached to it. I spoke to others, but received little encouragement. At last, in the autumn of 1845, Sir Stratford

Canning offered to incur, for a limited period, the expense of excavations in Assyria, in the hope that, should success attend the attempt, means would be found to carry it out on an adequate scale.

It was now in my power to prosecute a work which I had so long desired to undertake ; and the reader will not, I trust, be disinclined to join with me in feelings of gratitude toward one who, while he has maintained so successfully the honor and interests of England by his high character and eminent abilities, has acquired for his country so many great monuments of ancient civilization and art.* It is to Sir Stratford Canning we are mainly indebted for the collection of Assyrian antiquities with which the British Museum has been enriched ; without his liberality and public spirit the treasures of Nimroud would have been reserved for the enterprise of those who have appreciated the value and importance of the discoveries at Khorsabad.

It was deemed prudent that I should leave Constantinople without acquainting any one with the object of my journey. I was furnished with the usual documents given to travelers when recommended by the Embassy, and with letters of introduction to the authorities at Mosul and in the neighborhood. My preparations were soon completed, and I started from Constantinople by steamer to Samsoun in the middle of October. Anxious to reach the end of my journey, I crossed the mountains of Pontus and the great steppes of the Usun Yilak as fast as post-horses could carry me, descended the high lands into the valley of the Tigris, galloped over the vast plains of Assyria, and reached Mosul in twelve days.

---

* I need scarcely remind the reader that it is to Sir S. Canning we owe the marbles of Halicarnassus now in the British Museum. The difficulties which stood in the way of the acquisition of these valuable relics, and the skill which was required to obtain them, are not generally known. I can testify to the efforts and labor which were necessary for nearly three years before the repugnance of the Ottoman government could be overcome, and permission obtained to extract the sculptures from the walls of a castle, which was more jealously guarded than any similar edifice in the empire. Their removal, notwithstanding the almost insurmountable difficulties raised by the authorities and inhabitants of Budroon, was most successfully effected by Mr. Alison. The Elgin marbles, and all other remains from Turkey or Greece now in Europe, were obtained with comparative ease.

CHAPTER II.

MOHAMMED PASHAW.—HIS CRUELTIES.—THE STATE OF THE COUNTRY.—
START FOR NIMROUD.—AN ARAB FAMILY.—COMMENCE EXCAVATIONS.—
DISCOVERY OF A CHAMBER.—OF INSCRIPTIONS.—OF IVORY ORNAMENTS.
—RETURN TO MOSUL.—CONDUCT OF THE PASHAW.—EXCAVATIONS
COMMENCED AMONG VARIOUS RUINS.—RETURN TO NIMROUD.—FURTHER
DISCOVERIES.—SELAMIYAH.—DISCOVERY OF SCULPTURES.—DESCRIP-
TION OF BAS-RELIEFS.—INTERRUPTED BY THE PASHAW.—FURTHER DIS-
COVERY OF SCULPTURES.—DEPOSITION OF THE PASHAW.—DEPARTURE
FOR BAGHDAD.

MY first step on reaching Mosul was to present my letters to
Mohammed Pashaw, the governor of the province. Being a
native of Candia, he was usually known as Keritli Oglu (the
son of the Cretan), to distinguish him from his celebrated predecessor of the same name. The appearance of his excellency
was not prepossessing, but it matched his temper and conduct.
Nature had placed hypocrisy beyond his reach. He had one
eye and one ear ; he was short and fat, deeply marked by the
small-pox, uncouth in gestures and harsh in voice. His fame
had reached the seat of his government before him. On the
road he had revived many good old customs and impositions,
which the reforming spirit of the age had suffered to fall into
decay. He particularly insisted on *dish-parasi ;** or a compensation in money, levied upon all villages in which a man of
such rank is entertained, for the wear and tear of his teeth in
masticating the food he condescends to receive from the inhabitants. On entering Mosul, he had induced several of the principal aghas, who had fled from the town on his approach, to

* Literally, " tooth-money."

return to their homes; and having made a formal display of
oaths and protestations, cut their throats to show how much
his word could be depended upon. At the time of my arrival,
the population was in a state of terror and despair. Even the
appearance of a casual traveler led to hopes, and reports were
whispered about the town of the disgrace of the tyrant. Of
this the pashaw was aware, and hit upon a plan to test the
feelings of the people toward him. He was suddenly taken ill
one afternoon, and was carried to his harem almost lifeless.
On the following morning the palace was closed, and the attendants answered inquiries by mysterious motions, which
could only be interpreted in one fashion. The doubts of the
Mosuleeans gradually gave way to general rejoicings; but at
mid-day his excellency, who had posted his spies all over the
town, appeared in perfect health in the market-place. A general trembling seized the inhabitants. His vengeance fell principally upon those who possessed property, and had hitherto
escaped his rapacity. They were seized and stripped, on the
plea that they had spread reports detrimental to his authority.

The villages, and the Arab tribes, had not suffered less than
the townspeople. The pashaw was accustomed to give instructions to those who were sent to collect money, in three words—
" Go, destroy, eat ;"* and his agents were not generally backward in entering into the spirit of them. The tribes, who had
been attacked and plundered, were retaliating upon caravans
and travelers, or laying waste the cultivated parts of the pashawlic. The villages were deserted, and the roads were little frequented and very insecure.

Such was the pashaw to whom I was introduced two days
after my arrival by the British vice-consul, Mr. Rassam. He
read the letters which I presented to him, and received me with
that civility which a traveler generally expects from a Turkish
functionary of high rank. His anxiety to know the object of

---

* To eat money, i. e. to get money unlawfully or by pillage, is a common expression in the East.

my journey was evident, but his curiosity was not gratified for the moment.

Many reasons rendered it necessary that my plans should be concealed, until I was ready to put them into execution. Although I had always experienced from M. Botta the most friendly assistance, there were others who did not share his sentiments ; from the authorities and the people of the town I could only expect the most decided opposition. On the 8th of November, having secretly procured a few tools, I engaged a mason at the moment of my departure, and carrying with me a variety of guns, spears, and other formidable weapons, declared that I was going to hunt wild boars in a neighboring village, and floated down the Tigris on a small raft constructed for my journey. I was accompanied by Mr. Ross (a British merchant of Mosul*), my cawass, and a servant.

At this time of the year nearly seven hours are required to descend the Tigris, from Mosul to Nimroud. It was sunset before we reached the awai, or dam across the river. We landed and walked to the village of Naifa. No light appeared as we approached, nor were we even saluted by the dogs, which usually abound in an Arab village. We had entered a heap of ruins. I was about to return to the raft, upon which we had made up our minds to pass the night, when the glare of a fire lighted up the entrance to a miserable hovel. Through a crevice in the wall, I saw an Arab family crouching round a heap of half-extinguished embers. The dress of the man, the ample cloak and white turban, showed that he belonged to one of the tribes which cultivate a little land on the borders of the Desert, and are distinguished, by their more sedentary habits, from the Bedouins. Near him were three women, lean and haggard, their heads almost concealed in black handker-

---

* Mr. Ross will perhaps permit me to acknowledge in a note the valuable assistance I received from him, during my labors in Assyria. His knowledge of the natives, and intimate acquaintance with the resources of the country, enabled him to contribute much to the success of my undertaking; while to his friendship I am indebted for many pleasant hours, which would have been passed wearily in a land of strangers.

chiefs, and the rest of their persons enveloped in the striped
aba. Some children, nearly naked, and one or two mangy
greyhounds, completed the group. As we entered, all the
party rose, and showed some alarm at this sudden appearance
of strangers. The man, however, seeing Europeans, bid us
welcome, and spreading some corn-sacks on the ground, invited us to be seated. The women and children retreated
into a corner of the hut. Our host, whose name was Awad
or Abd-Allah, was a sheikh of the Jehesh. His tribe having
been plundered by the pashaw, and being now scattered in different parts of the country, he had taken refuge in this ruined village. He had learnt a little Turkish, and was intelligent and
active. Seeing, at once, that he would be useful, I acquainted
him with the object of my journey ; offering him the prospect
of regular employment in the event of the experiment proving
successful, and assigning him fixed wages as superintendent
of the workmen. He volunteered to walk, in the middle of the
night, to Selamiyah, a village three miles distant, and to some
Arab tents in the neighborhood, to procure men to assist in the
excavations.

I had slept little during the night. The hovel in which we
had taken shelter, and its inmates, did not invite slumber ; but
such scenes and companions were not new to me : they could
have been forgotten, had my brain been less excited. Hopes,
long cherished, were now to be realized, or were to end in disappointment. Visions of palaces under-ground, of gigantic
monsters, of sculptured figures, and endless inscriptions, floated
before me. After forming plan after plan for removing the
earth, and extricating these treasures, I fancied myself wandering in a maze of chambers from which I could find no outlet.
Then, again, all was reburied, and I was standing on the grass-
covered mound. Exhausted, I was at length sinking into sleep,
when hearing the voice of Awad, I rose from my carpet, and
joined him outside the hovel. The day already dawned ; he
had returned with six Arabs, who agreed for a small sum to
work under my direction.

· The lofty cone and broad mound of Nimroud broke like a distant mountain on the morning sky.   But how changed was the
scene since my former visit !   The ruins were no longer clothed
with verdure and many-colored flowers ; no signs of habitation,
not even the black tent of the Arab, were seen upon the plain.
The eye wandered over a parched and barren waste, across
which occasionally swept the whirlwind, dragging with it a
cloud of sand.   About a mile from us was the small village of
Nimroud, like Naifa, a heap of ruins.

Twenty minutes' walk brought us to the principal mound.
The absence of all vegetation enabled me to examine the
remains with which it was covered.   Broken pottery and
fragments of bricks, both inscribed with the cuneiform character, were strewed on all sides.   The Arabs watched my
motions as I wandered to and fro, and observed with surprise
the objects I had collected.   They joined, however, in the
search, and brought me handfuls of rubbish, among which I
found with joy the fragment of a bas-relief.   The material on
which it was carved had been exposed to fire, and resembled,
in every respect, the burnt gypsum of Khorsabad.   Convinced
from this discovery, that sculptured remains must still exist in
some part of the mound, I sought for a place where excavations
might be commenced with a prospect of success.   Awad led
me to a piece of alabaster which appeared above the soil.   We
could not remove it, and on digging downward, it proved to
be the upper part of a large slab.   I ordered all the men to
work around it, and they shortly uncovered a second slab.   Continuing in the same line, we came upon a third ; and, in the
course of the morning, discovered ten more, the whole forming
a square, with a slab missing at one corner.   It was evident
that we had entered a chamber, and that the gap was its entrance.   I now dug down the face of one of the stones, and an
inscription in the cuneiform character was soon exposed to view.
Similar inscriptions occupied the center of all the slabs, which
were in the best preservation ; but plain, with the exception of
the writing.   Leaving half the workmen to remove the rubbish

from the chamber, I led the rest to the S. W. corner of the mound, where I had observed many fragments of calcined alabaster.

A trench, opened in the side of the mound, brought me almost immediately to a wall, bearing inscriptions in the same character as those already described. The slabs, which had been almost reduced to lime by exposure to intense heat, threatened to fall to pieces as soon as uncovered.

Night interrupted our labors. I returned to the village well satisfied with their result. It was now evident that the remains of buildings of considerable extent existed in the mound; and that although some had been injured by fire, others had escaped the conflagration. As inscriptions, and the fragment of a bas-relief had been found, it was natural to conclude that sculptures were still buried under the soil. I determined, therefore, to explore the N. W. corner, and to empty the chamber partly uncovered during the day.

On returning to the village, I removed from the crowded hovel in which we had passed the night. With the assistance of Awad, who was no less pleased than myself with our success, we patched up with mud the least ruined house in the village, and restored its falling roof. We contrived at least to exclude, in some measure, the cold night winds; and to obtain a little privacy for my companion and myself.

Next morning my workmen were increased by five Turcomans from Selamiyah, who had been attracted by the prospect of regular wages. I employed half of them in emptying the chamber, and the rest in following the wall at the S. W. corner of the mound. Before evening, the work of the first party was completed, and I found myself in a room* paneled with slabs about eight feet high, and varying from six to four feet in breadth. Upon one of them, which had fallen backward from its place, was rudely inscribed, in Arabic characters, the name of Ahmed Pashaw, one of the former

---

* Chamber A, plan 3.

hereditary governors of Mosul. A native of Selamiyah remembered that some Christians were employed to dig into the
mound about thirty years before, in search of stone for the
repair of the tomb of Sultan Abd-Allah, a Mussulman saint,
buried on the left bank of the Tigris, a few miles below its
junction with the Zab. They uncovered this slab; but being
unable to move it, they cut upon it the name of their employer,
the pashaw. My informant further stated that, in another part
of the mound, he had forgotten the precise spot, they had found
sculptured figures, which they broke in pieces to carry away
the fragments.

The bottom of the chamber was paved with smaller slabs than
those which lined the walls. They were covered with inscriptions on both sides, and had been placed upon a layer of bitumen, which, having been used in a liquid state, had retained a
perfect impression in relief of the characters carved upon the
stone. The inscriptions on the upright slabs were about twenty
lines in length, and all were precisely similar.

In the rubbish near the bottom of the chamber, I found
several objects in ivory, upon which were traces of gilding;
among them were the figure of a king carrying in one hand
the Egyptian crux ansata, or emblem of life, part of a crouching
sphinx, and an elegant ornamental border of flowers. Awad,
who had his own suspicions of the object of my search, which
he could scarcely persuade himself was limited to mere stones,
carefully collected all the scattered fragments of gold leaf he
could find in the rubbish; and, calling me aside in a mysterious
and confidential fashion, produced them wrapped up in a piece
of dingy paper. "O bey," said he, "Wallah! your books are
right, and the Franks know that which is hid from the true be-
liever. Here is the gold, sure enough, and please God, we shall
find it all in a few days. Only don't say any thing about it to
those Arabs, for they are asses and can not hold their tongues.
The matter will come to the ears of the pashaw." The sheikh
was much surprised, and equally disappointed, when I generously
presented him with the treasures he had collected, and all such

as he might hereafter discover. He left me, muttering "Yia Rubbi!" and other pious ejaculations, and lost in conjectures as to the meaning of these strange proceedings.

At the foot of the slabs in the S. W. corner, we found a great accumulation of charcoal, proving that the building of which they had formed part had been destroyed by fire. I dug also in several directions in this part of the mound, and in many places came upon the calcined remains of walls.

On the third day, I opened a trench in the high conical mound, but found only fragments of inscribed bricks. I also dug at the back of the north side of the chamber first explored, in the expectation of coming upon other walls beyond, but unsuccessfully. As my chief aim was to ascertain the existence, as soon as possible, of sculptures, all my workmen were moved to the S. W. corner, where the many remains of walls already discovered evidently belonging to the same edifice, promised speedier success. I continued the excavations in this part of the mound until the 13th, still finding inscriptions, but no sculptures.

Some days having elapsed since my departure from Mosul, and the experiment having been so far successful, it was time to return to the town and acquaint the pashaw, who had, no doubt, already heard of my proceedings, with the object of my researches. I started, therefore, early in the morning of the 14th, and galloped to Mosul in about three hours.

I found the town in great commotion. In the first place, his excellency had, on the previous day, entrapped his subjects by the reports of his death, in the manner already described, and was now actively engaged in seeking pecuniary compensation for the insult he had received in the rejoicings of the population. In the second, the British vice-consul having purchased an old building to store his stock in trade, the cadi, a fanatic and a man of infamous character, had given out that the Franks had formed a design of buying up the whole of Turkey, and was endeavoring to raise a riot, which was to end in the demolition of the consulate and other acts of violence. I called on the pashaw, and, in the first place, congratulated him on his speedy recovery ; a compliment which he received with a grim smile of satisfaction. He then introduced the subject of the cadi, and the disturbance he had created. "Does that ill-conditioned fellow," exclaimed he, "think that he has Sheriff Pashaw (his excellency's immediate predecessor) to deal with, that he must be planning a riot in the town? When I was at Siwas the ulema tried to excite the people because I encroached upon a burying-ground. But I made them eat dirt ! Wallah! I took every gravestone and built up the castle walls with them." He pretended at first to be ignorant of the excavations at Nimroud ; but subsequently thinking that he would convict me of prevarication in my answers to his questions as to the amount of treasure discovered, pulled out of his writing tray a scrap of paper, as dingy as that produced by Awad, in which was also preserved an almost invisible particle of gold-leaf. This, he said, had been brought to him by the commander of the irregular troops stationed at Selamiyah, who had been watching my proceedings. I suggested that he should name an agent to be present as long as I worked at Nimroud, to take charge of all the precious metals that might be discovered. He promised to write on the subject to the chief of the irregulars ; but offered no objection to the continuation of my researches.

Reports of the wealth extracted from the ruins had already reached Mosul, and had excited the cupidity and jealousy of the cadi and principal inhabitants of the place. It was evident that I should have to contend against a formidable opposition ; but as the pashaw had not, as yet, openly objected to my proceedings, I hired some Nestorian Chaldeans, who had left their mountains for the winter to seek employment in Mosul, and sent them to Nimroud. At the same time I engaged agents to explore several mounds in the neighborhood of the town, hoping to ascertain the existence of sculptured buildings in some parts of the country, before steps were taken to interrupt me.

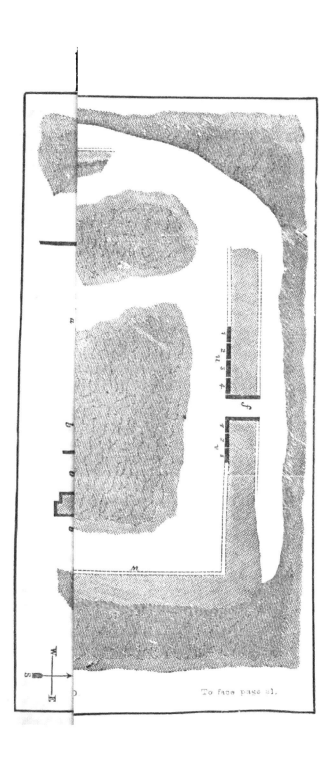

To face page 51.

While at Mosul, Mormous, an Arab of the tribe of Hadde-
deep, informed me that figures had been accidentally uncovered
in a mound near the village of Tel Kef. As he offered to take
me to the place, we rode out together ; but he .only pointed out
the site of an old quarry, with a few rudely hewn stones. Such
disappointments were daily occurring ; and I wearied myself
in scouring· the country to see remains which had been most
minutely described to me as sculptures, or slabs covered with
writing, and, which generally proved to be the ruin of some
modern building, or an early tombstone inscribed with Arabic
characters.

The mounds, which I directed to be opened, were those of
Baasheikha (of considerable size), Baazani, Karamles, Kara-
kush, Yara, and Jerraiyah.   Connected with the latter ruin
many strange tales were current in the country. It was said
that on its lofty conical mound formerly stood a temple of black
stone, held in great reverence by the Yezidis, or worshipers of
the devil ; its walls covered with all manner of sculptured figures,
and with inscriptions in an unknown language.   When the Bey
of Rowandiz fell upon the Yezidis, and massacred those who
were unable to escape, he destroyed this house of idols ; but the
ruins of the building, it was declared, had only been covered by
a small accumulation of rubbish. The lower part of an Assyrian figure, in relief on basalt, dug up, it was said, in the
mound, was actually brought to me ; but I had afterward reason to suspect that it was discovered at Khorsabad.   Excavations were carried on for some time at Jerraiyah, but no remains
of the Yezidi temple were brought to light.

Having finished my arrangements in Mosul, I returned to
Nimroud on the 19th.   During my absence, my cawass had
carried the excavations along the back of a wall, in the S. W.
corner of the mound,* and had discovered an entrance or doorway.† Being anxious to make as much progress as possible,
I increased my workmen to thirty, and distributed them in

---

* Wall *e*, plan 2.   † Entrance *d*, same plan.

three parties. By opening long trenches at right angles in
various directions, we came upon the top of a wall,* built of
slabs with inscriptions similar to those already described. One,
however, was reversed, and was covered with characters, exceeding in size any I had yet seen. On examining the inscription carefully I found that it corresponded with those of
the chamber in the N. W. corner; but as the edges of this, as
well as of all the other slabs hitherto discovered in the S. W.
ruins, had been cut away to make the stones fit into the wall,
several letters had been destroyed. From these facts it was evident that materials taken from another building had been used
in the construction of the one we were now exploring; but as
yet it could not be ascertained whether the face or the back of
the slabs had been uncovered; for the general plan of the edifice could not be determined until the heap of rubbish and earth
under which it was buried had been removed. The excavations were now carried on but slowly. The soil, mixed with
sun-dried and baked bricks, pottery, and fragments of alabaster, offered considerable resistance to the tools of the workmen; and when loosened, could only be removed in baskets to
be thrown over the edge of the mound. The Chaldeans from
the mountains, strong and hardy men, could alone wield the
pick; the Arabs were employed in carrying away the earth.
Spades could not be used, and there were no other means, than
those I had adopted, to clear away the rubbish from the ruins.
A person standing on the mound could see no remains of building until he approached the edge of the trenches, into which the
workmen descended by steps, where parts of the walls were exposed to view.

The Abou-Salman and Tai Arabs continuing their depredations in the plains of Nimroud and surrounding country, I
deemed it prudent to remove from Naifa, where I had hitherto
resided, to Selamiyah. This village is built on a rising ground
near the Tigris, and was formerly a place of some importance,

---

* Wall *m*, same plan.

being mentioned at a very early period as a market-town by the Arab geographers, who generally connect it with the ruins of Athur or Nimroud. It occupies an ancient site, and in long lines of mounds, inclosing the village, can be traced the walls of an Assyrian town, or more probably of one of the suburbs of the capital. Even five years ago Selamiyah was a flourishing place, and could furnish 150 well-armed horsemen. The pashaw had, however, plundered it; and the inhabitants had fled to the mountains or into the neighboring province of Baghdad. Ten miserable huts now stood in the midst of ruins of bazars and streets surrounding a kasr or palace, belonging to the old hereditary pashaws of Mosul, well built of alabaster, but rapidly falling into decay. I had intended to take possession of this building, which was occupied by a few hytas or irregular troops; but the rooms were in such a dilapidated condition that the low mud hut of the kiayah, or chief of the village, appeared to be both safer and warmer. I accordingly spread my carpet in one of its corners, and giving the owner a few piastres to finish other dwelling-places which he had commenced, established myself for the winter. The premises, which were speedily completed, consisted of four hovels, surrounded by a mud wall, and roofed with reeds and boughs of trees. I occupied half of the largest habitation, the other half being appropriated for beasts of the plow, and various domestic animals. We were separated by a wall; in which, however, numerous apertures served as a means of communication. These I studiously endeavored for some time to block up. A second hut was devoted to the wives, children, and poultry of my host; a third served as kitchen and servants' hall: the fourth was converted into a stall for my horses. In the inclosure formed by the buildings and outer wall, the few sheep and goats which had escaped the rapacity of the pashaw, congregated during the night, and kept up a continual bleating and coughing until they were milked and turned out to pasture at daybreak.

The roofs not being constructed to exclude the winter rains

now setting in, it required some exercise of ingenuity to escape the torrent which descended into my apartment. I usually passed the night on these occasions crouched up in a corner, or under a rude table which I had constructed. The latter, having been surrounded by trenches, to carry off the accumulating waters, generally afforded the best shelter. My cawass, who was a Constantinopolitan, complained bitterly of the hardships he was compelled to endure, and I had some difficulty in prevailing upon my servants to remain with me.

The present inhabitants of Selamiyah, and of most of the villages in this part of the pashawlic of Mosul, are Turcomans, descendants of tribes brought by the early Turkish sultans from the north of Asia Minor, to people a country which had been laid waste by repeated massacres and foreign invasions. In this portion of the Ottoman empire, there is scarcely, except in Mosul and the Mountains, a vestige of the ancient population. The great tribes which inhabit the Desert were brought from the Jebel Shammar, in Nedjd, within the memory of man. The inhabitants of the plains to the east of the Tigris are mostly Turcomans and Kurds, mixed with Arabs, or with Yezidis, who are strangers in the land, and whose origin can not easily be determined. A few Chaldean and Jacobite Christians, scattered in Mosul and the neighboring villages, or dwelling in the most inaccessible part of the mountains, their places of refuge from the devastating bands of Tamerlane, are probably the only descendants of that great people which once swayed, from these plains, the half of Asia.

The yuz-bashi, or captain of the irregular troops, one Daoud Agha, a native of the north of Asia Minor, called upon me as soon as I was established in my new quarters. Like most men of his class, acknowledged freebooters,* he was frank and

---

* The irregular cavalry (hytas as they are called in this part of Turkey, and bashi-bozuks in Roumelia and Anatolia) are collected from all classes and provinces. A man known for his courage and daring is named hyta-bashi, or chief of the hytas, and is furnished with teskérés or orders for pay and provisions for so many horsemen, from four or five hundred to a thousand or more. He collects all the vagrants and freebooters he can find to

intelligent.   He tendered me his services, entertained me with his adventures, and planned hunting expeditions.   A few presents secured his adherence, and he proved himself afterward a very useful and faithful ally.

I had now to ride three miles every morning to the mound; and my workmen, who were afraid, on account of the Arabs, to live at Naifa, returned, after the day's labor, to Selamiyah. The excavations were however carried on as actively as the means at my disposal would permit.   An entrance, or doorway, had now been completely cleared, and the backs of several inscribed slabs had been uncovered.*   A corner-stone which had evidently been brought from another building, was richly ornamented with flowers 'and scroll-work in relief; but there were no sculptures; nor could any idea be yet formed of the relative position of the walls.   I therefore ordered a trench to be opened from the doorway into the interior of the mound, presuming that we should ultimately come to the opposite side of the chamber, to which, it appeared probable, we had found the entrance.   After removing a large accumulation of earth mixed with charcoal, charred wood, and broken bricks, we reached the top of a new wall on the afternoon of the 28th November. In order to ascertain whether we were in the inside of a chamber, the workmen were directed to clear away the earth from both sides of the slabs.   The south face was unsculptured,

make up his number.   They must provide their own arms and horses, although sometimes they are furnished with them by the hyta-bashi, who deducts a part of their pay until he reimburses himself.   The best hytas are Albanians and Lazes, and they form a very effective body of irregular cavalry.   Their pay at Mosul is small, amounting to about eight shillings a month; in other provinces it is considerably more.   They are quartered on the villages, and are the terror of the inhabitants, whom they plunder and ill-treat as they think fit.   When a hyta-bashi has established a reputation for himself, his followers are numerous and devoted.   He wanders about the provinces, and like a condottiere of the middle ages, sells his services, and those of his troops, to the pashaw who offers most pay, and the best prospects of plunder.   Since the introduction of the *tanzimat*, or reformed system of government, the number of irregular troops has been greatly reduced, and the hytas are no longer able to ill-treat the inhabitants of villages as formerly.

* Wall and entrance *d*, plan 2.

but the first stroke of the pick on the opposite side, disclosed
the top of a bas-relief. The Arabs were no less excited than
myself by the discovery; and notwithstanding a heavy fall of
rain, working until dark, they completely exposed to view two
slabs.*

On each slab were two bas-reliefs, divided by an inscription.
In the upper compartment of the largest was a battle scene,
in which were represented two chariots, each drawn by richly
caparisoned horses at full speed, and containing a group of three
warriors, the principal of whom was beardless and evidently an
eunuch. This figure was clothed in a complete suit of mail
of metal scales, embossed in the center, and apparently attached to a shirt of felt or linen. This shirt was confined at
the waist by a girdle. On his head was a pointed helmet,
from which fell lappets, covered with scales, protecting the
ears, lower part of the face, and neck, the whole head-dress
resembling that of the early Normans. His left hand grasped
a bow at full stretch, while his right drew the string, with
the arrow ready to be discharged. The left arm was encircled by a guard, probably of leather, to protect it from the
arrow. His sword was in a sheath, the end of which was
elegantly adorned with the figures of two lions. In the same
chariot were a charioteer urging on the horses with reins and
whip, and a shield-bearer who warded off the shafts of the
enemy with a circular shield, which, like those of Solomon,
and of the servants or shield-bearers of Hadad-ezer, king of
Zobah, may have been of beaten gold.† The chariots were low,
rounded at the top, and edged by a rich molding or border,
probably inlaid with precious metals or painted. To the sides
were suspended two highly ornamented quivers, each containing, beside the arrows, a hatchet and axe. The wheels
had six spokes. The end of the pole, formed by the head
of a bull, was attached to the fore part of the chariot by
a singular contrivance, of which neither the use nor the

* Nos. 1 and 2, wall *f*, plan 2.
† 1 Kings x. 17; 2 Sam. viii. 7.

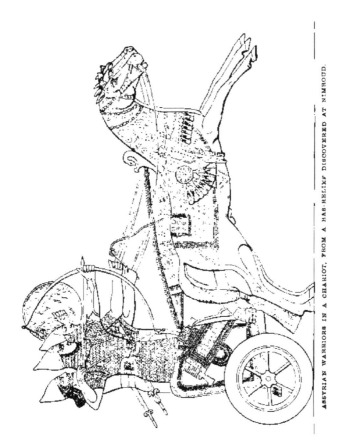

ASSYRIAN WARRIORS IN A CHARIOT, FROM A BAS-RELIEF DISCOVERED AT NIMROUD.

material can be determined from the sculptures. It appears to have been intended both as an ornament and as a support for the pole, and to have been a light frame-work, covered with linen or silk; its breadth almost precludes the idea of its having been of any other material. It was elaborately painted or embroidered with sacred emblems and elegant devices. The chariot, which was probably of wood and open behind, was drawn by three horses, whose trappings, decorated with a profusion of tassels and rosettes, must have been of the most costly description. They may have been of the looms of Dedan, whose merchants, in the days of old, supplied the East with "precious clothes for chariots."* The archer, who evidently belonged to the conquering nation, was pursuing a flying enemy. Beneath the chariot-wheels were scattered the conquered and the dying, and an archer, about to be trodden down, was represented as endeavoring to check the speed of the advancing horses. The costume of the vanquished differed entirely from that of the Assyrian warriors. They wore short tunics descending to their knees, and their hair was confined by a simple fillet round the temples.

I observed with surprise the elegance and richness of the ornaments, the faithful and delicate delineation of the limbs and muscles, both in the men and horses, and the knowledge of art displayed in the grouping of the figures, and in the general composition. In all these respects, as well as in costume, this sculpture appeared to me not only to differ from, but to surpass, the bas-reliefs of Khorsabad. I traced also, in the character used in the inscription, a marked difference from that on the monument discovered by M. Botta. Unfortunately, the slab had been exposed to fire, and was so much injured that its removal was hopeless. The edges had, moreover, been cut away, to the injury of some of the figures and of the inscription; and as the next slab was reversed, it was evident that both had been brought from another building.

* Ezekiel xxvii. 20.

The lower bas-relief on the same slab represented the siege of a castle, or walled city. To the left were two warriors, armed with a short sword and circular shield, and dressed in a tunic, edged by a fringe of tassels, and confined at the waist by a broad girdle. Each carried a quiver at his back, and a bow on his left arm. They wore the pointed helmets before described. The foremost warrior was ascending a ladder placed against the castle. Three turrets, with angular battlements, rose above walls similarly ornamented. In the first turret were two warriors, one in the act of discharging an arrow, the other raising a shield and casting a stone at the assailants, from whom the besieged were distinguished by their head-dress,— a simple fillet binding the hair above the temples. The second turret was occupied by a slinger preparing his sling. In the interval between this turret and the third, and over an arched gateway, was a female figure, known by long hair descending upon her shoulders in ringlets. Her right hand was raised as if in the act of asking for mercy. In the third turret were two more of the besieged, the first discharging an arrow, the second elevating his shield and endeavoring with a torch to burn an instrument resembling a catapult, which had been brought up to the wall by an inclined plane apparently built of boughs of trees and rubbish. These figures were out of all proportion when compared with the size of the building. A warrior with a pointed helmet, bending on one knee, and holding a torch in his right hand, was setting fire to the gate of the castle, while another in full armor was forcing stones from the walls with an instrument, probably of iron, resembling a blunt spear. Between them was a wounded man falling head- long from the battlements.

The adjoining slab, which was angular in shape and formed a corner, was much injured, the greater part having been cut away to reduce it to convenient dimensions. The upper part, or the lower as reversed, was occupied by two warriors; the foremost in a pointed helmet, riding on one horse and leading a second; the other, without helmet, standing in a chariot,

and holding the reins loosely in his hands.   The horses had
been destroyed, and the marks of the chisel were visible on
many parts of the slab, the sculpture having been in some
places carefully defaced.   The lower bas-relief represented the
battlements and towers of a castle.   A woman stood on the
walls tearing her hair in token of grief.   Beneath, by the side
of a stream, denoted by numerous undulating lines, crouched
a fisherman drawing a fish from the water.   This slab had been
exposed to fire like that adjoining, and had sustained too much
injury to be removed.

   As I was meditating in the evening over my discovery,
Daoud Agha entered, and seating himself near me, delivered
a long speech, to the effect, that he was a servant of the pashaw,
who was again the slave of the sultan; and that servants were
bound to obey the commands of their master, however disagreeable and unjust they might be.   I saw at once to what
this exordium was about to lead, and was prepared for the
announcement, that he had received orders from Mosul to stop
the excavations by threatening those who were inclined to
work for me.   On the following morning, therefore, I rode to
the town, and waited upon his excellency.   He pretended to
be taken by surprise, disclaimed having given any such orders,
and directed his secretary to write at once to the commander
of the irregular troops, who was to give me every assistance
rather than throw impediments in my way.   He promised to
let me have the letter in the afternoon before I returned to
Selamiyah; but an officer came to me soon after, and stated
that as the pashaw was unwilling to detain me he would forward
it during the night.   I rode back to the village, and acquainted
Daoud Agha with the result of my visit.   About midnight,
however, he returned to me, and declared that a horseman had
just brought him more stringent orders than any he had yet
received, and that on no account was he to permit me to carry
on the excavation.

   Surprised at this inconsistency, I returned to Mosul early
next day, and again called upon the pashaw.   " It was with deep

regret," said he, "I learnt, after your departure yesterday, that
the mound in which you are digging had been used as a burying-ground by Mussulmans, and was covered with their graves;
now you are aware that by the law it is forbidden to disturb
a tomb, and the cadi and mufti have already made representations to me on the subject." "In the first place," replied I,
"being pretty well acquainted with the mound, I can state
that no graves have been disturbed; in the second, after the
wise and firm 'politica' which your excellency exhibited at
Siwas, gravestones would present no difficulty. Please God,
the cadi and mufti have profited by the lesson which your
excellency gave to the ill-mannered ulema of that city."
"In Siwas," returned he, immediately understanding my meaning, "I had Mussulmans to deal with, and there was tanzimat,* but here we have only Kurds and Arabs, and Wallah!
they are beasts. No, I can not allow you to proceed ; you are
my dearest and most intimate friend; if any thing happens to
you, what grief should I not suffer; your life is more valuable
than old stones ; besides, the responsibility would fall upon my
head." Finding that the pashaw had resolved to interrupt my
proceedings, I pretended to acquiesce in his answer, and requested that a cawass of his own might be sent with me to
Nimroud, as I wished to draw the sculptures and copy the inscriptions which had already been uncovered. To this he consented, and ordered an officer to accompany me.

. On my return to Selamiyah there was little difficulty in
inducing the pashaw's cawass to permit a few workmen to
guard the sculptures during the day; and as Daoud Agha
considered that this functionary's presence relieved him from
any further responsibility, he no longer interfered with me.
Wishing to ascertain the existence of the graves, and also to
draw one of the bas-reliefs, which had been uncovered, I rode
to the ruins on the following morning, accompanied by the

* The reformed system, introduced into most provinces of Turkey, had
not yet been extended to Mosul and Baghdad.

hytas and their chief, who were going their usual rounds in
search of plundering Arabs. Daoud Agha confessed to me on
our way that he had received orders to make graves on the
mound, and that his troops had been employed for two nights
in bringing stones from distant villages for that purpose.*
" We have destroyed more real tombs of the true believers,"
said he, " in making sham ones, than you could have defiled
between the Zab and Selamiyah. We have killed our horses
and ourselves in carrying those accursed stones." A steady
rain setting in, I left the horsemen, and returned to the
village.

In the evening Daoud Agha brought back with him a prisoner
and two of his followers severely wounded. He had fallen in
with a party of horsemen under Sheikh Abd-ur-rahman of the
Abou-Salman Arabs, whose object in crossing the Zab had been
to plunder me as I worked at the mound. After a short engagement, the Arabs were compelled to recross the river.

I continued to employ a few men to open trenches by way of
experiment, and was not long in finding other sculptures.
Near the western edge of the mound were discovered the lower
part of several colossal figures, at the foot of the S. E. corner
a crouching lion, rudely carved in black basalt, and in the center
a pair of gigantic winged bulls, the head and half of the wings
of which had been destroyed. On the backs of the slabs, on
which the bulls were sculptured in high relief, were inscriptions in the arrow-headed character. The remains of two small-
winged lions forming the entrance into a chamber, and a bas-
relief nine feet in height, representing a human figure raising
the right hand, and carrying a branch with three flowers resembling the poppy, in the left, were also uncovered. But these
afforded no clew to the nature of the buildings, of which only
detached and unconnected walls had as yet been exposed.

The experiment had now been fairly made ; there was no
longer any doubt of the existence not only of sculptures and in

* In Arabia, the graves are merely marked by large stones placed upright at the head and feet, and in a heap over the body.

scriptions, but even of large edifices in the interior of the mound
of Nimroud.   I lost no time, therefore, in acquainting Sir Stratford Canning with my discovery, and in urging the necessity
of a firman, or order from the Porte, which would prevent any
future interference on the part of the authorities, or the inhabitants of the country.

It was now nearly Christmas, and as it was desirable to remove from the mound the tombs, which had been made by
the pashaw's orders, and others, more genuine, which had since
been found, I came to an understanding on the subject with
Daoud Agha.   I covered over the sculptures brought to light,
and withdrew altogether from Nimroud, leaving an agent at
Selamiyah.

On entering Mosul on the morning of the 18th of December,
I found the whole population in a ferment of joy.   A Tatar
had that morning brought from Constantinople the welcome news
that the Porte, at length alive to the wretched condition of the
province, and to the misery of the inhabitants, had disgraced the
governor, and had named Ismail Pashaw, a young major-gene-
ral of the new school, to carry on affairs until Hafiz Pashaw,
who had been appointed to succeed Keritli Oglu, could reach his
government.

Ismail Pashaw, who had been for some time in command of
the troops at Diarbekir, had gained a great reputation for justice
among the Mussulmans, and for tolerance among the Christians.
Consequently his appointment had given much satisfaction to
the people of Mosul, who were prepared to receive him with a
demonstration.   However, he slipped into the town during the
night, some time before he had been expected.   On the following
morning a change had taken place at the palace, and Mohammed
Pashaw, with his followers, were reduced to extremities.   The
dragoman of the consulate, who had business to transact with
the late governor, found him sitting in a dilapidated chamber,
through which the rain penetrated without hindrance.   " Thus
it is," said he, " with God's creatures.   Yesterday all those dogs

B*

were kissing my feet ; to-day every one, and every thing, falls upon me, even the rain !"

Meanwhile the state of the country rendering the continuation of my researches at Nimroud almost impossible, I determined to proceed to Baghdad, to make arrangements for the removal of the sculptures at a future period.

CHAPTER III.

On my return to Mosul in the beginning of January, I found
Ismail Pashaw installed in the government. He received me
with courtesy, offered no opposition to the continuation of my
researches at Nimroud, and directed the irregular troops stationed at Selamiyah to afford me every assistance and protection. The change since my departure had been as sudden
as great. A few conciliatory acts on the part of the new governor, an order from the Porte for an inquiry into the sums un-
justly levied by the late pashaw, with a view to their repay-
ment, and a promise of a diminution of taxes, had so far encouraged those who had fled to the mountains and the desert, that the
inhabitants of the villages were slowly returning to their homes ;
and even the Arab tribes, whose pasture-grounds are in the districts of Mosul, were again pitching their tents on the banks of
the Tigris.

During my absence my agents had not been inactive.
Several trenches had been opened in the great mound of Baasheikha ; and fragments of sculpture and inscriptions, with entire pottery and inscribed bricks, had been discovered there.
At Karamles a platform of brickwork had been uncovered,

and the Assyrian origin of the ruin proved by the inscription on the bricks, which contained the name of the Khorsabad king.

I rode to Nimroud on the 17th of January, having first engaged a party of Nestorian Chaldeans to accompany me.

The change that had taken place in the face of the country during my absence, was no less remarkable than that in the political state of the province. To me they were both equally agreeable and welcome. The rains, which had fallen almost incessantly from the day of my departure from Baghdad, had rapidly brought forward the vegetation of spring. The mound was no longer an arid and barren heap ; its surface and its sides were covered with verdure. From the summit of the pyramid my eye ranged, on one side, over a broad plain inclosed by the Tigris and the Zab ; on the other, over a low undulating country bounded by the snow-capped mountains of Kurdistan ; but it was no longer the dreary waste I had left a month before ; the landscape was clothed in green, the black tents of the Arabs checkered the plain of Nimroud, and their numerous flocks pastured on the distant hills. The Abou-Salman had re-crossed the Zab, and had sought their old encamping-grounds. The Jehesh and Shemutti Arabs had returned to their villages, around which the wandering Jebours had pitched their tents, and were now engaged in cultivating the soil. Even on the mound the plow opened its furrows, and corn was sown over the palaces of the Assyrian kings.

Security had been restored, and Nimroud offered a more convenient and agreeable residence than Selamiyah. Hiring, therefore, three huts, I removed to my new dwelling-place. A few rude chairs, a table, and a wooden bedstead, formed the whole of my furniture. My cawass spread his carpet, and hung his tobacco-pouch in the corner of a hovel, which he had appropriated, and spent his days in peaceful contemplation. The servants constructed a rude kitchen, and the grooms shared the stalls with the horses. Mr. Hormuzd Rassam, the brother of the British vice-consul, came to reside with me, and undertook the daily payment of the workmen and the domestic arrangements.

My agent, with the assistance of the chief of the hytas, had punctually fulfilled the instructions he had received on my departure. Not only were the counterfeit graves carefully removed, but even others, which possessed more claim to respect, had been rooted out. I entered into an elaborate argument with the Arabs on the subject of the latter, and proved to them that, as the bodies were not turned toward Mecca, they could not be those of true believers. I ordered the remains, however, to be carefully collected, and to be re-buried at the foot of the mound.

Since my last visit, a sculptured slab, divided into two compartments, had been discovered in the S. W. ruins.* The upper bas-relief had been destroyed; the lower contained four figures, carrying supplies for a banquet, or spoil taken from the enemy. The object carried by the foremost figure could not be determined; the second bore either fruit or a loaf of bread; the third a basket and a skin of wine; the fourth a similar skin, and a vessel of not inelegant shape. The four figures were clothed in long fringed robes, descending to the ankles, and wore the conical cap or helmet before described. The slab had been reduced in size, to the injury of the sculpture, and had evidently belonged to another building. It had on either side the usual inscription, and had been so much injured by fire that it could not be moved.

My labors had scarcely been resumed when I received information that the Cadi of Mosul was endeavoring to stir up the people against me, chiefly on the plea that I was carrying away treasure; and, what was worse, finding inscriptions proving that the Franks once held the country, and upon the evidence of which they intended immediately to resume possession of it, exterminating all true believers. These stories, however absurd they may appear, rapidly gained ground in the

---

* No. 12, wall *k*, plan 2.

town. Old Mohammed Emin Pashaw brought out his Yakuti, and confirmed, by that geographer's account of treasures anciently found at Khorsabad, the allegations of the cadi. A representation was ultimately made by the ulema to Ismail Pashaw; and as he expressed a wish to see me, I rode to Mosul. He was not, he said, influenced by the cadi or the mufti, nor did be believe the absurd tales which they had spread abroad. I should shortly see how he intended to treat these troublesome fellows, but he thought it prudent at present to humor them, and made it a personal request that I would, for the time, suspend the excavations. I consented with regret; and once more returned to Nimroud, without being able to gratify the ardent curiosity I felt to explore further the extraordinary building, the nature of which was still a mystery to me.

The Abou-Salman Arabs, who encamp around Nimroud, are known for their thievish propensities, and might have caused me some annoyance. Thinking it prudent, therefore to conciliate their chief, I rode over one morning to their principal encampment. Sheikh Abd-ur-rahman received me at the entrance of his capacious tent of black goat-hair, which was crowded with relations, followers, and strangers, enjoying his hospitality. He was one of the handsomest Arabs I ever saw; tall, robust, and well-made, with a countenance in which intelligence was no less marked than courage and resolution. On his head he wore a turban of dark linen, from under which a many-colored kerchief fell over his shoulders; his dress was a simple white shirt, descending to the ankles, and an Arab cloak thrown loosely over it. Contrary to the custom of the Arabs, he had shaved his beard; and, although he could scarcely be much beyond forty, I observed that the little hair which could be distinguished from under his turban was gray. He received me with every demonstration of hospitality, and led me to the upper place in the tent, which was divided by a goat-hair curtain from the harem. The place of reception for the guests was at the same time occupied by two favorite mares and a colt. A few camels were kneeling on the grass around, and the horses of the strangers were tied by their halters to the tent-pins. From the carpets and cushions, which were spread for me, stretched on both sides a long line of men of the most motley appearance, seated on the bare ground. The sheikh placed himself at the furthest end, as is the custom in some of the tribes, to show his respect for his guest; and could only be prevailed upon, after many excuses and protestations, to share the carpet with me. In the center of the group, near a small fire of camel's dung, crouched a half-naked Arab, engaged alternately in blowing up the expiring embers, and in pounding the roasted coffee in a copper mortar, ready to replenish the huge pots which stood near him.

After the customary compliments had been exchanged with all around, one of my attendants beckoned to the sheikh, who left the tent to receive the presents I had brought to him,—a silk gown and a supply of coffee and sugar. He dressed himself in his new attire and returned to the assembly. "Inshallah," said I, "we are now friends, although scarcely a month ago you came over the Zab on purpose to appropriate the little property I am accustomed to carry about me." "Wallah, Bey," he replied, "you say true, we are friends; but listen: the Arabs either sit down and serve his majesty the sultan, or they eat from others, as others would eat from them. Now my tribe are of the Zobeide, and were brought here many years ago by the pashaws of the Abd-el-Jelleel.* These lands were given us in return for the services we rendered the Turks in keeping back the Tai and the Shammar, who crossed the rivers to plunder the villages. All the great men of the Abou-Salman perished in encounters with the Bedouin,† and Injeh Bairakdar, Mohammed Pashaw, upon whom God has had mercy, acknowledged our fidelity and treated us with honor. When that blind dog, the son of the Cretan, may curses fall upon him! came to Mosul, I waited upon him, as it is usual for the sheikh; what did

---

* The former hereditary governors of Mosul.
† The father, uncles, and two or three brothers of Abd-ur-rahman, besides many of his other relations, had been slain as he described.

he do ? Did *he* give me the cloak of honor ? No ; he put me, an Arab of the tribe of Zobeide, a tribe which had fought with the prophet, into the public stocks. For forty days my heart melted away in a damp cell, and I was exposed to every variety of torture. Look at these hairs," continued he, lifting up his turban, " they turned white in that time, and I must now shave my beard, a shame among the Arabs. I was released at last ; but how did I return to the tribe ?—a beggar, unable to kill a sheep for my guests. He took my mares, my flocks, and my camels, as the price of my liberty. Now tell me, O Bey, in the name of God, if the Osmanlis have eaten from me and my guests, shall I not eat from them and theirs ?"

The fate of Abd-ur-rahman had been such as he described it ; and so had fared several chiefs of the desert and of the mountains. It was not surprising that these men, proud of their origin and accustomed to the independence of a wandering life, had revenged themselves upon the unfortunate inhabitants of the villages, who had no less cause to complain than themselves. However, the sheikh promised to abstain from plunder for the future, and to present himself to Ismail Pashaw, of whose conciliatory conduct he had already heard.

It was nearly the middle of February before I thought it prudent to make fresh experiments among the ruins. To avoid notice I employed only a few men, and confined myself to the examination of such parts of the mound as appeared to contain buildings. My first attempt was in the S. W. corner, where a new wall was speedily discovered, all the slabs of which were sculptured, and uninjured by fire, though they had, unfortunately, been half destroyed by long exposure to the atmosphere.* On three consecutive slabs was one bas-relief; on others were only parts of a subject. It was evident from the costume, the ornaments, and the general treatment, that these sculptures did not belong either to the same building, or to the same period as those previously discovered. I recognized in them the style of Khorsabad, and in the inscriptions certain characters, which

* Wall *q*, plan 2.

were peculiar to monuments of that age.   The slabs, like those
in other parts of the edifice, had been brought from elsewhere.

The most perfect of the bas-reliefs was, in many respects,
interesting.   It represented a king, distinguished by his high
conical tiara, raising his extended right hand and resting his
left upon a bow.   At his feet crouched a warrior, probably a
captive enemy or rebel, but more likely the latter as he wore the
pointed helmet peculiar to the Assyrians.   An eunuch held a fly-
flapper or fan over the head of the king, who appeared to be
conversing or performing some ceremony with an officer standing
in front of him,—probably his vizier or minister.*   Behind this
personage, who differed from the king by his head-dress,—a
simple fillet confining the hair,—were two attendants, the first
an eunuch, the second a bearded figure.   This bas-relief was separated from a second above, by an inscription ; the upper sculpture had been almost totally destroyed, and I could with difficulty
trace a wounded figure, wearing a helmet with a curved crest,
resembling the Greek, and horsemen engaged in battle.   Both
subjects were continued on the adjoining slabs, but they were
broken off near the bottom, and the feet of a row of figures,
probably other attendants, standing behind the king and his
minister, could alone be distinguished.

On the same wall, which had completely disappeared in some
places, could be traced a group resembling that just described,
and several colossal winged figures in low relief.

Several deep trenches led me to two new walls,† the sculptures
on which were not better preserved than those previously discovered in this part of the mound.   Of the lower parts of several
colossal figures, some had been purposely defaced by a sharp instrument, others, from long exposure, had been worn almost smooth.

* I shall in future designate this person, who is continually represented
in the Assyrian bas-reliefs, the king's vizier or minister.   It has been conjectured that he is a friendly or tributary monarch, but as he often occurs
among the attendants, aiding the king in his battles, or waiting upon him
at the celebration of religious ceremonies, with his hands crossed in front,
as is still the fashion in the East with dependents, it appears more probable that he was his adviser or some high officer of the court.

† s and t, plan 2.

These experiments were sufficient to prove that the building I was exploring had not been entirely destroyed by fire, but had been partly exposed to gradual decay. No sculptures had hitherto been discovered in a perfect state of preservation, and only one or two could bear removal. I determined, therefore, to abandon this corner, and to resume excavations in the north-west ruins near the chamber first opened, where the slabs were uninjured. The workmen were directed to dig behind the remains of the small lions, which appeared to have formed an entrance ; and after removing much earth, they discovered a few unsculptured slabs, fallen from their places, and broken in many pieces. The walls of the room of which they had originally formed part could not be traced.

As this part of the building stood on the very edge of the mound, it had probably been more exposed, and had consequently sustained more injury, than any other. I determined, therefore, to open a trench more in the center of the edifice, and choose for the purpose a deep ravine, which, apparently worn by the winter rains, extended far into the ruins. In two days the workmen reached the top of an entire slab, standing in its original position.* On one face of it I discovered, to my great satisfaction, two human figures, considerably above the natural size, in low relief, and in admirable preservation. In a few hours the earth and rubbish were completely removed from the sculpture. The ornaments delicately graven on the robes, the tassels and fringes, the bracelets and armlets, the elaborate curls of the hair and beard, were all entire. The figures were back to back, and from the shoulders of each sprang two wings. They appeared to represent divinities, presiding over the seasons, or over particular religious ceremonies. The one, whose face was turned to the east, carried a fallow deer on his right arm, and in his left hand a branch bearing five flowers. Around his temples was a fillet, adorned in front with a rosette. The other held a square vessel, or basket, in the left hand, and an object

* No. 30, chamber B, plan 8.

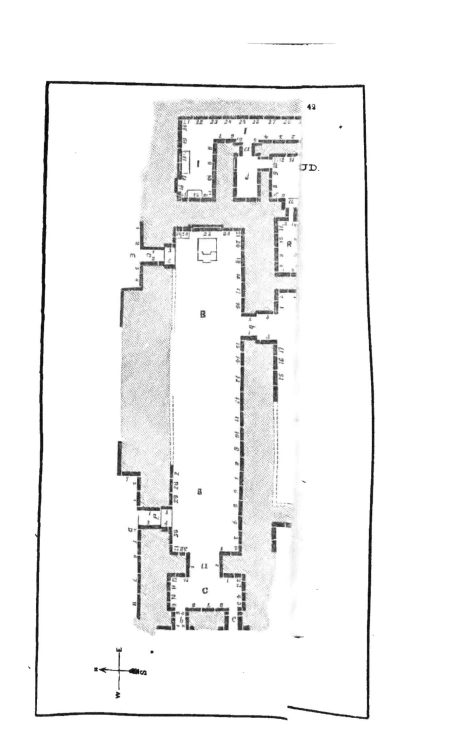

WINGED FIGURE. (N. W. Palace, Nimroud.)

resembling a fir-cone in the right.*   On his head he wore a

* This square vessel was probably of metal, sometimes made to resemble a basket. It may have contained water, as one of the sacred elements; while
the fir-cone, from its inflammable nature, may have
typified fire, another holy element. Such is the only
explanation I can give of the two objects so generally
seen in the Assyrian sculptures.

Vessel or Basket carried
by Winged Figures.

rounded cap, ornamented at the, lower part by a kind of horn curved upward in front. The garments of both, consisting of a stole falling from the shoulders to the ankles, and a short tunic underneath, descending to the knee, were richly and tastefully decorated with embroideries and fringes. Their hair fell in a profusion of ringlets on their shoulders, and their beards were elaborately arranged in alternate rows of curls. Although

SACRED TREE. (N. W Palace, Nimroud.)

the relief was lower, yet the outline was perhaps more careful, and true, than that of the sculptures of Khorsabad. The limbs were delineated with peculiar accuracy, and the muscles and bones faithfully, though somewhat too strongly, marked. In the center of the slab, and crossing the figures, was an inscription.

Adjoining this slab, was a second, cut so as to form a corner, sculptured with an elegant device, in which curved branches, springing from a kind of scroll-work, terminated in flowers of graceful form. As one of the figures last described was turned, as if act of adoration, toward this device, it was evidently a sacred emblem ; and I recognized in it the holy tree, or tree of life, so universally adored at the remotest periods in the East, and which was preserved in the religious systems of the Persians to the final overthrow of their empire by the Arabian conquerors.   The flowers were formed by seven petals springing from two tendrils, or a double scroll ; thus in all its details resembling that tasteful ornament of Ionic architecture known as the honeysuckle.   The alternation of this flower with an object resembling a tulip in the embroideries on the garments of the two winged figures just described, and in other bas-reliefs subsequently discovered, establishes, beyond a doubt, the origin of one of the most favorite and elegant embellishments of Greek art.   We are also reminded, by the peculiar arrangement of the intertwining branches, of the " network of

Assyrian Ornament.(Nimroud.)

Greek Honeysuckle Ornament.

Greek Honeysuckle Ornament.

pomegranates," which was one of the principal ornaments of the temple of Solomon.*   This sculpture and the two winged figures resembled in their style and details several of the fragments built into the S.W. palace, proving at once, from whence the greater part of the materials used in the construction of that building had been obtained.

Adjoining this corner-stone was a figure of singular form. A human body, clothed in robes similar to those of the winged

* 1 Kings vii. 41, 42. Similar trees, in which the flowers above described were replaced by pomegranates, were afterward discovered in the center palace of Nimroud. Mr. Fergusson, in his "Palace of Nineveh and Persepolis restored," has conjectured that this remarkable object represents the "grove" or "groves" which led the Israelites into idolatry. (Judges iii. 7 ; 1 Kings xiv. 23 ; 2 Kings xxi. 3, 7, &c.)   Mr. Fergusson also remarks, with regard to the connection between the ornaments mentioned in the text, and those of Greek architecture, " that it is now impossible to doubt that all that is Ionic in the arts of Greece is derived from the valleys of the Tigris and Euphrates." (P. 340.)

men already described, was surmounted by the head of an
eagle or of a vulture.*   The curved beak, of considerable

EAGLE-HEADED FIGURE.   (N.W. Palace, Nimroud.)

length, was half open, and displayed a narrow pointed tongue,
on which were still the remains of red paint.   On the shoulders

---

* It has been suggested that it is the head of a cock, but it is unques-
tionably that of a carnivorous bird of the eagle tribe.

fell the usual curled and bushy hair of the Assyrian images, and a comb of feathers rose on the top of the head. Two wings sprang from the back, and in either hand was the square vessel and fir-cone. In a kind of girdle were three daggers, the handle of one being in the form of the head of a bull. They may have been of precious metal, but more probably of copper, inlaid with ivory or enamel, as a few days before a copper dagger-handle, precisely similar in form to one of those carried by this figure, hollowed to receive an ornament of some such material, had been discovered in the S.W. ruins, and is now preserved in the British Museum.

This effigy, which probably typified by its mythic form the union of certain divine attributes, may perhaps be identified with the god Nisroch, in whose temple Sennacherib was slain by his sons* after his return from his unsuccessful expedition against Jerusalem; the word Nisr signifying, in all Semitic languages, an eagle.†

On all these figures were traces of color, particularly on the hair, beard, eyes, and sandals, and there can be no doubt that they had been originally painted. The slabs on which they were sculptured had sustained no injury, and they evidently formed part of a chamber, which could be completely explored by digging along the wall, now partly uncovered.

On the morning following these discoveries, I had ridden to the encampment of Sheikh Abd-ur-rahman, and was returning to the mound, when I saw two Arabs of his tribe urging their mares to the top of their speed. On approaching me they stopped. "Hasten, O Bey," exclaimed one of them—"hasten to the diggers, for they have found Nimrod himself. Wallah! it is wonderful, but it is true! we have seen him with our eyes. There is no God but God;" and both joining in this pious

---

* 2 Kings xix. 37.
† The form of this deity was conjectured to be that of an eagle long before the discovery of the Assyrian sculptures. (And. Beyeri ad Joh. Seldeni de Dis Syriis Syntag. addit. p. 325.)

exclamation, they galloped off, without further words, in the direction of their tents.

DISCOVERY OF THE GIGANTIC HEAD.

On reaching the ruins I descended into the new trench, and found the workmen, who had already seen me, as I approached, standing near a heap of baskets and cloaks. While Awad advanced and asked for a present to celebrate the occasion, the Arabs withdrew the screen they had hastily constructed, and disclosed an enormous human head sculptured in full out of the alabaster of the country. They had uncovered the upper part of a figure, the remainder of which was still buried in the earth. I saw at once that the head must belong to a winged lion or bull, similar to those of Khorsabad and Persepolis. It was in admirable preservation. The expression was calm, yet majestic, and the outline of the features showed a freedom and knowledge of art, scarcely to be looked for in works of so remote a period. The cap had three horns, and, unlike that of the human-headed bulls hitherto found in Assyria, was rounded and without ornament at the top.

I was not surprised that the Arabs had been amazed and terrified at this apparition. It required no stretch of imagination to conjure up the most strange fancies. This gigantic head, blanched with age, thus rising from the bowels of the earth, might well have belonged to one of those fearful beings which are pictured in the traditions of the country, as appearing to mortals, slowly ascending from the regions below. One of the workmen, on catching the first glimpse of the monster, had thrown down his basket and had run off toward Mosul as fast as his legs could carry him. I learned this with regret, as I anticipated the consequences.

While I was superintending the removal of the earth, which still clung to the sculpture, and giving directions for the continuation of the work, a noise of horsemen was heard, and presently Abd-ur-rahman, followed by half his tribe, appeared on the edge of the trench. As soon as the two Arabs had reached the tents, and published the wonders they had seen, every one mounted his mare and rode to the mound to satisfy himself of the truth of these inconceivable reports. When they beheld the head they all cried together, " There is no God but God, and Mohammed is his Prophet !" It was some time before the sheikh could be prevailed upon to descend into the pit, and convince himself that the image he saw was of stone. " This is not the work of men's hands," exclaimed he, "but of those infidel giants of whom the Prophet, peace be with him ! has said, that they were higher than the tallest date-tree ; this is one of the idols which Noah, peace be with him ! cursed before the flood." In this opinion, the result of a careful examination, all the by-standers concurred.

I now ordered a trench to be dug due south from the head

C

in the expectation of finding a corresponding figure, and before
night-fall reached the object of my search about twelve feet
distant.   Engaging two or three men to sleep near the sculptures, I returned to the village, and celebrated the day's discovery by a slaughter of sheep, of which all the Arabs near partook.   As some wandering musicians chanced to be at Selamiyah,
I sent for them, and dances were kept up during the greater
part of the night.   On the following morning Arabs from the
other side of the Tigris, and the inhabitants of the surrounding
villages, congregated on the mound.   Even the women could
not repress their curiosity, and came in crowds, with their children, from afar.   My cawass was stationed during the day in
the trench, into which I would not allow the multitude to
descend.

As I had expected, the report of the discovery of the
gigantic head, carried by the terrified Arab to Mosul, had
thrown the town into commotion.   He had scarcely checked
his speed before reaching the bridge.   Entering breathless into
the bazars, he announced to every one he met that Nimrod had
appeared.   The news soon got to the ears of the cadi, who
called the mufti and the ulema together, to consult upon this
unexpected occurrence.   Their deliberations ended in a procession to the governor, and a formal protest, on the part of the
Mussulmans of the town, against proceedings so directly contrary
to the laws of the Koran.   The cadi had no distinct idea whether
the bones of the mighty hunter had been uncovered, or only his
image; nor did Ismail Pashaw very clearly remember whether
Nimrod was a true-believing prophet, or an infidel.   I consequently received a somewhat unintelligible message from his
excellency, to the effect that the remains should be treated with
respect, and be by no means further disturbed; that he wished
the excavations to be stopped at once, and desired to confer with
me on the subject.

I called upon him accordingly, and had some difficulty in
making him understand the nature of my discovery.   As he
requested me to discontinue my operations until the sensation

in the town had somewhat subsided, I returned to Nimroud
and dismissed the workmen, retaining only two men to dig leisurely along the walls without giving cause for further interference. I ascertained by the end of March the existence of a
second pair of winged human-headed lions,* differing from
those previously discovered in form, the human shape being
continued to the waist, and being furnished with human arms,
as well as with the legs of the lion. In one hand each
figure carried a goat or stag, and in the other, which hung
down by the side, a branch with three flowers. They formed
a northern entrance into the chamber of which the lions
previously described were the western portal. I completely
uncovered the latter, and found them to be entire. They
were about twelve feet in height, and the same number in
length. The body and limbs were admirably portrayed ; the
muscles and bones, although strongly developed to display the
strength of the animal, showed at the same time a correct
knowledge of its anatomy and form. Expanded wings sprung
from the shoulder and spread over the back ; a knotted girdle,
ending in tassels, encircled the loins. These sculptures, forming an entrance, were partly in full and partly in relief. The
head and fore-part, facing the chamber, were in full ; but only
one side of the rest of the slab was sculptured, the back being
placed against the wall of sun-dried bricks. That the spectator
might have both a perfect front and side view of the figures,
they were furnished with five legs ; two were carved on the
end of the slab to face the chamber, and three on the side.
The relief of the body and limbs was high and bold, and the
slab was covered, in all parts not occupied by the image, with
inscriptions in the cuneiform character. The remains of color
could still be traced in the eyes—the pupils being painted black,
and the rest filled up with an opaque white pigment ; but on
no other parts of the sculpture. These magnificent specimens
of Assyrian art were in perfect preservation ; the most minute

---

* Entrance *d* to chamber B, plan 3.

lines in the details of the wings and in the ornaments had been retained with their original freshness.

I used to contemplate for hours these mysterious emblems, and muse over their intent and history. What more noble forms could have ushered the people into the temple of their gods? What more sublime images could have been borrowed from nature, by men who sought, unaided by the light of revealed religion, to embody their conception of the wisdom, power, and ubiquity of a Supreme Being? They could find no better type of intellect and knowledge than the head of the man; of strength, than the body of the lion; of ubiquity, than the wings of the bird. These winged human-headed lions were not idle creations, the offspring of mere fancy; their meaning was written upon them. They had awed and instructed races which flourished 3000 years ago. Through the portals which they guarded, kings, priests, and warriors had borne sacrifices to their altars, long before the wisdom of the East had penetrated to Greece, and had furnished its mythology with symbols recognized of old by the Assyrian votaries. They may have been buried, and their existence may have been unknown, before the foundation of the eternal city. For twenty-five centuries they had been hidden from the eye of man, and they now stood forth once more in their ancient majesty. But how changed was the scene around them! The luxury and civilization of a mighty nation had given place to the wretchedness and ignorance of a few half-barbarous tribes. The wealth of temples, and the riches of great cities, had been succeeded by ruins and shapeless heaps of earth. Above the spacious hall in which they stood, the plow had passed and the corn now waved. Egypt has monuments no less ancient and no less wonderful; but they have stood forth for ages to testify her early power and renown; while those before me had but now appeared to bear witness, in the words of the prophet, that once "the Assyrian was a cedar in Lebanon with fair branches and with a shadowing shroud of an high stature; and his top was among the thick boughs . . . . his height was exalted above all the trees of the field, and his

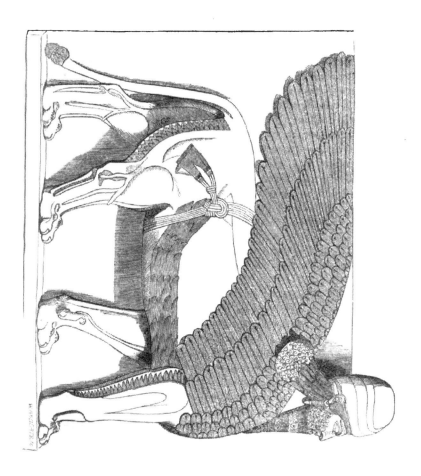

boughs were multiplied, and his branches became long, because of the multitude of waters when he shot forth. All the fowls of heaven made their nests in his boughs, and under his branches did all the beasts of the fields bring forth their young, and under his shadow dwelt all great nations;" for now is "Nineveh a desolation, and dry like a wilderness, and flocks lie down in the midst of her: all the beasts of the nations, both the cormorant and bittern, lodge in the upper lintels of it; their voice sings in the windows; and desolation is in the thresholds."*

The entrance formed by the human-headed lions led into a chamber round which were sculptured winged figures, such as I have already described. They were in pairs facing one another, and separated by the sacred tree. These bas-reliefs were inferior in execution, and finish, to those previously discovered.

During the month of March I received visits from the principal sheikhs of the Jebour Arabs, whose followers had now partly crossed the Tigris, and were pasturing their flocks in the neighborhood of Nimroud, or cultivating millet on the banks of the river. The Jebours are a branch of the ancient tribe of Obeid, and their pasture-grounds are on the banks of the Khabour, from its junction with the Euphrates,—from the ancient Carchemish or Circesium, to its source at Ras-el-Ain. Having been suddenly attacked and plundered a year or two before by the Aneyza, they had left their haunts, and taken refuge in the districts around Mosul. They were at this time divided into three branches obeying different sheikhs. The names of the three chiefs were Abd'rubbou, Mohammed-Emin, and Mohammed-ed-Dagher. Although all three visited me át Nimroud, it was the first with whom I was best acquainted, and who rendered me most assistance. I thought it necessary to give to each a few small presents, a silk dress, or an embroidered cloak, with a pair of capacious boots, as in case of any fresh disturbances in the country, it would be as well to be on friendly terms with the tribe.

The middle of March in Mesopotamia is the brightest epoch

* Ezekiel xxxi. 3. &c.; Zephaniah ii. 13 and 14.

of spring. A new change had come over the face of the plain of Nimroud. Its pasture lands, known as the "Jaif," are renowned for their rich and luxuriant herbage. In times of quiet, the studs of the pashaw and of the Turkish authorities, with the horses of the cavalry and of the inhabitants of Mosul, are sent here to graze. Day by day they arrived in long lines. The Shemutti and Jehesh left their huts, and encamped on the greensward which surrounded the villages. The plain, as far as the eye could reach, was studded with the white pavilions of the hytas and the black tents of the Arabs. Picketed around them were innumerable horses in gay trappings, struggling to release themselves from the bonds which restrained them from ranging over the green pastures.

Flowers of every hue enameled the meadows ; not thinly scattered over the grass as in northern climes, but in such thick and gathering clusters that the whole plain seemed a patchwork of many colors. The dogs, as they returned from hunting, issued from the long grass dyed red, yellow, or blue, according to the flowers through which they had last forced their way.

The villages of Naifa and Nimroud were deserted, and I remained alone with Said (my host) and my servants. The houses now began to swarm with vermin ; we no longer slept under the roofs, and it was time to follow the example of the Arabs. I accordingly encamped on the edge of a large pond on the outskirts of Nimroud. Said accompanied me ; and Salah, his young wife, a bright-eyed Arab girl, built up his shed, and watched and milked his diminutive flock of sheep and goats.

I was surrounded with Arabs, who had either pitched their tents, or, too poor to buy the black goat-hair cloth of which they are made, had erected small huts of reeds and dry grass.

In the evening, after the labor of the day, I often sat at the door of my tent, and giving myself up to the full enjoyment of that calm and repose which are imparted to the senses by such scenes as these, gazed listlessly on the varied groups before me. As the sun went down behind the low hills which separate the river from the desert—even their rocky sides had struggled to emulate the verdant clothing of the plain—its receding rays were gradually withdrawn, like a transparent vail of light, from the landscape. Over the pure, cloudless sky was the glow of the last light. The great mound threw its dark shadow far across the plain. In the distance, and beyond the Zab, Keshaf, another venerable ruin, rose indistinctly into the evening mist. Still more distant, and still more indistinct was a solitary hill over-looking the ancient city of Arbela. The Kurdish mountains, whose snowy summits cherished the dying sunbeams, yet strug-gled with the twilight. The bleating of sheep and lowing of cattle, at first faint, became louder as the flocks returned from their pastures, and wandered among the tents. Girls hurried over the greensward to seek their fathers' cattle, or crouched down to milk those which had returned alone to their well-remembered folds. Some were coming from the river bearing the replenished pitcher on their heads or shoulders; others, no less graceful in their form, and erect in their carriage, were carrying the heavy load of long grass which they had cut in the meadows. Sometimes a party of horsemen might have been seen in the distance slowly crossing the plain, the tufts of ostrich feathers which topped their long spears showing darkly against the evening sky. They would ride up to my tent, and give me the usual salutation, "Peace be with you, O Bey," or, "Allah Aienak, God help you." Then driving the end of their lances into the ground, they would spring from their mares, and fasten their halters to the still quivering weapons. Seating themselves on the grass, they related deeds of war and plunder, or specu-lated on the site of the tents of Sofuk, until the moon rose, when they vaulted into their saddles and took the way of the desert.

The plain now glittered with innumerable fires. As the night advanced, they vanished one by one until the landscape was wrapped in darkness and in silence, only disturbed by the bark-ing of the Arab dog.

Abd-ur-rahman rode to my tent one morning, and offered to take me to a remarkable cutting in the rock, which he described as the work of Nimrod, the giant. The Arabs call it "Ne-goub," or The Hole. We were two hours in reaching the

place, as we hunted gazelles and hares by the way. A tunnel
through the rock opens by two low arched outlets, upon the
river. It is of considerable length, and is continued for about
a mile by a deep channel, also cut in the rock, but open at the
top. I suspected at once that this was an Assyrian work, and on
examining the interior of the tunnel, discovered a slab covered
with cuneiform characters, which had fallen from its place, and
had been wedged in a crevice. With much difficulty I ascertained that an inscription had also been cut on the back of the
tablet. From the darkness of the place, I could scarcely copy
even the few characters which had resisted the wear of centuries. Some days after, others who had casually heard of my visit,
and conjectured that some Assyrian remains might have been
found there, sent a party of workmen to the spot; who, finding
the slab, broke it into pieces, in their attempt to displace it. This
wanton destruction of the tablet is much to be regretted; as,
from the fragment of the inscription copied, I can perceive that
it contained several royal names previously unknown.*

The tunnel of Negoub is undoubtedly a remarkable work, undertaken, as it would appear from the inscription, during the
reign of the builder of the palace at Kouyunjik. Its object is
doubtful. It may have led the waters of the Zab into the surrounding country for irrigation; or it may have been the termination of the great canal, which is still to be traced by a double
range of lofty mounds near the ruins of Nimroud, and which
may have united the Tigris with the neighboring river, and thus
fertilized a large tract of land. In either case, the level of the
two rivers, as well as the face of the country, must have changed
considerably since the period of its construction. At present
Negoub is above the Zab, except at the time of the highest floods
in spring, and then water is only found in the mouth of the tunnel; all other parts having been much choked up with rubbish
and river deposits.

* I have since been able to restore the greater part of the inscription
from the fragments of this tablet. It is of considerable importance, as it
gives us the names of the father, and perhaps grandfather of the Khorsabad king, with which we were not previously acquainted.

CHAPTER IV.

PREPARATIONS FOR A JOURNEY TO AL HATHER.—GATHERING OF THE
CARAVAN.—LEAVE MOSUL.—THE DESERT.—FLOCKS OF CAMELS.—THE
HADDEDEEN ARABS.—AN ARAB REPAST.—AN ENCAMPMENT.—AN ARAB
TRIBE MOVING.—THE TENTS OF SOFUK.—DESCRIPTION OF THE SHAMMAR
SHEIKH.—HIS HISTORY.—SOFUK'S HAREM AND WIVES.—HIS MARE.—
RIDE TO AL HATHER.—ARAB GUIDES.—THE RUINS OF AL HATHER.—
RETURN TO MOSUL.—MURDER OF NEJRIS—AND OF SOFUK.

THE operations at Nimroud having been completely suspended
until orders could be received from Constantinople, I thought the
time not inopportune to visit Sofuk, the sheikh of the great nomad Arab tribe of Shammar, which occupies nearly the whole
of Mesopotamia.   He had lately left the Khabour, and was now
encamped near the western bank of the Tigris, below its junction with the Zab, and consequently not far from Nimroud.   I
had two objects in going to his tents; in the first place I wished
to obtain the friendship of the chief of a powerful tribe of Bedouins, who would probably cross the river in the neighborhood
of the excavations during the summer, and might indulge, to my
cost, in their plundering propensities ; and, at the same time, I
was anxious to visit the remarkable ruins of Al Hather, which
I had only examined very hastily on my former journey.

Mr. Rassam (the vice-consul) and his wife, with several
native gentlemen of Mosul, Mussulmans and Christians, were
induced to accompany me ; and, as we issued from the gates of
the town, and assembled in the well-peopled burying-ground
opposite the governor's palace, I found myself at the head of a
formidable party.   Our tents, obtained from the pashaw, with our
provisions and necessary furniture, were carried by a string of
twelve camels.   Mounted above these loads, and on donkeys,
was an army of camel-drivers, tent-pitchers, and volunteers
ready for all services.   There were, moreover, a few irregular

horsemen, the cawasses, the attendants of the Mosul gentlemen, the Mosul gentlemen themselves, and our own servants, all armed to the teeth. Ali Effendi, chief of the Mosul branch of the Omeree, or descendants of Omar, which had furnished several pashaws to the province, was our principal Mussulman friend. He was mounted on the Hedban, a well-known white Arab, beautiful in form and pure in blood, but then of great age. Close at his horse's heels followed a confidential servant; who, perched on a pack-saddle, seemed to roll from side to side on two small barrels, the use of which might have been an enigma, had they not emitted a very strong smell of raki. A Christian gentleman was wrapped up in cloaks and furs, and appeared to dread the cold, although the thermometer was at 100. The English lady was equipped in riding-habit and hat. The two Englishmen, Mr. Ross and myself, wore a striking mixture of European and oriental raiments. Mosul ladies, in blue vails, their faces concealed by black horsehair sieves, had been dragged to the top of piles of carpets and cushions, under which groaned their unfortunate mules. Greyhounds in leashes were led by Arabs on foot; while others played with strange dogs, who followed the caravan for change of air. The horsemen galloped round and round, now dashing into the center of the crowd, throwing their horses on their haunches when at full speed, or discharging their guns and pistols into the air. A small flag with British colors was fastened to the top of a spear, and confided to a cawass. Such was the motley caravan which left Mosul by the Bab el Top, where a crowd of women had assembled to witness the procession.

We took the road to the ruins of the monastery of Mar Elias, a place of pilgrimage for the Christians of Mosul, which we passed after an hour's ride. Evening set in before we could reach the desert, and we pitched our tents for the night on a lawn near a deserted village, about nine miles from the town.

On the following morning we soon emerged from the low limestone hills; which, broken into a thousand rocky valleys, form a barrier between the Tigris and the plains of Mesopotamia.

We now found ourselves in the desert, or rather wilderness;
for at this time of the year, nature could not disclose a more
varied scene, or a more luxuriant vegetation. We trod on an
interminable carpet, figured by flowers of every hue. Nor was
water wanting; for the abundant rains had given reservoirs to
every hollow, and to every ravine. Their contents, owing to
the nature of the soil, were brackish, but not unwholesome.
Clusters of black tents were scattered, and flocks of sheep and
camels wandered, over the plain. Those of our party who
were well mounted urged their horses through the meadows,
pursuing the herds of gazelles, or the wild boar, skulking in the
long grass. Although such scenes as these may be described,
the exhilaration caused by the air of the desert in spring, and
the feeling of freedom arising from the contemplation of its
boundless expanse, must have been experienced before they can
be understood. The stranger, as well as the Arab, feels the
intoxication of the senses which they produce.

About mid-day we found ourselves in the midst of extensive
herds of camels. They belonged to the tribe of Haddedeen.
The sonorous whoop of the Arab herdsmen resounded from all
sides. A few horsemen were galloping about, driving back
the stragglers, and directing the march of the leaders of the
herd. Shortly after we came up with some families moving to
a new place of encampment, and at their head I recognized my
old antiquity-hunter, Mormous. He no sooner perceived us
than he gave orders to those who followed him, and of whom he
was the chief, to pitch their tents. We were now in the Wadi
Ghusub, formed by a small salt stream, forcing its sluggish way
through a dense mass of reeds and water shrubs, from which the
valley has taken its name. About fifteen tents having been
raised, a sheep was slaughtered in front of the one in which we
sat; large wooden bowls of sour milk, and platters of fresh
butter were placed before us; fires of camel's dung were lighted;
decrepit old women blew up the flames; the men cut the carcass into small pieces, and capacious caldrons soon sent forth
volumes of steam.

The sheep having been boiled, the Arabs pulled the fragments out of the caldron and laid them on the wooden platters
with their fingers. We helped ourselves after the same fashion.
The servants succeeded to the dishes, which afterward passed
through the hands of the camel-drivers and tent-pitchers; and
at last, denuded of all apparently edible portions, reached a
strong party of expectant Arabs. The condition of the bones
by the time they were delivered to a crowd of hungry dogs,
assembled on the occasion, may easily be imagined.

  We resumed our journey in the afternoon, preceded by
Mormous, who volunteered to accompany us. As we rode over
the plain, we fell in with the sheikh of the Haddedeen mounted
on a fine mare, and followed by a large concourse of Arabs,
driving their beasts of burden loaded with tents and furniture. He offered to conduct us to a branch of the Shammar,
whose encampment we could reach before evening. We gladly
accepted his offer, and he left his people to ride with us.

  We had been wandering to and fro in the desert, uncertain
as to the course we should pursue. The sheikh now rode in
the direction of the Tigris. Before nightfall we came to a
large encampment, and recognized in its chief one Khalaf, an
Arab who frequently came to Mosul, and whom Mr. Rassam
and myself had met on our previous journey to Al Hather.
He received us with hospitality; sheep were immediately
slaughtered, and we dismounted at his tent. Even his wives,
among whom was a remarkably pretty Arab girl, came to us
to gratify their curiosity by a minute examination of the Frank
lady. As the intimacy, which began to spring up, was somewhat inconvenient, we directed our tents to be pitched at a distance from the encampment, by the side of a small stream. It
was one of those calm and pleasant evenings, which in spring
make a paradise of the desert. The breeze, bland and per-
fumed by the odor of flowers, came calmly over the plain.
As the sun went down, countless camels and sheep wandered to
the tents, and the melancholy call of the herdsmen rose above
the bleating of the flocks. The Arabs led their prancing mares

to the water; the colts, as they followed, played and rolled on the grass. I spread my carpet at a distance from the group, to enjoy uninterrupted the varied scene. Rassam, now in his element, collected around him a knot of admiring Arabs, unscrewed telescopes, exhibited various ingenious contrivances, and described the wonders of Europe, interrupted by the exclamations of incredulous surprise, which his marvelous stories elicited from the hearers. Ali Effendi and his Mussulman friends, who preferred other pleasures and more definite excitement, hid themselves in the high rushes, and handed round a small silver bowl containing fragrant ruby-colored spirits, which might have rejoiced even the heart of Hafiz. The camel-drivers and servants hurried over the lawn, tending their animals or preparing the evening meal.

We had now reached the pasture-grounds of the Shammar, and Sheikh Khalaf declared that Sofuk's tents could not be far distant. A few days before they had been pitched almost among the ruins of Al Hather; but he had since left them, and it was not known where he had encamped. We started early in the morning, and took the direction pointed out by Khalaf. Our view was bounded to the east by a rising ground. When we reached its summit, we looked down upon a plain, which appeared to swarm with moving objects. We had come upon the main body of the Shammar. The scene caused in me feelings of melancholy, for it recalled many hours, perhaps unprofitably, though certainly happily spent; and many friends, some who now sighed in captivity for the joyous freedom which those wandering hordes enjoyed; others who had perished in its defense. We soon found ourselves in the midst of wide-spreading flocks of sheep and camels. As far as the eye could reach, to the right, to the left, and in front, still the same moving crowd. Long lines of asses and bullocks laden with black tents, huge caldrons and variegated carpets; aged women and men, no longer able to walk, tied on the heap of domestic furniture; infants crammed into saddle-bags, their tiny heads thrust through the narrow opening, balanced on the animal's back by kids or lambs tied on the opposite side ; young girls clothed only in the close-fitting Arab shirt, which displayed rather than

A SHAMMAR LADY ON A CAMEL.

concealed their graceful forms ; mothers with their children on their shoulders ; boys driving flocks of lambs ; horsemen armed

with long tufted spears, scouring the plain on their fleet mares;
riders urging their dromedaries with short hooked sticks, and
leading their high-bred steeds by the halter; colts galloping
among the throng; high-born ladies seated in the center of
huge wings, which extend like those of a butterfly from each
side of the camel's hump, and are no less gaudy and variegated.*
Such was the motley crowd through which we had to wend our
way for several hours. Our appearance created a lively sensation; the women checked our horses; the horsemen assembled
round us, and rode by our side; the children yelled and ran
after the Franks.

It was mid-day before we found a small party that had
stopped, and were pitching their tents. A young chestnut mare
belonging to the sheikh, was one of the most beautiful creatures
I ever beheld. As she struggled to free herself from the spear
to which she was tied, she showed the lightness and elegance of
the gazelle. Her limbs were in perfect symmetry: her ears
erect, slender, and transparent; her nostrils high, dilated, and
deep red; her neck gracefully arched, and her mane and tail of
the texture of silk. We all involuntarily stopped to gaze at her.
"Say Masha-Allah," exclaimed the owner, who, seeing not
without pride, that I admired her, feared the effect of an evil
eye. "That I will," answered I, "and with pleasure; for, O
Arab, you possess the jewel of the tribe." He brought us a
bowl of camel's milk, and directed us to the tents of Sofuk.

We had still two hours' ride before us, and when we reached
the encampment of the Shammar sheikh, our horses, as well as
ourselves, were exhausted by the heat of the sun, and the length
of the day's journey. The tents were pitched on a broad lawn

---

* These wings are formed by a light frame-work of cane, varying from
sixteen to twenty feet in length, covered with parchment. and ornamented,
as is also the body and neck of the camel, with tassels and fringes of worst-
ed of every hue, and with strings of glass beads and shells. The lady sits
in the center in a kind of pavilion, covered with gay carpets, by which she
is shaded from the sun. This singular contrivance sways from side to side,
and the motion is very disagreeable to one not accustomed to it.

in a deep ravine; they were scattered in every direction, and among them rose the white pavilions of the Turkish irregular cavalry. Ferhan, the son of Sofuk, and a party of horsemen, rode out to meet us as we approached, and led us to the tent of the chief, distinguished from the rest by its size, and the spears which were driven into the ground at its entrance. Sofuk advanced to receive us; he was followed by about three hundred Arabs, including many of the principal sheikhs of the tribe. In person he was short and corpulent, more like an Osmanli than an Arab; but his eye was bright and intelligent, his features regular, well formed and expressive. His dress differed but in the quality of the materials from that of his followers. A thick kerchief, striped with red, yellow, and blue, *x* and fringed with long plaited cords, was thrown over his head, and fell down his shoulders. It was held in its place, above the brow, by a band of spun camel's wool, tied at intervals by silken threads of many colors. A long white shirt, descending to the ankles, and a black and white cloak over it, completed his attire.

He led Rassam and myself to the top of the tent, where we seated ourselves on well-worn carpets. When all the party had found places, the words of welcome, which had been exchanged before we dismounted, were repeated. " Peace be with you, O Bey! upon my head you are welcome: my house is your house," exclaimed the sheikh, addressing the stranger nearest to him. " Peace be with you, O Sofuk! may God protect you!" was the answer, and similar compliments were made to every guest, and by every person, present. While this ceremony, which took nearly half an hour, was going on, I had leisure to examine those who had assembled to meet us. Nearest to me was Ferhan, the sheikh's eldest son, a young man of handsome appearance and intelligent countenance, although the expression was neither agreeable nor attractive. His dress resembled that of his father; but from beneath the kerchief thrown over his head hung his long black tresses plaited into many tails. His teeth were white as ivory, like those of most Arabs. Beyond

him sat a crowd of men of the most ferocious and forbidding
exterior—warriors who had passed their lives in war and
rapine, looking upon those who did not belong to their tribe as
natural enemies, and preferring their wild freedom to all the
riches of the earth.

Mrs. Rassam had been ushered into this crowded assembly.
The scrutinizing glance with which she was examined from
head to foot, by all present, not being agreeable, we requested
that she might be taken to the tent of the women. Sofuk called
two black slaves, who led her to the harem, scarcely a stone's
throw distant.

The compliments having been at length finished, we con-
versed upon general topics. Coffee, highly drugged with
odoriferous herbs found in the desert, and with spices, a mixture
for which Sofuk was celebrated, was handed round before we
retired to our own tents.

Sofuk's name was so well known in the desert, and he so
long played a conspicuous part in the politics of Mesopotamia,
that a few words on his history may not be uninteresting. He
was descended from the sheikhs, who brought the tribe from
Nedjd in Arabia Proper. At the commencement of his career
he had shared the chiefship with his uncle, after whose death
he became the great Sheikh of the Shammar. From an early
period he had been troublesome to the Turkish governors of the
provinces on the Tigris and Euphrates; but gained the confidence of the Porte by a spirited attack upon the camp of
Mohammed Ali Mirza, son of Feth Ali Shah, and governor of
Kirmanshah, when that prince was marching upon Baghdad
and Mosul. After this exploit, to which was mainly attributed
the safety of the Turkish cities, Sofuk was invested as Sheikh
of the Shammar. At times, however, when he had to complain
of ill-treatment from the Pashaw of Baghdad, or could not control
those under him, his tribes were accustomed to indulge their
love of plunder, to sack villages and pillage caravans. He thus
became formidable to the Turks, and was known as the King
of the Desert. When Mehemet Reshid Pashaw led his successful

expedition into Kurdistan and Mesopotamia, Sofuk was among
the chiefs whose power he sought to destroy. He knew that it
would be useless to attempt it by force, and he consequently
invited the sheikh to his camp on the pretense of investing
him with the customary robe of honor. He was seized and
sent a prisoner to Constantinople. There he remained some
months, until deceived by his promises, the Porte permitted
him to return to the tribe. From that time his Arabs had been
the terror of the pashawlics of Mosul and Baghdad, and had
even carried their depredations to the east of the Tigris. However, Nejris, the son of Sofuk's uncle, had appeared as his rival,
and many branches of the Shammar had declared for the new
sheikh. This led to dissensions in the tribe ; and, at the time
of our visit, Sofuk, who had forfeited his popularity by many
acts of treachery, was almost deserted by the Arabs. In this
dilemma he had applied to the pashaw of Mosul, and had promised to serve the Porte, and to control the Bedouins, if he were
assisted in re-establishing his authority. This state of things
accounted for the presence of the white tents of the hytas in
the midst of his encampment.

His intercourse with the Turkish authorities, who must be
conciliated by adequate presents before assistance can be expected from them, and the famine, which for the last two years
had prevailed in the countries surrounding the desert, were not
favorable to the domestic prosperity of Sofuk. The wealth
and display, for which he was once renowned among the
Arabs, had disappeared. A few months before, he had even
sent to Mosul the silver ankle-rings of his favorite wife—the
last resource—to be exchanged for corn. The furred cloaks,
and embroidered robe, which he once wore, had not been replaced. The only carpet in his tent was the rag on which sat
his principal guests ; the rest squatted on the grass, or on the
bare ground. He led the life of a pure Bedouin, from the com-
monest of whom he was only distinguished by the extent of his
female establishment—always a weak point with the sheikh.
But even in his days of greatest prosperity, the meanest Arab

looked upon him as his equal, addressed him as "Sofuk," and
seated himself unbidden in his presence. The system of patriarchal government, faithfully described by Burckhardt, still
exists, as it has done for 4000 years, in the desert.

The usual Arab meal was brought to us soon after our arrival
—large wooden bowls and platters filled with boiled fragments
of mutton swimming in melted butter, and sour milk; and when
we had eaten, Sofuk came to our tents, and remained with us
the greater part of the day. He was dejected and sad. He
bewailed his poverty, inveighed against the Turks, to whom he
attributed his ruin, and confessed, with tears, that his tribe was
fast deserting him. While conversing on these subjects, two
sheikhs rode into the encampment, and hearing that the chief
was with us, they fastened their high-bred mares at the door of
our tent, and seated themselves on our carpets. They had been
among the tribes to ascertain the feeling of the Shammar toward Sofuk, of whom they were the devoted adherents. One
was a man of forty, blackened by long exposure to the desert
sun, and of a savage and sanguinary countenance. His companion was a youth, whose features were so delicate and
feminine, and eyes so bright, that he might have been taken
for a woman; a profusion of black hair which fell, plaited
into numerous tresses, on his breast and shoulders, added to
his feminine appearance. An animated discussion took place
as to the desertion of the Nejm, a large branch of the Shammar
tribe. The young man's enthusiasm and devotedness knew no
bounds. He threw himself upon Sofuk, and clinging to his
neck, covered his cheek and beard with kisses. When the chief
had disengaged himself, his follower seized the edge of his garment, and sobbed violently as he held it to his lips. " I entreat
thee, O Sofuk!" he exclaimed, "say but the word; by thine
eyes, by thy beard, by the Prophet, order it, and this sword
shall find the heart of Nejris, whether he escape into the farthest
corner of the desert, or be surrounded by all the warriors of the
tribe." But it was too late, and Sofuk saw that his influence
was fast declining.

I must endeavor to convey to the reader some idea of the
domestic establishment of a great Arab sheikh. Sofuk, at the
time of our visit, was the husband of three wives, who were considered to have special claims to his affection and his constant
protection; for it was one of Sofuk's weaknesses, arising either
from a desire to impress the Arabs with a notion of his great-
ness and power, or from a partiality to the first stage of married
life, to take a new partner nearly every month; and at the end
of that period to divorce her, and marry her to one of his attendants. The happy man thus lived in a continual honeymoon.
Of the three ladies now forming his harem, the chief was
Amsha, a lady celebrated in the song of every Arab of the
desert for her beauty and noble blood. She was the daughter of
Hassan, Sheikh of the Tai, a tribe tracing its origin from the
remotest antiquity, and one of whose chiefs, Hatem, her ances-
tor, is a hero of Eastern romance. Sofuk had carried her away
by force from her father; but had always treated her with
great respect. From her rank and beauty, she had earned the
title of "Queen of the Desert." Her form, traceable through
the thin shirt which she wore like other Arab women, was well
proportioned and graceful. She was tall in stature, and fair in
complexion. Her features were regular, and her eyes large,
dark, and brilliant. She had undoubtedly claims to more than
ordinary beauty; to the Arabs she was perfection, for all the resources of their art had been exhausted to complete what nature
had begun. Her lips were dyed deep blue, her eyebrows were
continued in indigo until they united over the nose, her cheeks
and forehead were spotted with beauty-marks, her eyelashes
darkened by kohl; and on her legs and bosom could be seen the
tattooed ends of flowers and fanciful ornaments, which were
carried in festoons and network over her whole body. Hanging
from each ear, and reaching to her waist, was an enormous
ear-ring of gold, terminating in a tablet of the same material,
carved and ornamented with four turquoises. Her nose was
also adorned with a prodigious gold ring, set with jewels, of

such ample dimensions that it covered her mouth, and had to
be removed when she ate. Ponderous rows of strung beads,
Assyrian cylinders, fragments of coral, agates, and party-col-
ored stones, hung from her neck; silver rings encircled her
wrists and ankles, making a loud jingling as she walked. Over
her blue shirt was thrown, when she issued from her tent, a
coarse striped cloak, and a common black kerchief was bound
loosely round her temples by a rope of twisted camel's hair.

Her ménage combined, if the old song be true, the domestic
and the queenly, and was carried on with a nice appreciation of
economy. The immense sheet of black goat-hair canvas, which
formed the tent, was supported by twelve or fourteen stout
poles, and was completely open on one side. Being entirely
set apart for the women, it had no partitions, like the tent
of the common Arab, who is obliged to reserve a corner for
the reception of his guests. Between the center poles were
placed, upright and close to one another, large goat-hair sacks,
filled with rice, corn, barley, coffee, and other household stuff;
their mouths being, of course, upward. Upon them were
spread carpets and cushions, on which Amsha reclined. Around
her, squatted on the ground, were some fifty handmaidens, tending the wide caldrons, baking bread on the iron plates heated
over the ashes, or shaking between them the skins suspended
from three stakes, and filled with milk to be thus churned into
butter. It is the privilege of the head wife to prepare in her
tent the dinners of the sheikh's guests. Fires, lighted on all
sides, sent forth a cloud of smoke, which hung heavily under
the folds of the tent, and would have long before dimmed any
eyes less bright than those of Amsha. As supplies were asked
for by the women, she lifted the corner of her carpet, untied the
mouths of the sacks, and distributed their contents. Every thing
passed through her hands. To show her authority and rank, she
poured continually upon her attendants a torrent of abuse, and
honored them with epithets, of which I may be excused attempting to give a translation; her vocabulary equaling, if not
exceeding, in richness, that of the highly-educated lady of the

city.* The combination of the domestic and authoritative was thus complete. Her children, three naked little urchins, black with sun and mud, and adorned with long tails of plaited hair hanging from the crown of their heads, rolled in the ashes, or on the grass.

Amsha, as I have observed, shared the affections, though not the tent of Sofuk—for each establishment had a tent of its own —with two other ladies: Atouia, an Arab not much inferior to her rival in personal appearance ; and Ferrah, originally a Yezidi slave, who had no pretensions to beauty. Amsha, how-ever, always maintained her sway, and the others could not sit, without her leave, in her presence. To her alone were confided the keys of the larder—supposing Sofuk to have had either keys or larder—and there was no appeal from her authority on all subjects of domestic economy.

Mrs. Rassam was received with great ceremony by the ladies. To show the rank and luxurious habits of her hus-band, Amsha offered her guest a glass of " eau sucrée," which Mrs. Rassam, who is over-nice, assured me she could not drink, as it was mixed by a particularly dirty negro, in the absence of a spoon, with his fingers, which he sucked continually during the process.

In the evening, Amsha and Ferrah returned Mrs. Rassam's visit; Sofuk having, however, first obtained a distinct promise that they were to be received in a tent from-which gentlemen were to be excluded. They were very inquisitive, and their indiscreet curiosity could with difficulty be satisfied.

Sofuk was the owner of a mare of matchless beauty, called, as if the property of the tribe, the Shammeriyah. Her dam, who died about ten years ago, was the celebrated Kubleh, whose renown extended from the sources of the Khabour to the end of the Arabian promontory, and the day of whose death is an

---

* It may not perhaps be known that the fair inmate of the harem, whom we picture to ourselves conversing with her lover in language too delicate and refined to be expressed by any thing but flowers, uses ordinarily words which would shock the ears of even the most depraved among us.

epoch from which the Arabs of Mesopotamia date events concerning their tribe.   Mohammed-Emin, sheikh of the Jebours,
assured me that he had seen Sofuk ride down the wild ass
of the Sinjar on her back, and the most marvelous stories
are current in the desert of her fleetness and powers of endur-
ance.   Sofuk esteemed her and her daughter above all the
riches of the tribe ; for her he would have forfeited all his
wealth, and even Amsha herself.   Owing to the visit of the
irregular troops, the best horses of the sheikh and his followers
were concealed in a secluded ravine at some distance from the
tents.

Al Hather was about eighteen miles from Sofuk's encampment.   He gave us two well-known horsemen to accompany us
to the ruins.   Their names were Dathan and Abiram.   The
former was a black slave, to whom the sheikh had given his
liberty and a wife—two things, it may be observed, which are
in the desert perfectly consistent.   He was the most faithful
and brave of all the adherents of Sofuk, and the fame of his
exploits had spread through the tribes of Arabia.   As we rode
along, I endeavored to obtain from him some information concerning his people, but he would only speak on one subject.
"Ya Bej,"* said he, " the Arab only thinks of two things, war
and love: war, Ya Bej, every one understands; let us, therefore, talk of love."

As we rode to Al Hather, we passed large bodies of the Shammar moving with their tents, flocks, and families.   On all sides
appeared the huge expanding wings of the ladies' camel-saddle,
looking, as it rose above the horizon, like some stupendous
butterfly skimming slowly over the plain.   Dathan was known
to all.   As the horsemen approached, they dismounted and embraced him, kissing him, as is customary, on both cheeks, and
holding him by the hand until many compliments had been exchanged.

---

* "O my Lord:" he so prefaced every sentence.   The Shammar Arabs
pronounce the word Beg, which the Constantinopolitans soften into Bey,
Bej.

A dark thunder-cloud rose behind the time-worn ruins of Al Hather as we approached them. The sun, still throwing its rays upon the walls, lighted up the yellow stones until they shone like gold.* Mr. Ross and myself, accompanied by an Arab, urged our horses onward, that we might escape the coming storm; but it burst upon us in its fury ere we reached the palace. The lightning played through the vast buildings, the thunder re-echoed through its deserted halls, and the hail compelled us to rein up our horses, and turn our backs to the tempest. It was a fit moment to enter such ruins as these. They rose in solitary grandeur in the midst of a desert, "in mediâ solitudine positæ," as they stood fifteen centuries before, when described by the Roman historian.† On my previous visit, the first view I obtained of Al Hather was perhaps no less striking. We had been wandering for three days in the wilderness without seeing one human habitation. On the fourth morning a thick mist hung over the place. We had given up the search when the vapors were drawn up like a curtain, and we saw the ruins before us. At that time within the walls were the tents of some Shammar Arabs, but now as we crossed the confused heaps of fragments, forming a circle round the city, we saw that the place was tenantless. Flocks on a neighboring rising ground showed, however, that Arabs were not distant.

We pitched our tents in the great court-yard, in front of the palace, and near the entrance to the inner inclosure. During the three days we remained among the ruins I had ample time to take accurate measurements, and to make plans of the various buildings still partly standing within the walls. As Al Hather has already been described by others, and as the information I was able to collect has been placed before the public, ‡ I need

---

* The rich golden tint of the limestone, of which the great monuments of Syria are built, is known to every traveler in that country. The ruins of Al Hather have the same bright color; they look as if they had been steeped in the sunbeams.

† Ammianus Marcellinus, lib. xxv. cap. 8.

‡ See Dr. Ross's Memoir in the Geographical Society's Journal, and Dr. Ainsworth's Travels. A memoir on the place by me, accompanied by plans, &c., was read before the Institute of British Architects.

D

not detain the reader with a detailed account of the place.
Suffice it to mention, that the walls of the city, flanked by
numerous towers, form almost a complete circle, in the center of
which rises the palace, an edifice of great magnificence, solidly
constructed of squared stones, and elaborately sculptured with
figures and ornaments. It dates probably from the reign of one
of the Sassanian Kings of Persia, certainly not prior to the Arsacian dynasty, although the city itself was, I have little doubt,
founded at a very early period, being one of the great caravan
stations, like Palmyra, connecting the cities of Syria with those
on the banks of the Tigris. The singular marks upon the stones,
which appear to be either a builder's sign or to have reference to
some religious observance, are found in most of the buildings of
Sassanian origin in Persia, Babylonia, and Susiana.

With the exception of occasional alarms in the night, caused
by thieves attempting to steal our horses, we were not disturbed
during our visit. The Arabs from the tents in the neighborhood brought us milk, butter, and sheep. We drank the water
of the Thathar, which is, however, rather salt; and our servants and camel-drivers filled during the day many baskets with
truffles.

On our return we crossed the desert, reaching Wadi Ghusub
the first night, and Mosul on the following morning. Dathan
and Abiram, who had both distinguished themselves in recent forays, and had consequently accounts to settle with the
respectable merchants of the place, the balance being very much
against them, could not be prevailed upon to enter the town,
where they were generally known. We had provided ourselves
with two or three dresses of Damascus silk, and we invested
our guides as a mark of satisfaction for their services. Dathan
grinned a melancholy smile as he received his reward. "Ya
Bej," he exclaimed, as he turned his mare toward the desert;
"may God give you peace! Wallah! your camels shall be as
the camels of the Shammar. Be they laden with gold, they shall
pass through our tents, and our people shall not touch them."

A year after our visit the career of Sofuk was brought to its close. I have mentioned that Nejris, his rival, had obtained the support of nearly the whole tribe of Shammar. In a month Sofuk found himself nearly alone. His relations and immediate adherents, among whom were Dathan and Abiram, still pitched their tents with him; but he feared the attacks of his enemies, and retreated for safety into the territory of Beder Khan Bey, to the east of the Tigris, near Jezirah. He then sought the support of Nejib Pashaw of Baghdad, under whose authority the Shammar were supposed to be, and having succeeded in bringing back a considerable part of the tribe, proposed to Nejris, that they should meet at his tents, forget their differences, and share equally the sheikhship of the Shammar. The unfortunate sheikh was induced by Ferhan, the son of Sofuk, to enter the encampment of his rival, where he was perfidiously murdered, in violation of those laws of hospitality which are so much respected by the Arabs. The Shammar were amazed and disgusted by an act of perjury which brought disgrace upon the tribe. They withdrew a second time from Sofuk, and placed themselves under a new leader, a relation of the murdered sheikh. Sofuk again appealed to Nejib Pashaw, justifying his conduct by the dissensions which would have led to constant disorders in Mesopotamia had there still been rival candidates for the sheikhship. Nejib pretended to be satisfied, and agreed to send out a party of irregular troops to assist Sofuk in enforcing his authority throughout the desert.

The commander of the troops sent by Nejib was joyfully received by Sofuk, who immediately marched against the tribe. But he had scarcely left his tent, when he found that he had fallen into a snare such as he had more than once set for others. In a few hours after, his head was in the palace of the Pashaw of Baghdad.

Such was the end of one whose name will long be remembered in the wilds of Arabia; who, from his power and wealth, received the title of " the King of the Desert," and led the great tribe of Shammar from the banks of the Khabour to the ruins of Babylon. The tale of the Arab will turn for many years to come on the exploits and magnificence of Sofuk.

CHAPTER V.

ON my return to Mosul I hastened back to Nimroud. During
my absence little progress had been made, as only two men had
been employed in removing the rubbish from the upper part of
the chamber to which the great human-headed lions formed an
entrance. The lions to the east of them* had, however, been
completely uncovered; that to the right had fallen from its
place, and was sustained by the opposite sculpture. Between
them was a large pavement slab covered with cuneiform characters.

In clearing the earth from this entrance, and from behind the
fallen lion, many ornaments in copper, two small ducks in baked
clay, and tablets of alabaster inscribed on both sides were discovered.† Among the remains in copper were the head of a
ram or bull, ‡ several hands (the fingers closed and slightly
bent), and a few flowers. The hands may have served as a
casing to similar objects in baked clay, frequently found among
the ruins, and having an inscription, containing the names,
titles, and genealogy of the king, graved upon the fingers.
The heads of the ducks are turned and rest upon the back,
which bears an inscription in cuneiform characters. Objects

* Entrance d, plan 8.
† All these objects are now in the British Museum.
‡ This head probably belonged to a throne or seat.

somewhat similar have been found in Egypt. The inscribed
tablets appear to have been built into the walls of sun-dried
bricks, to record the foundation of the edifice. The inscription upon them resembled that on all the slabs in the N. W.
palace.

It is remarkable that while such parts of the great hall as
had been uncovered were paved with baked bricks, and the
smaller entrance to it with a large slab of alabaster, between
the two great lions there were only sun-dried bricks. In the
middle of this entrance, near the fore-part of the lions, were
a few square stones carefully placed. I expected to find under
them small figures in clay, similar to those discovered by M.
Botta in the doorways at Khorsabad; but nothing of the kind
existed.

As several of the principal Christian families of Mosul were
anxious to see the sculptures, whose fame had spread over the
town and province, I was desirous of gratifying their curiosity
before the heat of summer had rendered the plain of Nimroud almost uninhabitable. An opportunity, at the same time,
presented itself of securing the good-will of the Arab tribes
encamped near the ruins, by preparing an entertainment which
might gratify all parties. The Christian ladies, who had never
before been out of sight of the walls of their houses, were eager
to see the wonders of Nimroud, and availed themselves joyfully
of the permission, with difficulty extracted from their husbands,
to leave their homes. The French consul and his wife, and Mr.
and Mrs. Rassam, joined the party. On the day after their
arrival I issued a general invitation to all the Arabs of the district, men and women.

White pavilions, borrowed from the pashaw, had been pitched
near the river, on a broad lawn still carpeted with flowers.
These were for the ladies, and for the reception of the sheikhs.
Black tents were provided for some of the guests, for the attendants, and for the kitchen. A few Arabs encamped around us to
watch the horses, which were picketed on all sides. An open
space was left in the center of the group of tents for dancing,

and for various exhibitions provided for the entertainment of the, company.

Early in the morning came Abd-ur-rahman, mounted on a tall white mare. He had adorned himself with all the finery he possessed. Over his keffiah or head-kerchief, was folded a white turban, edged with long fringes which fell over his shoulders, and almost concealed his handsome features. He wore a long robe of red silk and bright yellow boots, an article of dress much prized by Arabs. He was surrounded by horsemen carrying spears tipped with tufts of ostrich feathers.

As the sheikh of the Abou-Salman approached the tents, I rode out to meet him. A band of Kurdish musicians advanced at the same time to do honor to the Arab chief. As he drew near to the encampment, the horsemen, led by Schloss, his nephew, urged their mares to the utmost of their speed, and engaging in mimic war, filled the air with their wild war-cry. Their shoutings were, however, almost drowned by the Kurds, who belabored their drums, and blew into their pipes with redoubled energy. Sheikh Abd-ur-rahman, having dismounted, seated himself with becoming gravity on the sofa prepared for guests of his rank; while his Arabs picketed their mares, fastening the halters to spears driven into the ground.

The Abou-Salman were followed by the Shemutti and Jehesh, who came with their women and children, on foot, except the sheikhs, who rode on horseback. They also chanted their peculiar war-cry as they advanced. When they reached the tents, the chiefs placed themselves on the divan, while the others seated themselves in a circle on the greensward.

The wife and daughter of Abd-ur-rahman, mounted on mares, and surrounded by their slaves and hand-maidens, next appeared. They dismounted at the entrance of the ladies' tents, where an abundant repast of sweetmeats, halwa, parched peas, and lettuces had been prepared for them.

Fourteen sheep had been roasted and boiled to feast the crowd that had assembled. They were placed on large wooden platters, which, after the men had satisfied themselves, were

passed on to the women. The dinner having been devoured to
the last fragment, dancing succeeded. Some scruples had to
be overcome before the women would join, as there were other
tribes, besides their own, present; and when, at length, by the
exertions of Mr. Hormuzd . Rassam, this difficulty was overcome, they made up different sets. Those who did not take an
active share in the amusements seated themselves on the grass,
and formed a large circle round the dancers. The sheikhs remained on the sofas and divans. The dance of the Arabs, the
Debkè, as it is called, resembles in some respects that of the
Albanians, and those who perform in it are scarcely less vehe-
ment in their gestures, or less extravagant in their excitement,
than those wild mountaineers. They form a circle, holding one
another by the hand, and, moving slowly round at first, go
through a shuffling step with their feet, twisting their bodies
into various attitudes. As the music quickens, their movements
are more active ; they stamp with their feet, yell their war-cry,
and jump as they hurry round the musicians. The motions of
the women are not without grace ; but as they insist on wrap-
ping themselves in their coarse cloaks before they join in the
dance, their forms, which the simple Arab shirt so well displays,
are entirely concealed.

When those who formed the debkè were completely exhausted by their exertions, they joined the lookers-on, and
seated themselves on the ground. Two warriors of different
tribes, furnished with shields and naked cimiters, then entered
the circle, and went through the sword-dance. As the music
quickened the excitement of the performers increased. The
bystanders at length were obliged to interfere and to deprive
the combatants of their weapons, which were replaced by stout
staves. With these they belabored one another unmercifully,
to the great enjoyment of the crowd. On every successful hit,
the tribe, to which the one who dealt it belonged, set up their
war-cry and shouts of applause, while the women deafened us
with the shrill *tahlehl*, a noise made by a combined motion
of the tongue, throat, and hand vibrated rapidly over the

mouth.   When an Arab or a Kurd hears this tahlehl he almost
loses his senses through excitement, and is ready to commit any
desperate act.

A party of Kurdish jesters from the mountains entertained the
Arabs with performances and imitations, more amusing than refined.   They were received with shouts of laughter.   The
dances were kept up by the light of the moon, the greater part
of the night.

On the following morning Abd-ur-rahman invited us to his
tents, and we were entertained with renewed debkès and sword-
dances.   The women, undisturbed by the presence of another
tribe, entered more fully into the amusement, and danced with
greater animation.   The sheikh insisted upon my joining with
him in leading off a dance, in which we were followed by some
five hundred warriors, and Arab women.

The festivities lasted three days, and made the impression I
had anticipated.   They earned me a great reputation and no
small respect, the Arabs long afterward talking of their reception and entertainment.   When there was occasion for their
services, I found the value of the feeling toward me, which a
little show of kindness to these ill-used people had served to produce.

Hafiz Pashaw, who had been appointed to succeed the last
governor, having received a more lucrative post, the province
was sold to Tahyar Pashaw, who made his public entry into
Mosul early in May, followed by a large body of troops, and by
the cadi, mufti, ulema, and principal inhabitants of the town.
The Mosuleeans had not been deceived by the good report of
his benevolence and justice which had preceded him.   He was
a perfect specimen of the Turkish gentleman of the old school,
of whom few are now left in Turkey : venerable in his appearance, bland and polished in his manners, courteous to
Europeans, and well informed on subjects connected with the
literature and history of his country.   I had been furnished
with serviceable letters of introduction to him ; he received me
with every mark of attention, and at once permitted me to con-

tinue the excavations. As a matter of form, he named a ca
wass, to superintend the work on his part. I willingly concurred
in this arrangement, as it saved me from any further inconve-
nience on the score of treasure ; for which, it was still believed,
I was successfully searching. This officer's name was Ibrahim
Agha. He had been many years with Tahyar Pashaw, and was
a kind of favorite. He served me during my residence in Assyria, and on my subsequent journey to Constantinople, with
great fidelity ; and as is very rarely the case with his fraternity
with great honesty.

The support of Tahyar Pashaw relieved me from some of my
difficulties ; for there was no longer cause to fear any interrup.
tion on the part of the authorities. But my means were very
limited, and my own resources did not enable me to carry on
the excavations as I wished. I returned, however, to Nimroud,
and formed a small but effective body of workmen, choosing
those who had already proved themselves equal to the work.

The heats of summer had now commenced, and it was no
longer possible to live under a white tent. The huts were
equally uninhabitable, and still swarmed with vermin. In this
dilemma I ordered a recess to be cut into the bank of the river
where it rose perpendicularly from the water's edge. By
screening the front with reeds and boughs of trees, and cover
ing the whole with similar materials, a small room was formed
I was much troubled, however, with scorpions and other rep-
tiles, which issued from the earth forming the walls of my
apartment ; and later in the summer by the gnats and sandflies,
which hovered on a calm night over the river. Similar rooms
were made for my servants. They were the safest that could
be invented, should the Arabs take to stealing after dark. My
horses were picketed on the edge of the bank above, and the
tents of my workmen were pitched in a semicircle behind
them.

The change to summer had been as rapid as that which
ushered in the spring. The verdure of the plain had perished
almost in a day. Hot winds, coming from the desert, had

D*

burnt up and carried away the shrubs; flights of locusts, darkening the air, had destroyed the few patches of cultivation, and had completed the havoc commenced by the heat of the sun. The Abou-Salman Arabs, having struck their black tents, were now living in *ozailis*, or sheds constructed of reeds and grass, along the banks of the river. The Shemutti and Jehesh had returned to their villages, and the plain presented the same naked and desolate aspect that it wore in the month of November. The heat, however, was now almost intolerable. Violent whirlwinds occasionally swept over the face of the country. They could be seen as they advanced from the desert, carrying along with them clouds of sand and dust. Almost utter darkness prevailed during their passage, which lasted generally about an hour, and nothing could resist their fury. On returning home one afternoon after a tempest of this kind, I found no traces of my dwellings; they had been completely carried away. Ponderous wooden frame-works had been borne over the bank, and hurled some hundred yards distant; the tents had disappeared, and my furniture was scattered over the plain. When on the mound, my only secure place of refuge was beneath the fallen lion, where I could defy the fury of the whirlwind: the Arabs ceased from their work, and crouched in the trenches, almost suffocated and blinded by the dense cloud of fine dust and sand which nothing could exclude.*

Although the number of my workmen was small, the excavations were carried on as actively as possible. The two human-headed lions, at the small entrance to the great hall, already described, led into another chamber, or to sculptured walls, forming an outward facing to the build-

---

* Storms of this nature are frequent during the early part of summer throughout Mesopotamia, Babylonia, and Susiana. It is difficult to convey an idea of their violence. They appear suddenly, and without any previous sign, and seldom last above an hour. It was during one of them that "the Tigris" steamer, under the command of Colonel Chesney, was wrecked in the Euphrates; and so darkened was the atmosphere that, although the vessel was within a short distance of the bank of the river, several persons who were in her are supposed to have lost their lives from not knowing in what direction to swim.

ing.* The slabs to the right and left, had fallen from their original position, and, with the exception of one, were broken. I
had some difficulty in raising the pieces from the ground. As
the face of the slabs was downward, the sculpture had been well
preserved.

To the right was represented the king holding a bow in
one hand and two arrows in the other. He was followed by
his attendant eunuch, who bore a second 'bow and a quiver
for his use, and a mace, with a head in the form of a rosette,
which may have been one of the wooden clubs, topped with
iron, mentioned by Herodotus as a weapon used by the Assyrians, or one of those staffs adorned with an apple, a rose,
a lily, or an eagle, described by the same historian as carried
by the Babylonians.† Standing before him were his vizier and
an eunuch, their hands crossed before them, a posture still
assumed in the East as one of respect and submission by
inferiors in the presence of persons of rank. It is interesting thus to trace the observance of the same customs in the
same countries, after the lapse of so many centuries. In the bas-
relief representing a similar subject discovered in the S. W.
ruins, the vizier raises his right hand before the king—an attitude, apparently denoting an oath or homage, in which dependents are seen on the later monuments of the Achæmenian and
Sassanian dynasties. Dejoces, who was the successor of the
Assyrian monarchs, permitted no one to see him, except certain privileged individuals ; and the person of the Persian king,
as we learn from the story of Esther, was considered so sacred,
that even the queen, who ventured before him without being
bidden, was punished with death, "except the king might
hold out the golden scepter that she might live."‡ It might
be expected, therefore, that in the Assyrian sculptures those
who stand in the royal presence would be portrayed in the
humblest posture of submission. These figures were about

* Wall D, plan 3.
† Herod. lib. vii. c. 68, and lib. i. c. 195.
‡ Herod. lib. i. c. 99; Esther iv. 11.

G 2

eight feet high ; the relief very low, and the ornaments rich
and elaborate.   The bracelets, armlets, and weapons were all

adorned with the heads of horses,
bulls, and rams, the style of which
would not have been unworthy of
the exquisite chasing of the middle
ages ; color still remained on the
hair, beard, and sandals.

The adjoining slab, forming a wall
at right angles with these bas-reliefs,
was of enormous dimensions, but had
been broken in two : the upper part
had fallen, the lower was still standing in its place.   It was only after

Handles of three Daggers carried in the Girdle.   (N. W.
Palace, Nimroud.)

many ineffectual attempts that I
succeeded in raising the fallen half
sufficiently to see the sculpture upon it.   It was a winged
giant about sixteen and a half feet high in low relief, carrying the fir-cone and square utensil ; in other respects similar
to those already described, except that it had four wings, two
rising from each shoulder, and almost completely encircling the
figure.

On the opposite side of the entrance, were also a vizier and
his attendant ; but they were followed by figures, differing
altogether in dress from those previously discovered, and apparently resembling people of another race ; some carrying
presents or offerings, consisting of armlets, bracelets, and ear-
rings on trays ; others elevating their clenched hands, probably
in token of submission.   They were evidently captives and
tribute-bearers from a conquered nation ushered into the presence of the monarch by his minister.   Among the objects of
tribute were two monkeys, held by ropes ; one raising itself
on its hind legs, the other sitting on the shoulders of its
keeper.*   The costume of these figures consisted of high boots

* This bas-relief is in the British Museum.

turned up at the toes, resembling those still in use in Turkey
and Persia; conical caps, apparently formed by bands, or folds
of felt or linen; and loose shirts descending to the ankles, ornamented down the center and at the bottom with fringes. The
figure with the monkey was clothed in a short tunic, scarcely
reaching to the calf of the leg, and his hair was simply bound up
by a fillet. There were traces of black paint on the face, but it
is probable that it had been washed down from the hair, as no
remains of color have been found on the face of any other figure,
although it is possible that the Assyrians, like the Egyptians,
may have denoted races, sexes, and the orders of the priesthood
by various tints.

To the south of the colossal lions forming the principal entrance* to the great hall, the wall was continued by an eagle-
headed figure resembling that on the opposite side. Adjoining
it was a corner-stone bearing the sacred tree—beyond, the slabs
ceased altogether; but I soon found that they had only fallen
from their places, and that although broken, the sculptures upon
them representing battles, sieges, and other historical subjects,
were, as far as it could be ascertained by the examination of
one or two, in admirable preservation. The wall of sun-dried
bricks, against which they had stood, was still distinctly visible
to the height of twelve or fourteen feet. This wall served as my
guide in digging onward, to the distance of about one hundred
feet.

The first sculpture discovered still standing in its original
position, was a winged human-headed bull of yellow limestone.
On the previous day we had found the detached human head
now in the British Museum. The bull, to which it belonged,
and which had formed one side of an entrance, had been broken
into several pieces by falling against the opposite sculpture. I
lifted the body with difficulty; and discovered under it sixteen
copper lions, of admirable execution, forming a regular series,
diminishing in size from the largest, which was above one foot

---

* Entrance *a*, chamber B, plan 3.

in length, to the smallest, which scarcely exceeded an inch. A ring attached to the back of each, gave them the appearance of weights. In the same place were the fragments of an earthen vase, on which were represented two figures, with the wings and claws of a bird, the breasts of a woman, and the tail of a scorpion.*

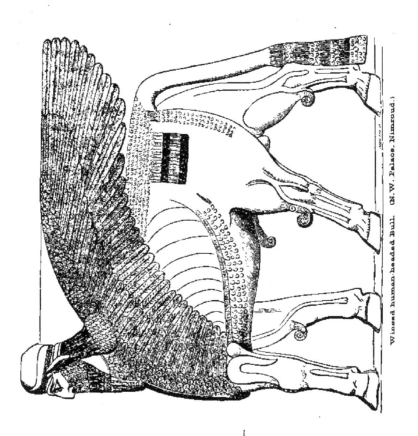

Winged human-headed Bull. (N.W. Palace, Nimroud.)

* All these remains are now in the British Museum.

Beyond the winged bulls the slabs were still upright and entire. On the first was sculptured a winged human figure carrying a branch with five flowers in the raised right hand, and the usual square vessel in the left. Around his temples was a fillet adorned with three rosettes. On each of the four following slabs were two bas-reliefs, divided by the usual inscription. The upper, on the first slab, represented a castle apparently built on an island in a river. One tower was defended by an armed man, on two others were females. Three warriors, probably escaping from the enemy, were swimming across the stream; two of them supporting themselves on inflated skins, in the mode practiced to this day by the Arabs inhabiting the banks of the rivers of Assyria and Mesopotamia; except that, in the bas-relief, the swimmers were

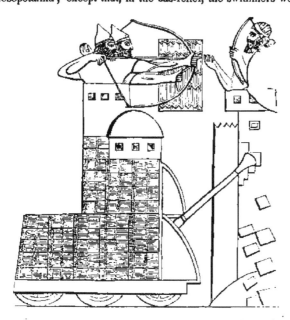

Battering Ram with movable Tower containing Warriors. (N. W. Palace, Nimroud)

pictured as retaining in their mouths the aperture through which the skin is filled with air. The third, pierced by the arrows of two warriors kneeling on the shore, was struggling without any support against the current. Three rudely designed trees completed the background.

The upper compartment of the next slab represented the siege of a city, in which the king, followed by his shield-bearer and attendants, was seen discharging an arrow against the enemy. A battering-ram of wicker-work, on wheels, and attached to a movable tower, occupied by two warriors, had been drawn up to the walls, from which several stones had already been dislodged. The besieged, apparently anticipating the fall of their city, were asking for quarter.

Beneath the two bas-reliefs just described was one subject. The king, followed by his eunuchs and by his chariot, from which he had dismounted, was receiving a line of prisoners brought before him by his vizier. Some bore objects of spoil or tribute, such as vases, shawls, and elephants' tusks; others were bound together by ropes, and were driven forward by Assyrian warriors with drawn swords.

The upper compartments of the third and fourth slabs contained hunting scenes. The king was represented as discharging an arrow against a lion springing upon his chariot, while a second, already pierced by many shafts, had fallen beneath the feet of the horses. Two warriors with drawn swords appeared to be running to the assistance of the monarch. This bas-relief, from the knowledge of art displayed in the treatment and composition, the correct and effective delineation of the men and animals, and the spirit of the grouping, is one of the finest specimens yet discovered of Assyrian sculpture. The rage of the fallen animal, who is struggling to extricate the arrow from his neck, is admirably portrayed; while the majesty and power conveyed in the form of the springing lion is worthy of a very high order of art. In the other bas-relief the king in his chariot was seen piercing a wild bull with a short sword; a second bull wounded by arrows being beneath the horses. A horseman following the chariot led a second horse, apparently for the use of the king. The animal represented in this sculpture was probably a wild ox, once inhabiting the Assyrian plains, and long since extinct, as neither tradition nor history records its existence in this part of Asia. It may have roved through Assyria at a very early period, and may have been exterminated when an increasing population covered the face of the country with cities and villages.* It is distinguished from the domestic ox by a number of small marks covering the body, and apparently intended to denote long and shaggy hair, and is represented with one horn, as horses are frequently with only two legs or one ear, because the Assyrian sculptor did not attempt to give both in a side view of the animal. Beneath these bas-reliefs was represented the king on his return from the chase, pouring a libation or drinking out of the sacred cup above the fallen lion and bull. His attendants stood around him, and musicians celebrated, on stringed instruments, his victories over the wild beasts of the desert.†

The frequent representations of hunting scenes, in which the king is the principal actor, is a proof of the high estimation in which the chase was held by the primitive inhabitants of Assyria. A conqueror and the founder of an empire was, at the same time, a great hunter. His courage, wisdom, and dexterity were as much shown in encounters with wild animals as in martial exploits ; he rendered equal services to his subjects, whether he cleared the country of beasts of prey, or repulsed an enemy. The scriptural Nimrod, who laid the foundation of the Assyrian

* I have found no representation of this animal in any sculptures of a later date than those of the N. W. palace of Nimroud, the earliest Assyrian edifice with which we are acquainted. Had it inhabited the plains of Mesopotamia in the time of Xenophon, he would probably have described it when speaking of the wild animals of that province. The wild ox is mentioned in Deut. xiv. 5, among the animals whose flesh may be eaten by the Jews. The " wild bull in a net" is also alluded to in Isaiah li. 20; · The Hebrew word is rendered " wild bull" in the Targums, and " oryx" in the Vulgate ; some, however, believe the animal meant to be a kind of antelope. (Gesenius, Lex. in voce.)

† All the bas-reliefs here described are now in the British Museum.

monarchy was " a mighty hunter before the Lord;" and the
Ninus of history and tradition, the builder of Nineveh, and the
greatest of the Assyrian kings, was as renowned for his encounters with the lion and the leopard, as for his triumphs over
warlike nations.   The Babylonians, as well as the Assyrians,
ornamented the walls of their temples and palaces with pictures
and sculptures representing the chase; and similar subjects were
introduced even in the embroidery of garments.   The Assyrians
were probably also the inventors of the parks, or paradises,
which were afterward maintained at so vast a cost by the
Persian kings of the Achæmenian and Sassanian dynasties.   In
these spacious preserves wild animals of various kinds were con
tinually kept for the diversion of the king and of those who
were privileged to join with him in the chase.   They contained lions, tigers, wild boars, antelopes, and many varieties
of birds.   The sculptures just described may represent the
king hunting in one of those royal paradises.

The Assyrian, like the Persian youths, were probably trained
to the chase at an early age.   Xenophon gives an interesting
account of the hunting expeditions of the Persians in the time
of Cyrus.   The king was accompanied by half his guard,
each man being armed as if he were going to battle, with a
bow, quiver, sword, shield, and two javelins,—hunting being,
as Xenophon declares, the truest method of practicing all such
things as relate to war.*   Such it would appear from the bas-
reliefs was also the practice among the Assyrians, for the king
is represented as accompanied by warriors fully equipped for
the fight.

On the flooring, below the sculptures, were discovered
remains of painted plaster still adhering to the sun-dried bricks,
which had formed the upper part of the wall above the sculptured slabs.   The colors, particularly the blues and reds, were as
brilliant and vivid when the earth was removed from them, as
they could have originally been; but on exposure to the air

* Cyrop. lib. i. c. 2.

they faded rapidly. The designs were elegant and elaborate. It was found almost impossible to preserve any portion of these ornaments, the earth crumbling to pieces when an attempt was made to raise them.

About this time I received from Sir Stratford Canning, the vizirial letter authorizing the continuation of the excavations and the removal of such objects as might be discovered. I was sleeping in the tent of Sheikh Abd-ur-rahman, who had invited me to hunt gazelles with him before dawn on the following morning, when an Arab awoke me. He was the bearer of letters from Mosul; and I read by the light of a small camel-dung fire, the document which secured to the British nation the records of Nineveh, and a collection of the earliest monuments of Assyrian art.

The vizirial order was as comprehensive as could be desired; and having been granted on the departure of the British embassador, was the highest testimony the Turkish government could give of their respect for the character of Sir Stratford Canning, and of their appreciation of the eminent services he had rendered them.

One of the difficulties, and not one of the least which had to be encountered, was now completely removed. Still, however, pecuniary resources were wanting, and in the absence of the necessary means, extensive excavations could not be carried on. I hastened, nevertheless, to communicate the letter of the Grand Vizier to the pashaw, and to make arrangements for pursuing the researches as effectually as possible.

Not having yet examined the great mound of Kouyunjik, believed by travelers to mark the true site of Nineveh, I determined to open trenches in it. I had not previously done so, as from the vicinity of the ruins to Mosul, the inhabitants of the town would have been able to watch my movements, and to cause me continual interruptions before the sanction of the authorities could be obtained to my proceedings. A small party of workmen having been organized, excavations were commenced on the southern face, where the mound was highest;

as sculptures, if any still existed, would probably be found in the best state of preservation under the largest accumulation of rubbish. My researches, however, were not attended with much success. A few fragments of sculpture and inscriptions were discovered, which enabled me to assert with some confidence that the remains were those of a building cotemporary or nearly so, with Khorsabad, and consequently of a more recent epoch than the most ancient palace of Nimroud. All the bricks dug out bore the name of the same king, but I could not find any traces of his geneaology. After excavating for about a month, I discontinued my researches until a better opportunity might offer.

On my return to Nimroud, about thirty men, chiefly Arabs, were employed to dig in the N. W. palace.

On excavating beyond the five sculptured slabs last described, a corner-stone with the sacred tree was discovered, which formed the eastern end of a great hall, 154 feet in length, and only 33 feet in breadth. These proportions, the length so far exceeding the width, are peculiar to Assyrian interior architecture, and may probably be attributed to the difficulty experienced in roofing over a larger span. Adjoining this corner-stone was a winged figure; beyond it a slab 14 feet in length cut into a recess, in which were four figures. Two kings stood face to face, their right hands raised in prayer or adoration. Between them was the oft-recurring sacred tree, above which hovered that emblem of the supreme deity —a human figure, with the wings and tail of a bird, inclosed in a circle,—which was adopted by the Persians, and is the type of Ormuzd, or the great God of the Zoroastian system, on the monuments of Persepolis. In the right hand of this figure was a ring. The kings, who were either different monarchs, or were but a double representation of the same person, appeared to be attired for the performance of some religious ceremony. Their waists were encircled by knotted zones, the ends of which fell almost to their feet. Around their necks were suspended certain mystic emblems, and in their hands they carried a kind of mace, terminating in a disk or globe. Each king was followed by a winged figure with the fir-cone and basket.*

To the left of this slab was a winged figure similar to that on the right, and a second corner-stone, with the sacred tree, completed the eastern end of the hall. Part of both the winged figures adjoining the center slab, as well as the lower part of that slab, which advanced beyond the sculpture, had been purposely destroyed, and still bore the marks of the chisel.

Subsequent excavations disclosed in front of the large bas-relief of the two kings, a slab of alabaster, 10 feet by 8, and about 2 feet thick, cut into steps or gradines on the side facing the grand entrance, and covered on both sides with inscriptions. On raising it, a process of considerable difficulty from its great weight and size, I found beneath a few pieces of gold-leaf and some fragments of bone, which crumbled into dust as soon as exposed to the air. In a corner of the same part of the chamber, were two square stones, slightly hollowed in the center, and round the large slab was a conduit in alabaster, apparently intended to carry off some fluid, perhaps the blood of the sacrifice.

On the first slab of the northern wall, adjoining the corner-stone, was a human figure with four wings ; the right hand raised, and the left holding a mace. Beyond were two lions,† corresponding with those forming the other entrance on this side of the hall, from which, however, they differed somewhat in form, the hands being joined in front instead of bearing an animal. They, also, led to an outer wall, on which was sculptured a procession of figures, similarly clothed to those already described, bearing tribute or spoil. The corner was likewise formed by a colossal winged figure, which was connected with the corresponding sculpture by four or more winged bulls and lions, of enormous proportions. Two of these gigantic sculptures had fallen on their faces and were broken in several

---

* This bas-relief is in the British Museum.
† Entrance c, chamber B, plan 3.

pieces. This assemblage of winged human-headed lions and bulls appears to have formed the grand entrance into the palace, and must have been truly magnificent.

As the edge of a ravine had now been reached, the workmen were directed to return to the yellow bulls, which formed the entrance into a further chamber,* paneled with bas-reliefs rep-

resenting eagle-headed deities facing one another, and separated by the sacred tree, except on the east side, where a king stood between the same mythic figures. Around the monarch's neck were suspended the five sacred emblems.

Sacred Emblems suspended round the Neck of the King. (N.W. Palace, Nimroud.)

They consist of the sun, a star, a half-moon, a bident, and a horned cap similar to that worn by the human-headed bulls.†

An entrance, formed by four slabs, two with bas-reliefs of human figures carrying a mystic flower,‡ led me into a new chamber, remarkable for the elaborate and careful finish of its sculptures. I uncovered the northern wall, and the eastern as far as a second entrance.§

The northern end of the chamber was occupied by one group, the principal figure in which was that of the king, seated on a throne or stool, holding in his right hand a cup, and resting his left upon his knee. In front of the monarch stood an eunuch, raising with one hand a fan, and holding in the other the cover or stand of the cup from which the king was drinking or pouring a libation. Over the shoulder of this attendant was thrown an embroidered towel, resembling that still presented by servants in the East to one who has drunk, or performed his ablutions. He was followed by a winged figure with the fir-cone and basket. Behind the king

* Ch. F, plan 3.
† It is worthy of remark that, with the exception of the horned cap, these symbols are found on the sacred monuments of India, which, accompanied as they are by the sacred bull, bear a striking resemblance to the Assyrian.
‡ Entrance a, ch, F. pl. 3.   § Entrance e, ch. G.

were two eunuchs bearing his arms, and a second winged figure similar to that in front of the throne. The whole group probably represented the celebration, after a great victory, of some

Ornament on the Dress of Eunuchs.

religious ceremony, in which the presiding divinities of Assyria, or priests assuming their form, ministered to the king. This very fine bas-relief was remarkable for the extreme delicacy and beauty of the details. The robes of the monarch

Ornament on the Robe of King.

together with those of his attendants, were covered with the most elaborate designs. In the center of his breast were represented two kings in act of adoration before the emblem of the supreme God. Around were engraved figures of winged deities, and the king performing different religious ceremonies. Borders of similar groups, including various forms of animals

Ornament on the
robe of winged
figure.

and monsters, winged horses, gryphons and sphinxes, adorned the front, and were carried round the skirts of the dress. The embroideries on the garments of the priests and eunuchs were of the same nature and equally beautiful. They consisted chiefly of men struggling with winged monsters, ostriches, standing before the sacred tree, and numerous elegant devices, in which the seven-petaled flower was always the most conspicuous ornament.

These elaborate designs were probably intended to represent embroideries on silk, linen, or woolen stuffs, in the manufacture and dyeing of which the Assyrians had obtained so great a perfection that their garments were still a proverb many centuries after the fall of the empire. Among those who traded "in blue clothes and embroidered work" with Tyre were the merchants of Ashur, or Assyria; and Achan confessed to Joshua that "when he saw among the spoils *a goodly Babylonish garment* and two hundred shekels of silver, and a wedge of gold of fifty shekels weight," he coveted and took them.[*] Robes such as are seen in these sculptures may have been "the dyed attire and embroidered work" so frequently mentioned in the Bible as the garments of princes and the most costly gifts of kings. The ornaments and figures upon them may either have been dyed, wove in the loom, or embroidered with the needle like "the prey of divers colors of needlework, of divers colors of needlework on both sides."[†]

---

[*] Ezekiel xxvii. 24; Joshua vii. 21.
[†] Judges v. 30. We learn from Pliny (lib. viii. c. 48), that gold threads were introduced into the Assyrian woof of many hues.

In the bas-relief I am describing, the dress of the king consisted of a long flowing garment, edged with fringes and tassels descending to his ankles, and confined at the waist by a girdle.

Over this robe a second, similarly ornamented, and open in front, appears to have been thrown.   From his shoulders fell a cape, or hood, also adorned with tassels, and to it were attached two long ribbons or lappets.   He wore the conical miter, or tiara, which distinguishes the monarch in Assyrian bas-reliefs, and appears to have been reserved for him alone.   It is impossible to determine from the sculptures the nature of the material of which it was made, but it

Head-Dress of the King. (N.W. Palace, Nimroud.)

may be conjectured that it consisted of bands or folds of linen or silk.   It was adorned with flowers and other ornaments, and was surmounted by a small cone.*   Around the neck of the king was a necklace.   He wore ear-rings, and his arms, which were bare from a little above the elbow, were encircled by armlets and bracelets remarkable for the beauty of their forms.   The clasps were formed by the heads of animals, and the center by stars and rosettes, probably inlaid with precious stones.†   His beard was elaborately plaited, and his hair, which fell in ringlets on his shoulders, may have been partly artificial like that of the Persian monarchs, who, according to Xenophon,‡ wore a wig. Both the hair and beard were probably dyed, and the eyes black-

---

* Such was the head-dress of the Persian monarchs, called the "cidaris," which appears to have resembled the Phrygian bonnet, or the French cap of liberty.   That worn by Darius was of blue and white, or purple and white.   (Quint. Curt. lib. iii. ch. iii. and lib. vi. ch. 6.)

† The dress of the Assyrian king appears to have been similar to that of his successors in the empire of the East.   Xenophon describes Astyages as clothed in a purple coat and rich habit, with necklaces round his neck and bracelets on his arms.   (Cyrop. lib. i. ch. 8.)   Darius wore a tunic of white and purple, embroidered robes, golden girdle, and sword adorned with jewels.   (Quint. Curt. lib. iii. ch. 3.)

‡ Cyrop. lib. i. c. 3.

ened with some preparation, resembling the *kohl* or *surma* still
used by persons of both sexes in the East. His sandals covered

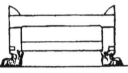

The King's Sandal. (N.W. Palace,
Nimroud.)

The King's Footstool.
(N.W. Palace, Nimroud.)

the back part of the foot, leaving the fore part exposed, and were
fastened by bands crossing the instep and passing round the great
toe.   The soles appear to have been of wood or thick leather.

The eunuchs and winged figures wore robes and ornaments
similar in most respects to those of the king. The eunuchs, however, had no other head-dress than the carefully curled ringlets.

The arms, carried by the eunuchs for their own use, as well
as for that of the king, were richly ornamented with the heads
of lions: the beaks of eagles held the strings of their bows, and
their quivers were covered with groups of human figures
and animals.   The king's throne and his footstool were in

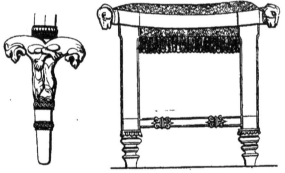

End of a Sword Sheath.
(N.W. Palace, Nimroud.)

The King's Throne.
(N.W. Palace, Nimroud.)

keeping with the rest of the details.   The throne or rather
stool, for it had neither back nor arms, was tastefully carved, and

adorned with the heads of rams; the legs of the footstool terminated in lions' paws. They may have been of wood or copper, inlaid with ivory and other precious materials, or of solid gold, like the tables and couches in the temple of Belus at Babylon.

The figures in these fine bas-reliefs were about eight feet high. They were in an extraordinary state of preservation, the most delicate chasings being still distinct, and the outline retaining all its original sharpness.* On the other slabs forming the walls of this chamber were alternate groups, representing the king holding his bow in one hand and two arrows in the other, standing between winged figures; and the king also erect, raising the sacred cup, and attended by eunuchs. The details in these sculptures were similar in character to those already described. They furnished, however, many new and interesting groups; such as the combats of winged figures with monsters of various forms, scenes of the chase, goats and bulls kneeling before the sacred tree, and the king performing certain religious ceremonies.

The Arabs marveled at these strange figures. As each head was uncovered they showed their amazement by extravagant gestures, or exclamations of surprise. If it were a bearded man, they concluded at once that it was an idol or a Jin, and   x cursed, or spat upon it. If an eunuch, they declared that it was the likeness of a beautiful female, and kissed or patted the cheek. They soon felt as much interest as I did in the discoveries, and worked with renewed ardor when their curiosity was excited by the appearance of a fresh sculpture. On such occasions stripping themselves almost naked, throwing the kerchief from their heads, and letting their matted hair stream in the wind, they would rush like madmen into the trenches to carry off the baskets of earth, shouting, at the same time, the war-cry of the tribe.

Passing through an entrance formed by the usual winged figures, I reached a chamber paneled by slabs, on which was

---

* They are now in the British Museum; but, unfortunately, owing to the extreme neglect shown in their transport to this country, they have been much injured.

sculptured the king, raising a richly ornamented cup and standing between two divinities wearing fillets adorned with rosettes
round their temples.*

I quitted this chamber, after uncovering the upper part of
four or five bas-reliefs; and returning to the western wall
of that previously explored, discovered another pair of human-
headed lions, similar to, but smaller than, those forming the
grand entrance to the great hall. So perfect was the preservation of even the smallest details, that had not the slabs been
slightly cracked, I could have fancied they had issued but the
day before from the hand of the sculptor. The accumulation
of earth and rubbish above this part of the ruins was very considerable, and it is not improbable that it was owing to this the
sculptures had been so completely guarded from injury.

I was now anxious to send to Baghdad, or Busrah, for transport to Bombay, such sculptures as I could move with the
means at my disposal. Major Rawlinson had obligingly proposed that, for this purpose, the small steamer navigating the
lower part of the Tigris should be sent up to Nimroud, and I
expected the most valuable assistance, both in removing the
slabs and in forming plans for future excavations, from her
able commander, Lieutenant Jones. The Euphrates, one of
the two vessels originally constructed for the navigation of
the rivers of Mesopotamia, had some years before succeeded in
reaching the tomb of Sultan Abd-Allah, a few miles below
Nimroud. Impediments, not more serious than those she had
already surmounted, occurring in this part of the bed of the
stream, she returned to Baghdad. A vessel even of her size,
and with engines of the same power, could have reached, I have
little doubt, the bund or dam of the Awai, which would probably have been a barrier to a further ascent of the Tigris. It
was found, however, that the machinery of the Nitocris was
either too much out of repair, or not sufficiently powerful to
impel the vessel over the rapids, which occur in the river.

* Ch. H, plan 8.

After ascending some miles above Tekrit the attempt was given up, and she returned to her station.

Without proper materials it was impossible to move the colossal lions, or even any entire slab. The ropes of the country were so ill-made that they could not support any considerable weight. I determined, therefore, to saw the slabs containing double bas-reliefs into two pieces, and to lighten them as much as possible by cutting from the back. The inscriptions being a mere repetition of the same formula, I did not consider it necessary to preserve them, as they added to the weight. With the help of levers of wood, and by digging away the wall of sun-dried bricks, I was able to move the sculptures into the center of the trenches, where they were reduced to the requisite size. They were then packed and transported from the mound upon rude buffalo-carts belonging to the pashaw, to the river, where they were placed upon a raft, constructed of inflated skins and beams of poplar wood. They were floated down the Tigris as far as Baghdad, were there transferred to boats of the country, and reached Busrah in the month of August. The sculptures sent home on this occasion formed the first collection exhibited to the public in the British Museum.

While I was moving these bas-reliefs, Tahyar Pashaw visited me. He was accompanied, for his better security, by a large body of regular and irregular troops, and three guns. His Diwan Effendesi, seal-bearer, and all the dignitaries of his household, were also with him. I entertained this large company for two days. The pashaw's tents were pitched on an island in the river near my shed. He visited the ruins, and expressed no less wonder at the sculptures than the Arabs; nor were his conjectures as to their origin and the nature of the subjects represented much more rational than those of the sons of the desert. The colossal human-headed lions terrified, as well as amazed, his Osmanli followers. " La Illahi il Allah" (there is no God but God), was echoed from all sides. " These are the idols of the infidels," said one, more knowing than the rest. "I saw many such when I was in Italia with Reshid Pashaw, the embassador. Wallah! they have them in all the churches, and the papas (priests) kneel and burn candles before them." "No, my lamb," exclaimed a more aged and experienced Turk. "I have seen the images of the infidels in the churches of Beyoglu; they are dressed in many colors; and although some of them have wings, none have a dog's body and a tail; these are the works of the Jin, whom the holy Solomon, peace be upon him! reduced to obedience and imprisoned under his seal." "I have seen something like them in your apothecaries' and barbers' shops," said I, alluding to the well-known figure, half woman and half lion, which is met with so frequently in the bazars of Constantinople. "Istafer Allah" (God forbid), piously ejaculated the pashaw; "that is a sacred emblem of which true believers speak with reverence, and not the handywork of infidels." "There is no infidel living," exclaimed the engineer, who was looked up to as an authority on these subjects, "either in Frangistan or in Yenghi Dunia (America), who could make any thing like that; they are the work of the Majus (Magi), and are to be sent to England to form a gateway to the palace of the queen." "May God curse all infidels and their works!" observed the cadi's deputy, who accompanied the pashaw; "what comes from their hands is of Satan: it has pleased the Almighty to let them be more powerful and ingenious than the true believers in this world, that their punishment and the reward of the faithful may be greater in the next."

The heat had now become so intense that my health began to suffer from continual exposure to the sun, and from the labor entailed upon me by the excavations. In the trenches, where I daily passed many hours, the thermometer generally ranged from 112° to 115° in the shade, and on one or two occasions even reached 117°. Hot winds swept like blasts from a furnace over the desert during the day, and drove away sleep by night. I resolved, therefore, to take refuge for a week in the sardaubs or cellars of Mosul; and, in order not to lose time, to try further excavations in the Mound of Kouyunjik.

Leaving a superintendent, and a few guards to watch over the uncovered sculptures, I rode to the town.

The houses of Baghdad and Mosul are provided with under- ground apartments, in which the inhabitants pass the day during the summer months.   They are generally ill-lighted, and the air is close and frequently unwholesome ; still they offer a welcome retreat during the hot weather, when it is impossible to sit in a room.   At sunset the people emerge from these subterraneous chambers and congregate on the roofs, where they spread their carpets, eat their evening meal, and pass the night.

After many fruitless inquiries after the bas-relief, described by Rich* as having been discovered in one of the mounds forming the large quadrangle in which are included Nebbi Yunus and Kouyunjik, I met with an aged stone-cutter, who declared that he had not only been present when the sculpture was found, but that he had been employed to break it up. He pointed out the spot, in the northern line of ruins, and I at once commenced excavations.   The workmen were not long in coming upon fragments of sculptured alabaster, and after two or three days' labor, an entrance was discovered, formed by two winged figures, which had been purposely destroyed.   The legs and the lower part of the tunic were alone preserved.   The pro- portions were colossal, and the relief higher than that of any sculpture hitherto discovered in Assyria.   This entrance led into a chamber, the lower part of the walls of which was paneled with limestone slabs about five feet high and three broad.   There were marks of the chisel upon them all as if something had been effaced ; but from their size it appeared doubtful whether figures had ever been sculptured upon them. The upper part of the walls was of sun-dried bricks.   In the rub- bish filling up the chamber were discovered numerous baked bricks, bearing the name of the Kouyunjik king.   The pave- ment was of limestone.   After tracing the walls of one chamber, I renounced a further examination of the ruin, as no traces of

* Residence in Kurdistan and Nineveh, vol. ii. p. 89.

sculpture were to be found, and the accumulation of rubbish was very considerable.

This mound appears to cover either an entrance to the city, or a small temple or tower forming part of the walls. From its height, it would seem that the building had two or more stories.

The comparative rest obtained in Mosul so far restored my strength, that I returned to Nimroud in the middle of August, and again attempted to renew the excavations. I uncovered the top of many of the slabs in the chamber last discovered, and found two chambers leading out of it.* The sculptures were similar to those already described; the king standing between two winged figures, and hold in one hand a cup, and in the other a bow. The only new feature was a recess cut out of the upper part of one of the slabs. I am at a loss to account for its use; from its position it might have been taken for a window, opening into the adjoining room, in which, however, there was no corresponding aperture. It may have been used as a place of deposit for sacred vessels and instruments, or as an altar for sacrifice, as a large square stone slightly hollowed in the center, probably to contain a fluid, was generally found in front of similar slabs.

The walls of the small chamber to the west were unsculptured. The pavement was formed by inscribed slabs of alabaster. The further entrance† led me into a long narrow room surrounded by double bas-reliefs separated by the usual inscription; the upper (similar on all the slabs) representing two winged human figures, kneeling before the mystic tree; the lower eagle-headed figures facing each other in pairs, and separated by the same symbol.

The state of my health again compelled me to renounce, for the time, my labors at Nimroud. As I required a cooler climate, I determined to visit the Tiyari mountains, inhabited by the Chaldean Christians, and to return to Mosul in September, when the violence of the heat had abated.

---

* Chambers I and R, plan 8.
† Entrance b, Ch. H.

CHAPTER VI.

DEPARTURE FOR THE TIYARI MOUNTAINS.—KHORSABAD.—SHEIKH ADI.—
A KURDISH ENCAMPMENT. — A CHALDEAN VILLAGE. — AMADIYAH. — A
TURKISH GOVERNOR.—ALBANIAN IRREGULARS.—AN ALBANIAN CHIEF.—
THE VALLEY OF BERWARI.—CHALDEAN VILLAGES.—A KURDISH BEY.—
ASHEETHA.

THE preparations for my journey were completed by the 28th
August, and on that day I started from Mosul.   My party consisted of Mr. Hormuzd Rassam, Ibrahim Agha, two Albanian
irregulars, who were to accompany me as far as Amadiyah,
a servant, a groom, and one Ionan, or Ionunco, as he was
familiarly called, a half-witted Nestorian, whose drunken frolics
were reserved for the entertainment of the patriarch, and who
was enlisted into our caravan for the amusement of the company.   We rode our own horses.   As Ionunco pretended to
know all the mountain-roads, and volunteered to conduct us,
we placed ourselves under his guidance.   I was provided with
Bouyourouldis, or orders, from the pashaw to the authorities as
far as Amadiyah, and with a letter to Abd-ul-Summit Bey, the
Kurdish chief of Berwari, through whose territories we had to
pass.   Mar Shamoun, the patriarch, gave me a very strong letter
of recommendation to the meleks and priests of the Nestorian
districts.

As I was anxious to visit the French excavations at Khorsabad
on my way to the mountains, I left Mosul early in the afternoon,
notwithstanding the great heat of the sun.   It was the sixth day
of Ramazan, and the Mohammedans were still endeavoring to
sleep away their hunger when I passed through the gates, and
crossed the bridge of boats.   Leaving my baggage and servants
to follow leisurely, I galloped on with the Albanians, and reached
Khorsabad in about two hours.

E*

The mound is about fourteen miles N. N. E. of Mosul. A small village* formerly stood on its summit, but the houses were purchased and removed by M. Botta, when excavations were undertaken by the French government. It has been rebuilt in the plain at the foot of the mound. The Khausser, a small stream issuing from the hills of Makloub, is divided into numerous branches as it approaches Khorsabad, and irrigates extensive rice-grounds. The place is consequently very unhealthy, and the few squalid inhabitants who appeared were almost speechless from ague. M. Botta's workmen suffered greatly from fever, and many fell victims to it.

The excavations were carried on as at Nimroud; and the general plan of the building is the same as that of the Assyrian edifices already described. It has, however, more narrow passages, and the chambers are inferior in size; though the sculptured slabs are in general higher. The relief of the larger figures is bolder, that of the smaller about the same. The human-headed bulls differ principally in the head-dress from those at Nimroud; the horned cap is not rounded off, but is high and richly ornamented, like that of the winged monsters of Persepolis. The faces of several of the bulls are turned inward, which gives them an awkward appearance.

Since M. Botta's departure the sides of the trenches have fallen in, and have filled up the greater part of the chambers; the sculptures are rapidly perishing; and, shortly, little will remain of this remarkable monument. Scarcely any part of the building had escaped the fire which destroyed it, and consequently very few bas-reliefs could be removed. Of exterior architecture I could find no trace except a curious cornice, and a flight of steps, flanked by solid masonry, apparently leading to a small temple of black stone or basalt, the foundations of

---

* In the drawing of this village engraved in M. Botta's large work on Nineveh, the houses are represented with shelving roofs and as of considerable size. Such roofs are never seen in this part of the East, and the village, like all others in Assyria, was a mere collection of miserable mud huts.

which still remain. At the foot of the mound lies an altar or tripod, similar to that now in the Louvre.

Altar, or Tripod. (From Khorsabad.)

Khorsabad, or Khishtabad, is mentioned by the early Arab geographers. It is described as a village occupying the site of an ancient Assyrian city called "Saraoun," or "Saraghoun;" and Yakuti declares, that soon after the Arab conquest considerable treasures were found among the ruins. It was generally believed at Mosul, where a copy of Yakuti's very rare work exists, that it was in consequence of this notice, and in the hopes of finding further riches, M. Botta excavated in the mound—hence much of the opposition encountered from the authorities.

I had finished my examination of the ruins by the time the baggage reached the village. The sun had set, but being unwilling to expose my party to fever by passing the night on this unhealthy spot, I rode on to a small hamlet about two miles distant. It was dark when we reached it, and we found ourselves in the midst of a marsh, even more extensive than that of Khorsabad. As there was no village beyond, I was obliged to stop here, and clambering up to a platform of branches of trees elevated upon poles, I passed the night free from the attacks of the swarms of gnats which infested the stagnant water below.

We left the hamlet long before sunrise, and soon reached some of the springs of the Khausser, a small stream which rises at the northern extremity of the Jebel Maklub, irrigates the lands of numerous villages on its course toward Mosul, and falls into the Tigris, near Kouyunjik, after traversing the large quadrangle, of which that mound forms a part.

Our road crossed the northern spur of Jebel Maklub, and then stretched over an extensive plain to the first range of the Kurdish hills. The heat soon became intense, the soil was parched and barren; a few mud walls marked here and there the ruins of a village, and the silence and solitude were only broken by parties of Kurds, lazily driving before them, toward Mosul, donkeys laden with rich clusters of grapes from the mountains.

A weary ride brought us to the Yezidi village of Ain Sifni. Its white houses and conical tombs had long been visible on the declivity of a low hill; its cleanliness was a relief after the filth of Mussulman and Christian habitations. I had expected to find Sheikh Naser, the religious chief of the Yezidis. As he was absent, I partook of the hospitality of the head of the village, and continued my journey to the tomb of Sheikh Adi. After a further ride of two hours through a pleasant ravine watered by a mountain torrent, whose banks were concealed by flowering oleanders, we reached a well-wooded valley, in the center of which rose the white spire of the tomb of the great Yezidi saint.

Stretching myself by a fountain in the cool shade, flung over the tomb by a cluster of lofty trees, I gave myself up to a full flow of gratitude, at this sudden change from the sultry heat and salt streams of the plains, to the verdure and sweet springs of the Kurdish Hills. There were "pleasure-places" enough for all my party, and each eagerly seized his tree, and his fountain.   The guardians of the tomb, and a few wanderers from a neighboring village, gathered round me, and satisfied my curiosity as far as their caution and prejudices would allow.

We passed the night on the roof of one of the buildings within the precincts of the sacred edifice, and continued our journey at dawn on the following morning.

Quitting the Yezidi district, we entered the mountains inhabited by the large Kurdish tribe of Missouri.   The valleys were well wooded; many-shaped rocks towered above our heads or rose in the streams of the Gomel,* which almost cut off our passage through the narrow defiles.   A few villages were scattered on the declivities, but their inhabitants had deserted them for rude huts, built of branches of trees,—their summer habitations.

In four hours we reached the large village of Kaloni, or Kalah-oni, rising among vineyards, and hanging over the bed of the Gomel.   The houses, well constructed of stone, were empty. Huge horns of the ibex ornamented the lintels of the gateways, and the corners of the buildings.   The inhabitants were at some distance, on the banks of the stream, living under the trees in their temporary sheds.

These Kurds were of the Badinan branch of the Missouri tribe.   Their chief, whose hut was in the midst of this group of simple dwellings, was absent; but his wife received me with hospitality.   Carpets, the work of her own women, were spread under a mulberry-tree; and large bowls of milk and cream, wooden platters filled with boiled rice, slices of honey-comb, and baskets of new-gathered fruit, were speedily placed before us.   The men sat at a respectful distance, and readily gave me such information as I asked for.   The women, unembarrassed by the vail, brought straw to our horses, or ran to and fro with their pitchers.   Their hair fell in long tresses down their backs, and their foreheads were adorned with rows of coins and beads;

---

* Or Gomer; this stream forms the principal branch of the Ghazir or Bumadas.

many were not unworthy of the reputation for beauty which the
women of Missouri enjoy.

The spot was rich in natural beauties. The valley, shut in
by lofty rocks, was well wooded with fruit trees—the mulberry,
the peach, the fig, the walnut, the olive, and the pomegranate;
beneath them sprang the vine, or were laid out plots of Indian
corn, sesame, and cotton. The sheds were built of boughs; and
the property of the owners,—carpets, horse-cloths, and domestic
utensils,—were spread out before them. From almost every
door, mingling with the grass and flowers, stretched the many-
colored threads of the loom, at which usually sat one female of
the family. There was a cleanliness, and even richness, in the
dresses of both women and men, an appearance of comfort and
industry, which contrasted strikingly with the miserable state of
the people of the plain; and proved that these Kurds had been
sufficiently fortunate to escape the notice of the last governor of
Mosul, and were reserved for some scrutinizing pashaw.

I acknowledged the hospitality of the Kurdish lady by a present to her son, and rode up to the small Chaldean village of
Bebozi, standing on the summit of a high mountain. The
ascent was most precipitous, and the horses could with difficulty
reach the place. We found a group of ten houses, built on the
edge of a cliff overhanging the valley, at so great a height, that
the stream below was scarcely visible. The inhabitants were
poor, but received us with unaffected hospitality. I had left
the usual road to Amadiyah for the purpose of visiting an inscription, said to exist near this village. A guide was soon
found to conduct me to the spot of which I had heard; but
after toiling up a very difficult pathway, I was shown a rock on
which were only a few rude marks, bearing no resemblance
to any writing that had ever been invented. I was accustomed
to such disappointments, and always prepared for them. I returned to the village and visited the small church. The people
of Bebozi are among those Chaldeans who have been recently
brought over to the Roman Catholic faith. They furnish but
a too common instance of the mode in which such proselytes

are made. In the church I saw a few miserable Italian prints,
dressed up in all the horrors of red, yellow, and blue, miracles
of saints, and of the blessed Virgin.

Having rested in the village, we resumed our journey, and
crossed a range of hills, covered by a forest of dwarf oak.
We descended into the valley of Cheloki, reaching, about sunset, the large Kurdish village of Spandareh, so called from its
poplar-trees.

We were now separated from the valley of Amadiyah by a
range of high and well-wooded mountains called Ghara. This
we crossed by a road little frequented, and of so precipitous a
nature, that our horses could scarcely keep their footing—one,
indeed, carrying part of our baggage, suddenly disappeared over
the edge of a rock, and was found some hundred feet below, on
his back, firmly wedged between two rocks; how he got there
with nothing but the bone of his tail broken, was a mystery beyond the comprehension of our party. The valley of Amadiyah
is cut up into innumerable ravines by the torrents, which rush
down the mountains, and force their way to the river Zab. It
is, however, well wooded with oaks, producing in abundance
the galls for which this district is celebrated. The peasants
were now picking this valuable article of export.

The town and fort of Amadiyah had been visible from the
crest of the Ghara range; but we had a long ride before us,
and it was nearly mid-day ere we reached the foot of the lofty
isolated rock on which they are built. We rested in the small
Chaldean village of Bebadi, one of the few in the district which
still retain the Nestorian faith. The inhabitants were miserably
poor, and I had to listen to a long tale of wretchedness and oppression. The church was hung with a few tattered cotton
handkerchiefs, and the priest's garments were to match. I gave
him two or three pieces of common print, out of which he made
a turban for himself, and beautified the altar.

Some half-clothed, fever-stricken Albanians were slumbering
on the stone benches as we entered the gates of the fort, which,
certainly, during the season of Ramazan, if not at all others,

might be taken by surprise by a few resolute Kurds. We found
ourselves in the midst of a heap of ruins—porches, bazars,
baths, habitations, all laid open to their inmost recesses. Falling
walls would have threatened passers-by, had there been any;
but the place was a desert. We had some difficulty in finding
our way to a crumbling ruin, honored with the name of Serai
—the Palace. Here the same general sleep prevailed. Neither guards nor servants were visible, and we wandered through
the building until we reached the room of the governor. His
hangers-on were indulging in comfort and sleep upon the divans,
and we had some trouble in rousing them. We were at length
taken to a large, gaudily-painted room, in a tower, built on the
very edge of the rock, and overlooking the whole valley—the
only remnant of the state of the old hereditary pashaws of Amadiyah. A refreshing breeze came down from the mountain, the
view was extensive and beautiful, and I forgot the desolation and
misery which reigned around.

A few miserable Nestorian Chaldeans, and one or two half-
starved Jews came to me with the usual melancholy tale of distress; and, shortly after, Kasha Mendi, a worthy ecclesiastic,
who ministered to the spiritual wants of half the villages in the
valley, hearing of my arrival, joined the party. The priest was,
of course, better informed than the rest; and from him I obtained the information I required as to the state of the Chaldeans
in the district, and as to the means of reaching Tiyari. The
Albanian irregulars were to leave me here, the authority of the
Pashaw of Mosul not extending beyond Amadiyah. We were
now to enter the territories of Kurdish chiefs, who scarcely
admitted any dependence upon the Porte. I determined upon
hiring mules for the rest of my journey, and sending all my
horses, except one, with the Albanians to Dohuk, there to await
my return.

It was the hour of afternoon prayer before Selim Agha, the
mutesellim, or governor, emerged from his harem; which, however, as far as the fair sex were concerned, was empty. The
old gentleman, who was hungry, half asleep, and in the third

stage of the ague, hurried through the ordinary salutations, and asked at once for quinine. His attendants exhibited illustrations of every variety of the fever; some shivered, others glowed, and the rest sweated. He entreated me to go with him into the harem; his two sons were buried beneath piles of cloaks, carpets, and grain-sacks, but the whole mass trembled with the violence of their shaking. I dealt out emetics and quinine with a liberal hand, and returned to the Salamlik, to hear from Selim Agha a most doleful history of fever, diminished revenues, arrears of pay, and rebellious Kurds. The tears ran down his cheeks as he recapitulated his manifold misfortunes, and entreated me to intercede with the governer of Mosul for his advancement or recall. I left him with his watch in his hand, anxiously looking for sunset, that he might console himself with a dose of tartar-emetic.

Amadiyah was formerly a place of considerable importance and strength, containing a very large and flourishing population. It was governed by hereditary pashaws—feudal chiefs, who traced their descent from the Abbaside caliphs, and were always looked up to, on that account, with religious respect by the Kurds. The ladies of this family were no less venerated, and enjoyed the very peculiar title, for a woman, of "Khan." The last of these hereditary chiefs was Ismail Pashaw; who long defied, in his almost inaccessible castle, the attempts of Injeh Bairakdar Mohammed Pashaw to reduce him. A mine was at length sprung under a part of the wall, which, from its position, the Kurds had believed safe from attack, and the place was taken by assault. Ismail Pashaw was sent a prisoner to Baghdad, where he still remains; and his family, among whom was his beautiful wife, Esma Khan, not unknown to the Europeans of Mosul, together with Mohammed Seyyid Pashaw of Akra,* a member of the same race, long lived upon the bounty of Mr. Rassam. Amadiyah is frequently mentioned by the early Arab geographers and historians, and its foundation dates, most prob-

* A district to the east of Amadiyah.

ably, from a very early epoch. Kasha Mendi casually confirmed the assertion of Rich, that the town was once called Ecbatana, by saying, that he had seen it so designated in a very
early Chaldean MS. The only ancient remains that I could
discover, were a defaced bas-relief on the rock near the northern
gate, of which sufficient alone was distinguishable to enable me
to assign to it an approximate date—the time of the Arsacian
kings; and some excavations in the rock within the walls,
which appear to have been used at an early period as a Christian
church. Amadiyah is proverbially unhealthy, notwithstanding
its lofty and exposed position. At this time of the year, the
inhabitants leave the town for the neighboring mountains, in
the valleys of which they construct " ozailis," or sheds, with
boughs.

I made my way through the deserted street to a small inclosure, in which were the quarters of the Albanians. The
disposable force may have consisted of three men; the rest
were stretched out on all sides, suffering under every stage of
fever, amid heaps of filth, and skins of water-melons, showing
the nature and extent of their commissariat. One of their chiefs
boasted that he had braved the fever, and insisted upon my
drinking coffee, and smoking a narguileh of no very prepossessing appearance, with him. He even indulged so far in mirth
and revelry, that he disturbed a shivering youth basking in the
last rays of the sun, and brought him to play upon a santour,
which had lost the greater number of its strings. An air of his
native mountains brought on a fit of melancholy, and he dwelt
upon the miseries of an irregular's life, when there was neither
war nor plunder. The evening gun announced sunset while I
was sitting with the chief; and I left the garrison as they were
breaking their fast on donkey-loads of unripe water-melons.

On my return to the serai, I found the governor recovering
from the effects of his emetic, and anxious for his dinner. As
the month of Ramazan is, during the nights, one of festivity
and open house, Ismail Agha of Tepelin (the Albanian chief in
command of the garrison), the cadi, the collector of the revenue,

a Kurdish chief, and one or two others came as guests. Our meal gave undoubted proofs either of the smallness of the means of Selim Agha, or of the limited resources of the country. When the dinner was over, I introduced a theological subject as becoming the season, and the cadi entered deeply into the subject of predestination and free-will. The reckless way in which the Albanian threw himself into the argument, astonished the. company, and shocked the feelings of the expounder of the law. His views of the destinies of man were bold and original ; he appealed to me for a confirmation of his opinions, and assuming that I fully concurred with him, and that he had silenced the cadi, who was ejaculating a pious "Istaffer Allah" (may God forgive him), he finished by asking me to breakfast.

Next morning, I left my guards and the attendants of the governor to collect mules for my journey from the peasants who had brought provisions to the town, and after some difficulty found my way to the quarters of Ismail Agha. They were in a small house, the only habitable spot in the midst of a heap of ruins. His room was hung round with guns, swords, and yataghans, and a few dirty Albanians, armed to the teeth, were lounging at the door. The chief had adorned himself most elaborately. His velvet jacket was covered with a maze of gold embroidery, his arms were of the most costly description, and ample fur cloaks were spread over the dingy divans. It was a strange display of finery in the midst of misery. He received me with great cordiality ; and when he found that I had been to his old haunts in his native land, and had known his friends and kindred, his friendship exceeded all reasonable bounds. " We are all brothers, the English and the Tosques" (an Albanian tribe), exclaimed he, endeavoring to embrace me ; " we are all Framasouns ;* I know nothing of these Turks and their Ramazan, thank God! Our stomachs were given us to be

* The term Framasoun (or Freemason), as well as Protestant, are in the East, I am sorry to say, equivalent to infidel. The Roman Catholic missionaries have very industriously spread the calumny.

filled, and our mouths to take in good things." He accompanied these words with a very significant signal to one of his followers, who, at no loss to understand his meaning, set about forming a pyramid of cushions, to the top of which he mounted at the imminent risk of his neck, and reached down from a shelf a huge bottle of wine, with a corresponding pitcher of raki. Ismail Agha then dived into the recesses of a very capacious but ill-looking purse, out of which he pulled twenty paras,* its sole contents, and dispatched without delay one of his attendants to the stall of a solitary grocer, who was apparently the only commercial survivor in the wreck around him. The boy soon returned with a small parcel of parched peas, a few dates, and three lumps of sugar, which were duly spread on a tray, and placed before us as zests to the wine and brandy. It was evident that Ismail Agha had fully made up his mind to a morning's debauch, and my position was an uncomfortable one. After drinking a few glasses of raki in solitary dignity, he invited his followers to join him. Messengers were dispatched in all directions for music; a Jew with the ague, the band of the regiment, consisting of two cracked dwarf kettle-drums and a fife, and two Kurds with a fiddle and a santour, were collected together. I took an opportunity of slipping out of the room unseen, amid the din of Albanian songs, and the dust of Palicari dances.

On my return to the serai, I found the mules ready, the owners having been, after much discussion, brought to understand that it was my intention to pay for their hire. Every thing being settled, and the animals loaded, I wished the mutesellim good day, and promised to bring his miserable condition to the notice of the pashaw.

Accompanied by a Kurdish chief, we left Amadiyah by the gate opposite to that by which we had entered. We were obliged to descend on foot the steep pathway leading to the valley below. Crossing some well-cultivated gardens, we com-

* About one penny.

menced the ascent of the mountains through a wooded ravine,
and came suddenly upon the Yilaks, or summer quarters of the
population of Amadiyah. The spot was well chosen. The torrent was divided into a thousand streams, which broke over the
rocks, falling in cascades into the valley below. Fruit trees
and oaks concealed the huts and tents, and creepers of many
hues almost covered the sides of the ravine. All our party
enjoyed the delicious coolness and fragrance of the place; and
we did not wonder that the people of Amadiyah had left the
baneful air of the town for these pleasant haunts. An hour's
ride brought us to the summit of the pass, from which a
magnificent view of the Tiyari mountains opened before us.
Ionunco became eloquent when he beheld his native Alps, and
named one by one the lofty peaks which sprang out of the
confused heaps of hills; that of Asheetha and several others
were covered with snow. Below us was the long valley of
Berwari, which separates the range of Amadiyah from the
Nestorian country. At a short distance from the crest of the
pass we found a small barren plain, called Nevdasht, in which
stands the Kurdish village of Maglana. We reached Hayis, a
Nestorian hamlet, about sunset. There were but four families
in the place, so destitute, that we could only procure a little
boiled meal, and some dried mulberries for our supper. The
poor creatures, however, did all they could to make us comfortable, and gave us what they had.

The valley of Berwari is well wooded with the gall-bearing
oak; and the villages are surrounded by gardens and orchards.
The present chief of the district, Abd-ul-Summit Bey, is a
fanatic, and has almost ruined the Christian population. In all
the villages through which we passed, we saw the same scene,
and heard the same tale of wretchedness. Yet the land is
rich, water plentiful, and the means of cultivation easy.
Fruit trees of many descriptions abound; and tobacco, rice,
and grain of various kinds could be extensively cultivated.
Even the galls afford but a scanty gain to the villagers, as
those who collect them are obliged to sell them to the chief at a

very small price. The villages are partly inhabited by Kurds
and partly by Nestorian Chaldeans; there are no Catholics
among them.   Many of the Christian villages have been reduced
to five or six houses, and some even to two or three. We
stopped at several during our day's journey. The men, with
the priests, were generally absent picking galls; the women
were seated in circles under the trees, clipping the grapes, and
immersing them in boiling water, previous to drying them for
raisins. We were everywhere received with the same hospitality, and everywhere found the same poverty. Even Ibrahim
Agha, who had been inured to the miseries of misgovernment,
grew violent in his expressions of indignation against Abd-ul-
Summit Bey, and indulged in a variety of threats against all the
male and female members of his family.

The castle of Kumri or Gumri, the residence of Abd-ul-
Summit Bey, stands on the pinnacle of a lofty isolated rock, and
may be seen from most parts of the valley of Berwari. It is a
small mud fort, but it is looked upon as an impregnable place by
the Kurds. The chief had evidently received notice of my approach, and probably suspected that the object of my visit was
an inspection, for no friendly purposes, of his stronghold; for as
we came near to the foot of the hill, we saw him hastening down
a precipitous pathway on the opposite side, as fast as his horse
could carry him. A mullah, one of his hangers-on, having been
sent to meet us on the road, informed me that his master had left
the castle early in the morning, for a distant village, whither we
could follow him. Not having any particular wish to make a
closer inspection of Kalah Kumri, I struck into the hills, and took
the pathway pointed out by the mullah.

We rode through several Kurdish villages, surrounded by
gardens, and well watered by mountain streams. A pass of
some elevation had to be crossed before we could reach the
village of Mia, our quarters for the night. Near its summit we
found a barren plain on which several Kurdish horsemen, who
had joined us, engaged with my own party in the Jerid. The
mimic fight soon caused general excitement, and old habits

getting the better of my dignity, I joined the *mêlée*. A severe
kick in the leg from a horse soon put an end to my manœuvers,
and the party was detained until I was sufficiently recovered from
the effects of the blow to continue our journey. It was consequently sunset before we reached Mia. There are two villages
of this name; the upper, inhabited by Mohammedans, the lower
by Nestorian Chaldeans. A Kurd met us as we were entering
the former, with a message from Abd-ul-Summit Bey, to the
effect that, having guests, he could not receive me there, but had
provided a house in the Christian village, where he would join us
after his dinner. I rode on to the lower Mia, and found a party
of Kurds belaboring the inhabitants, and collecting old carpets and
household furniture. Understanding that these proceedings were
partly meant as preparations for my reception, though the greater
share of the objects collected was intended for the comfort of the
Bey's Mussulman guests, I at once put a stop to the pillaging,
and released the sufferers. We ascended a spacious and cleanly
roof; and with the assistance of the people of the house, who
were ready enough to assist when they learned we were Christians, established ourselves there for the night.

　　Soon after dark another messenger came from Abd-ul-Summit
Bey, to say that as the cadi and other illustrious guests were
with him, he could not visit me before the morning. I had
from the first suspected that these delays and excuses had an
object, and that the chief wished to give a proof of his dignity
to the Kurds, by treating me in as unceremonious a manner as
possible; so, calling the Kurd, and addressing him in a loud
voice, that the people who had gathered round the house
might hear, I requested him to be the bearer of a somewhat
uncivil answer to his master, and took good care that he should
fully understand its terms. Ionunco's hair stood on end at
the audacity of this speech, and the Nestorians trembled
at the results. Ibrahim Agha tittered with delight; and
pushing the Kurd away by the shoulders, told him to be particular in delivering his answer. The message had the effect I
had anticipated; an hour afterward, shuffling over the house-

tops at the great risk of his shins, and with a good chance of disappearing down a chimney, came the bey.   He was enveloped in a variety of cloaks;. and wore, after the manner of the Bohtan chiefs, a turban of huge dimensions—about four feet in diameter—made up of numberless kerchiefs and rags of every hue of red, yellow, and black, and a jacket and wide trowsers, richly embroidered; in his girdle were all manner of weapons.   In person he was tall and handsome; his eyes were dark, his nose aquiline, and his beard black; but the expression of his face was far from prepossessing.   I left him to open the conversation, which. he did by a multiplicity of excuses and apologies for what had passed, not having, by the Prophet, been aware, he said, of the rank of the guest by whose presence he had been honored.   I pointed out to him one or two fallacies in his assertions; and we came to a distinct understanding on the subject, before we proceeded to general topics.   He sat with me till midnight, and entered, among other things, into a long justification of his conduct toward Christians, which proved that his authority was not established as well as he could desire.

In the morning the bey sent me a breakfast, and gave me a party of Kurdish horsemen as an escort as far as the Tiyari frontier, which was not far distant.   Beyond Mia we passed through Bedou, the largest and most populous Kurdish village I had seen.

Our guards would not venture into the territories of the Tiyari, between whom and the Kurds there are continual hostilities, but quitted us in a narrow desolate valley, up which our road to Asheetha now led.   I lectured my party on the necessity of caution during our future wanderings; and reminded my cawass and Mohammedan servants that they had no longer the quiet Christians of the plains to deal with.   Resigning ourselves to the guidance of Ionunco, who now felt that he was on his own soil, we made our way with difficulty over the rocks and stones with which the valley is blocked up, and struck into what our guide represented to be a short cut to

Asheetha. The pathway might certainly, on some occasions, have been used by the mountain goats; but the passage of horses and mules was a miracle. After a most tedious walk, we reached the top of the pass and looked down on the village. From this spot the eye rested upon a scene of great beauty. In front rose the lofty peak, with its snows and glaciers, visible even from Mosul. At our feet the village spread over the whole valley; and detached houses, surrounded by gardens and orchards, were scattered over the sides of the mountains. To the right ran the valley which leads to the Zab. We had little difficulty in descending through the loose stones and detritus which cover the face of the mountain, although both our mules and ourselves had frequent falls. On reaching the entrance of the valley, we rode at once to the house of Yakoub, the rais or chief of Asheetha, who received us with grateful hospitality.

F

CHAPTER VII.

WE had no sooner reached the house of Yakoub Rais, than a
cry of " The bey is come," spread rapidly through the village,
and I was surrounded by a crowd of men, women, and boys.
My hand was kissed by all, and I had to submit for some time
to this tedious process. As for my companion, he was almost
smothered in the embraces of the girls, nearly all of whom had
been liberated from slavery after the great massacre, and had
been supported in their distress by his brother for some months
in Mosul.* Among the men were many of my old workmen,
who were distinguished from the rest of the inhabitants of
Asheetha by their gay dresses and arms, the fruits of their

---

* It may be remembered that Beder Khan Bey, in 1843, invaded the
Tiyari districts, massacred in cold blood nearly 10,000 of their inhabitants,
and carried away as slaves a large number of women and children. But it
is, perhaps, not generally known, that the release of the greater part of the
captives was obtained through the humane interference and generosity of Sir
Stratford Canning, who prevailed upon the Porte to send a commissioner into
Kurdistan, for the purpose of inducing Beder Khan Bey and other Kurdish chiefs to give up the slaves they had taken, and who advanced himself
a considerable sum toward their liberation. Mr. Rassam also obtained the
release of many slaves, and maintained and clothed, at his own expense and
for many months, not only the Nestorian Patriarch, who had taken refuge in
Mosul, but many hundred Chaldeans who had escaped from the mountains.

industry during the winter. They were anxious to show their
gratitude, and their zeal in my service. The priests came too ;
Kasha Ghioorghis, Kasha Hormuzd, and others. As they entered
the room, the whole assembly rose ; and lifting their turbans
and caps reverentially from their heads, kissed the hand extended to them. In the meanwhile the girls had disappeared ; but
soon returned, each bearing a platter of fruit which they placed
before me. My workmen also brought large dishes of boiled
garas swimming in butter. There were provisions enough
for the whole company.

The first inquiries were after Mar Shamoun, the patriarch.
I produced his letter, which the priests first kissed and placed
to their foreheads. They afterward passed it to the principal
men, who went through the same ceremony. Kasha Ghioorghis
then read the letter aloud, and at its close, those present uttered
a pious ejaculation for the welfare of their patriarch, and
renewed their expressions of welcome to us.

These preliminaries having been concluded, we had to satisfy
all present as to the object, extent, and probable duration of
our journey. The village was in the greatest alarm at a threatened invasion from Beder Khan Bey. The district of Tkhoma,
which had escaped the former massacre, was now the object of
his fanatical vengeance. He was to march through Asheetha,
and orders had already been sent to the inhabitants to collect
provisions for his men. As his expedition was not to be undertaken before the close of Ramazan, there was full time to see
the proscribed districts before the Kurds entered them. I
determined, however, to remain a day in Asheetha, to rest
our mules.

On the morning following our arrival, I went with Yakoub
Rais to visit the village. The trees and luxuriant crops had
concealed the desolation of the place, and had given to Asheetha,
from without, a flourishing appearance. As I wandered, however, through the lanes, I found little but ruins. A few houses
were rising from the charred heaps ; still the greater part of
the sites were without owners, the whole family having perished.

Yakoub pointed out, as we went along, the former dwellings of wealthy inhabitants, and told me how and where they had been murdered. A solitary church had been built since the massacre; the foundations of others was seen among the ruins. The pathways were still blocked up by the trunks of trees cut down by the Kurds. Water-courses, once carrying fertility to many gardens, were now empty and dry; and the lands which they had irrigated were left naked and unsown. I was surprised at the proofs of the industry and activity of the few surviving families, who had returned to the village, and had already brought a large portion of the land into cultivation.

The houses of Asheetha are not built in a group, but are scattered over the valley like those of the Tiyari districts.* Each dwelling stands in the center of the land belonging to its owner; consequently, the village occupies a much larger space than would otherwise be required, but has a cheerful and pleasing appearance. The houses are simple, and constructed so as to afford protection and comfort, during winter and summer. ` The lower part is of stone, and contains two or three rooms inhabited by the family and their cattle during the cold months. Light is admitted by the door, and by small holes in the wall. There are no windows, as in the absence of glass, a luxury as yet unknown in Kurdistan, the cold would be very great during the winter, when the inhabitants are frequently snowed up for many days together. The upper floor is constructed partly of stone and partly of wood, the whole side facing the south being open. Enormous beams, resting on wooden pillars and on the walls, support the roof. This is the summer habitation, and here all the members of the family reside. · During July and August they usually sleep on the roof, upon which they erect stages of boughs and grass resting on high poles. By thus raising themselves as much as possible, they avoid the vermin which swarm in the rooms, and

---

* Asheetha and Zaweetha were formerly looked upon as half-independent districts, each having its own rais or head. They were neither within the territories, nor under the authority of the Meleks of Tiyari.

catch the night winds which carry away the gnats. Sometimes
they build these stages in the branches of high trees around
the houses. The winter provision of dried grass and straw
for the cattle is stacked near the dwelling, or is heaped on
the roof.

A Nestorian House in the District of Tiyari.

As this was the first year that the surviving inhabitants of
Asheetha, about 200 families, had returned to the village and
had cultivated the soil, they were almost without provisions of
any kind. We were obliged to send to Zaweetha for meat and
rice; and even milk was scarce, the flocks having been carried
away by the Kurds. Garas was all we could find to eat. They
had no corn and very little barley. Their bread was made of
this garas, and upon it alone they lived, except when on holydays they boiled the grain, and soaked it in melted butter.

The men were now busy in irrigating the land; and seemed
to be rewarded by the promise of ample crops of their favorite
garas, and of wheat, barley, rice, and tobacco. The boys kept

up a continued shrill shriek or whistle to frighten away the
small birds, which had been attracted in shoals by the ripe
corn. When tired of this exercise, they busied themselves with
their partridges. Almost every youth in the country carries
one of these birds at his back, in a round wicker cage. Indeed,
while the mountains and the valleys swarm with wild partridges, the houses are as much infested by the tame. The
women, too, were not idle. The greater part of them, even
the girls, were beating out the corn, or employed in the fields.
A few were at the doors of the houses working at the loom, or
spinning wool for the clothes of the men. I never saw more
general or cheerful industry; even the priests took part in the
labors of their congregation.

I walked to the ruins of the school and dwelling-house, built
by the American missionaries during their short sojourn in the
mountains. These buildings had been the cause of much
jealousy and suspicion to the Kurds. They stand upon the
summit of an isolated hill, commanding the whole valley. A
position less ostentatious and proportions more modest might
certainly have been chosen; and it is surprising that persons,
so well acquainted with the characters of the tribes among
whom they had come to reside, should have been thus indiscreet. They were, however, most zealous and worthy men;
and had their plans succeeded, I have little doubt that they
would have conferred signal benefits on the Nestorian Chaldeans. I never heard their names mentioned by the Tiyari,
and most particularly that of Dr. Grant, without expressions of
profound respect, amounting almost to veneration.*

During the occupation of Asheetha by the Kurds, Zeinel

* Dr. Grant, who published an account of his visit to the mountains, fell
a victim to his humane zeal for the Chaldeans in 1844. After the massacre,
his house in Mosul was filled with fugitives, whom he supported and clothed.
Their sufferings, and the want of common necessaries before they reached
the town, had brought on a malignant typhus fever, of which many died,
and which Dr. Grant caught while attending the sick in his house. Mosul
holds the remains of most of those who were engaged in the American missions to the Chaldeans.

Bey fortified himself with a few men in the house constructed by the Americans; and the position was so strong, that, holding it against all the attempts of the Tiyari to dislodge him, he kept the whole of the valley in subjection.

Yakoub Rais, who was naturally of a lively and joyful disposition, could not restrain his tears as he related to me the particulars of the massacre. He had been among the first seized by Beder Khan Bey; and having been kept by that chief as a kind of hostage, he had been continually with him, during the attack on the Tiyari, and had witnessed all the scenes of bloodshed which is so graphically described. The descent upon Asheetha was sudden and unexpected. The greater part of the inhabitants fell victims to the fury of the Kurds, who endeavored to destroy every trace of the village. We walked to the church, which had been newly constructed by the united exertions and labor of the people. The door was so low, that a person, on entering, had to bring his back to the level of his knees. The entrances to Christian churches in the East are generally so constructed, that horses and beasts of burden may not be lodged by Mohammedans within the sacred building. A few rituals, a book of prayer, and the Scriptures, all in manuscript, were lying upon the rude altar; but the greater part of the leaves were wanting, and those which remained were either torn into shreds, or disfigured by damp and water. The manuscripts of the churches were hid in the mountains, or buried in some secure place, at the time of the massacre; and as the priests, who had concealed them, were mostly killed, the books have not been recovered. A few English prints and handkerchiefs from Manchester were hung about the walls; a bottle and a glass, with a tin plate for the sacrament, stood upon the table; a curtain of coarse cloth hung before the inner recess, the Holy of Holies; and these were all the ornaments and furniture of the place.

I visited my former workmen, the priests, and those whom I had seen at Mosul; and as it was expected that I should partake of the hospitality of each, and eat of the dishes they

had prepared for me—generally garas floating in melted rancid
butter, with a layer of sour milk above—by the time I reached
Yakoub's mansion, my appetite was abundantly satisfied. At
the door, however, stood Sarah, and a bevy of young damsels
with baskets of fruits mingled with ice, fetched from the
glacier; nor would they leave me until I had tasted of every
thing.

We lived in a patriarchal way with the rais. My bed was
made in one corner of the room. The opposite corner was
occupied by ·Yakoub, his wife and unmarried daughters; a
third was appropriated to his son and daughter-in-law, and all
the members of his son's family; the fourth was assigned to
my companion; and various individuals, whose position in our
household could not be very accurately determined, took possession of the center. We slept well nevertheless, and no one
troubled himself about his neighbor. Even Ibrahim Agha,
whose paradise was Chanak Kalassi, the Dardanelles, to which
he always disadvantageously compared every thing, confessed
that the Tiyari mountains were not an unpleasant portion of
the sultan's dominions.

Yakoub volunteered to accompany me during the rest of my
journey through the mountains; and as he was generally
known, was well acquainted with the by-ways and passes, and
a very merry companion withal, I eagerly accepted his offer.
We left part of our baggage at his house, and it was agreed
that he should occasionally ride one of the mules. He was a
very portly person, gayly dressed in an embroidered jacket
and striped trowsers, and carrying a variety of arms in his
girdle.

The country through which we passed, after leaving
Asheetha, could scarcely be surpassed in the beauty and sublimity
of its scenery. The patches of land on the declivities of the
mountains were cultivated with extraordinary skill and care.
I never saw greater proofs of industry. Our mules, however,
were dragged over places almost inaccessible to men on foot,
but we forgot the toils and dangers of the way in gazing upon

the magnificent prospect before us. Zaweetha is in the same
valley as Asheetha. The stream formed by the eternal snows
above the latter village, forces its way to the Zab. On the
mountain-sides is the most populous and best cultivated district in Tiyari. The ravine below Asheetha is too narrow to
admit of the road being carried along the banks of the torrent;
and we were compelled to climb over a mass of rocks, rising to a
considerable height above it. Frequently the footing was so insecure that it required the united force of several men to carry
the mules along by their ears and tails. We, who were unac-
customed to mountain paths, were obliged to have recourse to the
aid of our hands and knees.

I had been expected at Zaweetha; and before we entered the
first gardens of the village, a party of girls, bearing baskets
of fruit, advanced to meet me. Their hair, neatly plaited and
adorned with flowers, fell down their backs. On their heads
they wore colored kerchiefs loosely tied, or an embroidered cap.
Many were pretty, and the prettiest was Aslani, a liberated slave,
who had been for some time under the protection of Mrs. Rassam; she led the party, and welcomed me to Zaweetha. My
hand having been kissed by all, they simultaneously threw themselves upon my companion, and saluted him vehemently on both
cheeks; such a mode of salutation, in the case of a person of my
rank and distinction, not being, unfortunately, considered either
respectful or decorous. The girls were followed by the rais
and the principal inhabitants, and I was led by them into the
village.

The Rais of Zaweetha had fortunately rendered some service
to Beder Khan Bey, and on the invasion of Tiyari his village
was spared. It had not even been deserted by its inhabitants,
nor had its trees and gardens been injured. It was, consequently, at the time of my visit, one of the most flourishing
villages in the mountains. The houses, neat and clean, were
still overshadowed by the wide-spreading walnut-tree; every
foot of ground which could receive seed, or nourish a plant,
was cultivated. Soil had been brought from elsewhere, and

F*

built up in the terraces on the precipitous sides of the mountains.
A small pathway among the gardens led us to the house of the
rais.

We were received by Kasha Kana of Lizan, and Kasha Yusuf
of Siatha ; the first, one of the very few learned priests left
among the Nestorian Chaldeans. Our welcome was as unaffected and sincere as it had been at Asheetha. Preparations
had been made for our reception, and the women of the chief's
family were congregated around huge caldrons at the door
of the house, cooking an entire sheep, with rice and garas.
The liver, heart, and other portions of the entrails, were immediately cut into pieces, roasted on ramrods, and brought on
these skewers into the room. The fruit, too, melons, pomegranates, and grapes, all of excellent quality, spread on the
floor, before us, served to allay our appetites until the breakfast
was ready.

Mar Shamoun's letter was read with the usual solemnities
by Kasha Kana, and we had to satisfy the numerous inquiries
of the company. Their patriarch was regarded as a prisoner
in Mosul, and his return to the mountains was expected
with deep anxiety. Everywhere, except in Zaweetha, the
churches had been destroyed to their foundations, and the
priests put to death. Some of the holy edifices had been rudely
rebuilt ; but the people were unwilling to use them until they
had been consecrated by the patriarch. There were not priests
enough indeed to officiate, nor could others be ordained until
Mar Shamoun himself performed the ceremony. These wants
had been the cause of great irregularities and confusion in
Tiyari ; and the Nestorian Chaldeans, who are naturally a
religious people, and greatly attached to their churches and
ministers, were more alive to them than to any of their misfortunes.

Kasha Kana was making his weekly rounds among the villages which had lost their priests. He carried under his arm a
bag full of manuscripts, consisting chiefly of rituals and copies
of the Scriptures ; but he had also one or two volumes on profane

subjects, which he prized highly; among them was a grammar by Rabba Iohannan bar Zoabee, to which he was chiefly indebted for his learning.* He read to us—holding as usual the book upside down—a part of the introduction, treating of the philosophy and nature of languages, and illustrated the text by various attempts at the delineation of most marvelous alphabets. A taste for the fine arts seemed to prevail generally in the village, and the walls of the rais's house were covered with sketches of wild goats and snakes in every variety of posture. The young men were eloquent on the subject of the chase, and related their exploits with the wild animals of the mountains. A cousin of the chief, a handsome youth, very gayly dressed, had shot a bear a few days before, after a hazardous encounter. He brought me the skin, which measured seven feet in length. The two great subjects of complaint I found to be the Kurds and the bears, both equally mischievous; the latter carrying off the fruit both when on the trees and when laid out to dry; and the former the provisions stored for the winter. In some villages in Berwari the inhabitants pretended to be in so much dread of the bears, that they would not venture out alone after dark.

The rais, finding that I would not accept his hospitality for the night, accompanied us, followed by the principal inhabitants, to the outskirts of the village. His frank and manly bearing, and

---

* Although few works on other subjects than those connected with theology and the church services now exist among the Nestorians, it must be remembered that, at the time of the Arab invasion, the learning of the East was still chiefly to be found with the Chaldeans. We are indebted to them for the preservation of numerous precious fragments of Greek learning, as the Greeks were, many centuries before, to their ancestors, the Chaldees of Babylon, for the records of astronomy and the elements of Eastern science. They had translated at an early period the works of Greek physicians and philosophers. and. at the request of the caliphs. who were the encouragers and patrons of learning, had re-translated them into the Arabic langaage. The Caliph Al Mamoun sent learned Nestorians into Syria, Armenia. and Egypt to collect manuscripts. and confided for translation to his Chaldean subjects, among other treatises. those of Aristotle and Galen. Alexander Von Humboldt (Cosmos. vol. ii. ch. 5) admits and commends the influence of the Nestorian Chaldeans in the civilization of the East.

simple kindness, had made a most favorable impression upon
me, and I left him with regret. Kasha Kana, too, fully merited
the praise which he received from all who knew him. His
appearance was mild and venerable ; his beard, white as snow,
fell low upon his breast ; but his garments were in a very advanced stage of rags. I gave him a few handkerchiefs, some
of which were at once gratefully applied to the bettering of his
raiment ; the remainder being reserved for the embellishment
of his parish church. The kasha is looked up to as the physi-
cian, philosopher, and sage of Tiyari, and is treated with great
veneration by the people. As we walked through the village,
the women left their thresholds, and the boys their sports, to kiss
his hand—a mark of respect, however, which is invariably
shown to the priesthood.

We had been joined by Mirza, a confidential servant of Mar
Shamoun, and our party was further increased by several men
returning to villages on our road. Yakoub Rais kept every
one in good-humor by his anecdotes, and the absurdity of the
gesticulations. Ionunco, too, dragging his mare over the projecting rocks, down which he continually contrived to tumble,
added to the general mirth, and we went laughing through the
valley.

From Zaweetha to the Zab, there is almost an unbroken line
of cultivation on both sides of the valley. The two villages of
Miniyanish and Murghi are buried in groves of walnut-trees,
and their peaceful and flourishing appearance deceived me until
I wandered among their dwellings, and found the same scenes
of misery and desolation as at Asheetha. But nature was so
beautiful that we almost forgot the havoc of man, and envied
the repose of these secluded habitations. In Miniyanish, out
of seventy houses, only twelve had risen from their ruins ;
the families to which the rest belonged having been totally
destroyed. Yakoub pointed out a spot where above three
hundred persons had been murdered in cold blood ; and all
our party had some tale of horror to relate. Murghi was not
less desolate than Miniyanish, and eight houses alone had been

resought by their owners.   We found an old priest, blind and
gray, bowed down by age and grief, the solitary survivor of
six or eight of his order.   He was seated under the shade of
a walnut-tree, near a small stream.   Some children of the village were feeding him with grapes, and on our approach his
daughter ran into the half-ruined cottage, and brought out a
basket of fruit and a loaf of garas bread.   I endeavored to glean
some information from the old man as to the state of his flock ;
but his mind wandered to the cruelties of the Kurds, or dwelt
upon the misfortunes of his patriarch, over whose fate he shed
many tears.   None of our party being able to console the kasha,
I gave some handkerchiefs to his daughter, and we resumed our
journey.

Our road lay through the gardens of the villages, and through
the forest of gall-bearing oaks which clothe the mountains above
the line of cultivation.   But it was everywhere equally difficult
and precipitous, and we tore our way through the matted boughs
of overhanging trees, or the thick foliage of creepers which hung
from every branch.   Innumerable rills, leading the mountain
springs into the terraced fields, crossed our path and rendered
our progress still more tedious.   We reached Lizan, however,
early in the afternoon, descending to the village through scenery
fo extraordinary beauty and grandeur.

Lizan stands on the river Zab, which is crossed near the village by a rude bridge.   I need not weary or distress the reader
with a description of desolation and misery, hardly concealed by
the most luxuriant vegetation.   We rode to the grave-yard of a
roofless church slowly rising from its ruins—the first edifice in
the village to be rebuilt.   We spread our carpet among the
tombs ; for as yet there were no habitable houses.   The melek,
with a few who had survived the massacre, was living during
the day under the trees, and sleeping at night on stages of grass
and boughs, raised on high poles, fixed in the very bed of the
Zab.   By this latter contrivance they succeeded in catching
any breeze that might be carried down the narrow ravine of

the river, and in freeing themselves from the gnats and sandflies abounding in the valley.

It was near Lizan that occurred one of the most terrible
incidents of the massacre ; and an active mountaineer offering
to lead me to the spot, I followed him up the mountain.
Emerging from the gardens we found ourselves at the foot of
an almost perpendicular detritus of loose stones, terminated,
about one thousand feet above us, by a wall of lofty rocks.   Up
this ascent we toiled for above an hour, sometimes clinging
to small shrubs whose roots scarcely reached the scanty soil
below : at others crawling on our hands and knees ; crossing
the gullies to secure a footing, or carried down by the stones
which we put in motion as we advanced.   We soon saw evidences of the slaughter.   At first a solitary skull rolling down
with the rubbish ; then heaps of blanched bones ; further up
fragments of rotten garments.   As we advanced, these remains
became more frequent—skeletons, almost entire, still hung to
the dwarf shrubs.   I was soon compelled to renounce an attempt
to count them.   As we approached the wall of rock, the declivity became covered with bones, mingled with the long plaited
tresses of the women, shreds of discolored linen, and well-worn
shoes.   There were skulls of all ages, from the child unborn to
the toothless old man.   We could not avoid treading on the
bones as we advanced, and rolling them with the loose stones
into the valley below.   " This is nothing," exclaimed my guide,
who observed me gazing with wonder on these miserable heaps ;
" they are but the remains of those who were thrown from
above, or sought to escape the sword by jumping from the rock.
Follow me !"   He sprang upon a ledge projecting from the preci-
pice that rose before us, and clambered along the face of the
mountain overhanging the Zab, now scarcely visible at our feet.
I followed him as well as I was able to some distance ; but when
the ledge became scarcely broader than my hand, and frequently
disappeared for three or four feet altogether, I could no longer
advance.   The Tiyari, who had easily surmounted these difficulties, returned to assist me, but in vain.   I was still suffering

severely from the kick received in my leg four days before; and was compelled to return, after catching a glimpse of an open recess or platform covered with human remains.

When the fugitives who had escaped from Asheetha, spread the news of the massacre through the valley of Lizan, the inhabitants of the villages around collected such part of their property as they could carry, and took refuge on the platform I have just described, and on the rock above; hoping thus to escape the notice of the Kurds, or to be able to defend, against any numbers, a place almost inaccessible. Women and young children, as well as men, concealed themselves in a spot which the mountain goat could scarcely reach.* Beder Khan Bey was not long in discovering their retreat; but being unable to force it, he surrounded the place with his men, and waited until they should be compelled to yield. The weather was hot and sultry, the Christians had brought but small supplies of water and provisions; after three days the first began to fail them, and they offered to capitulate. The terms proposed by Beder Khan Bey, and ratified by an oath on the Koran, were their lives on the surrender of their arms and property. The Kurds were then admitted to the platform. After they had disarmed their prisoners, they commenced an indiscriminate slaughter; until, weary of using their weapons, they hurled the few survivors from the rocks into the Zab below. Out of nearly one thousand souls, who are said to have congregated here, only one escaped.

We had little difficulty in descending to the village; a moving mass of stones, skulls, and rubbish carried us rapidly down the declivity. The melek, who had but recently been raised to

---

* When among the Bakhtiyari, I saw a curious instance of the agility of the women of the mountains. I occupied an upper room in a tower, forming one of the corners in the yard of the chief's harem. I was accustomed to lock my door on the outside with a padlock. The wife of the chief advised me to secure the window also. As I laughed at the idea of any one being able to enter by it, she ordered one of her handmaidens to convince me, which she did at once, dragging herself up in the most marvelous way by the mere irregularities of the bricks. After witnessing this feat, I could believe any thing of the activity of the Kurdish women.

that rank, his predecessor having been killed by the Kurds, prepared a simple meal of garas and butter—the only provisions
that could be procured.   The few stragglers who had returned
to their former dwellings collected round us, and made the usual
inquiries after their patriarch, or related their misfortunes.   As
I expressed surprise at the extent of land already cultivated, they
told me that the Kurds of some neighboring villages had taken
possession of the deserted property, and had sown grain and tobacco in the spring, which the Tiyari were now compelled to
irrigate and look after.

The sun had scarcely set, when I was driven by swarms of
insects to one of the platforms in the river.   A slight breeze
came from the ravine, and I was able to sleep undisturbed.

The bridge across the Zab at Lizan is of basket-work.   Stakes
are firmly fastened together with twigs, forming a long hurdle,
reaching from one side of the river to the other.   The two ends

A Wicker Bridge across the Zab near Lizan.

are laid upon beams, resting upon piers on the opposite bank,
and kept in their places by heavy stones heaped upon them.

Animals, as well as men, are able to cross over this frail structure, which swings to and fro, and seems ready to give way at every step. These bridges are of frequent occurrence in the Tiyari mountains.

As some of the beams had been broken, the bridge of Lizan formed an acute angle with the stream below, and was scarcely to be crossed by a man on foot. We had consequently to swim the mules and horses, a labor of no slight trouble and difficulty, as the current was rapid, and the bed of the river choked with rocks. More than an hour was wasted in finding a spot sufficiently clear of stones, and in devising means to induce the animals to enter the water. We resumed our journey on the opposite side of the valley. But before leaving Lizan I must mention the heroic devotion of ten Tiyari girls from the village of Serspeetho, who, as they were led across the bridge by the Kurds, on their return from the great massacre,—preferring death to captivity and conversion, threw themselves simultaneously into the Zab, and were drowned in its waters.

We now entered a valley formed by a torrent which joins the Zab below Lizan. On the opposite side, but far in the distance, were the Kurdish villages of the district of Chal, surrounded by trees and gardens. We passed through the small Chaldean village of Shoordh, now a heap of ruins, inhabited by a few wretched families, whose priest had been recently put to death by Nur-Ullah Bey, the chief of the Hakkiari tribes. From Shoordh we descended into a wild and rocky ravine, opening into the once rich and populous valley of Raola. We soon found ourselves on the outskirts of cultivation. A few feet of soil were rescued from the bed of the torrent, and sown with tobacco and garas. These straggling plots led us into a series of orchards and gardens, extending to the district of Tkhoma.

We were nearly two hours in reaching the house of the melek.* My party having gradually increased as we rode among the scattered cottages, I was followed by a large com-

---

* Literally, King, the title given to the chiefs of Tiyari.

pany. Melek Khoshaba* had been apprised of my intended visit; for he met us with the priests, and principal inhabitants at some distance from his dwelling. I was much struck by his noble carriage and handsome features. He wore, like the other chiefs, a dress of very gay colors, and a conical cap of felt, slightly embroidered at the edges, and ornamented with an eagle's feather. The men who accompanied him were mostly tall and well made, and were more showily dressed than the inhabitants of other villages through which we had passed. Their heads were shaved, as is customary among the Tiyari tribes, a small knot of hair being left uncut on the crown, and allowed to fall in a plait down the back. This tail, with the conical cap, gives them the appearance of Chinese. The boys, in addition to their inseparable partridges, carried cross-bows, with which they molested every small bird that appeared, and almost every one had an eagle's feather in his cap.

We followed the melek to his house, which stood high above the torrent on the declivity of the mountain. The upper, or summer room, was large enough to contain all the party. The melek and priests sat on my carpets; the rest ranged themselves on the bare floor against the walls. The girls brought me, as usual, baskets of fruit, and then stood at the entrance of the room. Many of them were very pretty; but the daughter of the chief, a girl of fourteen, excelled them all. I have seldom seen a more lovely form. Her complexion was fair; her features regular; her eyes and hair as black as jet; a continual smile played upon her mouth; and an expression of mingled surprise and curiosity stole over her face, as she examined my dress, or followed my movements. Her tresses, unconfined by the colored kerchief bound loosely round her head, fell in disorder down her back, reaching to her waist. Her dress was more gay, and neater, than that of the other women, who evidently confessed her beauty and her rank. I motioned to her to sit down; but that was an honor only re-

---

* A corruption of Khath Shaba, Sunday.

served for the mother of the melek, who occupied a corner of the room. At length she approached timidly to examine more closely a pocket compass, which had excited the wonder of the men.

The threatened invasion of Tkhoma by Beder Khan Bey, was the chief subject of conversation, and caused great excitement among the inhabitants of Raola. They calculated the means of defense possessed by the villagers of the proscribed district; but while wishing them success against the Kurds, they declared their inability to afford them assistance; for they still trembled at the recollection of the former massacre, and the very name of the Bohtan chief struck terror into the hearts of the Tiyari. They entreated me to devise some mode of delivering them from the danger. "It is true," said the melek, "that when Nur-Ullah Bey joined Beder Khan Bey in the great massacre, the people of Tkhoma marched with the Kurds against us; but could they do otherwise?—for they feared the chief of Hakkiari. They are our brothers, and we should forgive them; for the Scriptures tell us to forgive even our enemies." This pious sentiment was re-echoed by all the company.

Several men, whose wives and daughters were still in slavery, came to me, thinking that I could relieve them in their misfortune; and there was scarcely any one present who had not some tale of grief to relate. Several members of the family of Melek Khoshaba, including his cousin, to whom he had succeeded in the chiefship, had been killed in the massacre. The villages in the valley of Raola having, however, suffered less than those we had previously visited, were fast returning to their former prosperity.

The melek insisted upon accompanying us, with the priests and principal inhabitants, to the end of the valley. As we passed through the village we saw the women bathing at almost every door; nor did they appear at all conscious that we were near them. This simple and primitive mode of washing is thus publicly practiced among all the Chaldean tribes, particularly on the Saturday.

Melek Khoshaba accompanied me to a rude monument raised
over the bodies of fifty prisoners, who had been murdered at
the time of the invasion, and left me at the entrance of the
village. We had to pass through a narrow and barren ravine,
and a rocky gorge, before entering the district of Tkhoma.
Our path was the bed of the torrent; and the mountains,
rising precipitously on either side, shut in a scene of extraordinary wildness and solitude. This was the only road by which
we could reach Tkhoma, without crossing the lofty ranges of
rocks surrounding it on all other sides. A resolute body of
men might have held the ravine against any numbers. This
was one of the most dangerous tracts we had to traverse during
our journey. On the heights above are one or two villages,
inhabited by the Apenshai* Kurds, who are always engaged in
hostilities with the Tiyari, and fall upon such as are crossing
the frontiers of Tkhoma. My party was numerous and well
armed, and keeping close together we traveled on without appre-
hension.

  We emerged suddenly from this wilderness, and saw a richly
cultivated valley before us. Flocks of sheep and goats were
browsing on the hill-sides, and herds of cattle wandered in the
meadows below. These were the first domestic animals we had
seen in the Chaldean country, and they showed that hitherto
Tkhoma had escaped the hand of the spoiler. Two villages
occupied opposite sides of the valley; on the right, Ghissa,
on the left, Birijai. We rode to the latter. The houses
are built in a cluster, and not scattered among the gardens,
as in Tiyari. We were surrounded by the inhabitants as
soon as we entered the streets, and they vied with one another in expressions of welcome and offers of hospitality.
Kasha Hormuzd, the principal priest, prevailed upon me to
accompany him to a house he had provided, and on the roof of
which carpets were speedily spread. The people were in great
agitation at the report of Beder Khan Bey's projected march

* By the Kurds they are called Pinianish.

upon Tkhoma. They immediately flocked round us, seeking for news. The men were better dressed than any Nestorian Chaldeans I had yet seen. The felt cap was replaced by turbans of red and black linen, and these two favorite colors of the Kurds were conspicuous in their ample trowsers and embroidered jackets. As they carried pistols and daggers in their girdles, and long guns in their hands, they could scarcely be distinguished from the Mussulman inhabitants of the mountains. The women wore small embroidered skull-caps, from beneath which their hair fell loose or in plaits. Their shirts were richly embroidered, and round their necks and bosoms were hung coins and beads. They were happy in having escaped so long the fanaticism and rapacity of the Kurds. But they foresaw their fate. All was bustle and anxiety; the women were burying their ornaments and domestic utensils in secure places; the men preparing their arms, or making gunpowder. I walked to the church, where the priests were collecting their books, and the holy vessels to be hid in the mountains. Among the manuscripts I saw many ancient rituals, forms of prayer, and versions of the Scripture; the Acts of the Apostles, and the Epistles on vellum, the first and last leaves wanting, and without date, but evidently of a very early period; and a fine copy of the Gospels, Acts, and Epistles also on vellum, entire, with numerous illuminations, written in the year of the Seleucidæ 1552*, in the time of "Mar Audishio, Patriarch of the East, and of the Chaldeans."

I was much touched by the unaffected hospitality and simple manners of the two priests, Kashas Hormuzd, and Khoshaba, who entertained me; a third was absent. Their dress, torn and soiled, showed that they were poorer than their congregation. They had just returned from the vineyards, where

---

* The era of the Seleucidæ (the Greek or Alexandrian year, or the era of contracts, as it is sometimes called), was once in general use among the Christians, Jews and Mussulmans of the East, and is to this day always employed by the Chaldeans. It commences in October, B. C. 312; according to the Chaldeans one year later.

they had been toiling during the day; yet they were treated with reverence and respect; the upper places were given to them, they were consulted on all occasions, and no one drew nigh without kissing the hand, scarred by the plow and the implements of the field.

Almost every house furnished something toward our evening repast; and a long train of girls and young men brought us in messes of meat, fowls, boiled rice, garas and fruit. The priests and the principal inhabitants feasted with us, and there remained enough for my servants, and for the poor who were collected on the roof of a neighboring house. After our meal, many of the women came to me, and joined with the men in debating on their critical position, and in forming schemes for the security of their families, and the defense of their village. It was past midnight before the assembly separated.

The following day being Sunday, we were roused at dawn to attend the service of the church. The two priests officiated in white surplices. The ceremonies were short and simple; a portion of Scripture was read and then interpreted by Kasha Hormuzd in the dialect in use in the mountains—few understanding the Chaldean of the books.* His companion chanted the prayers—the congregation kneeling or standing, and joining in the responses. There were no idle forms or salutations; the people used the sign of the cross when entering, and bowed when the name of Christ occurred in the prayers. The Sacrament was administered to all present—men, women, and children partaking of the bread and wine, and my companion

---

* The language of the Chaldeans is a Semitic dialect allied to the Hebrew, Arabic, and Syriac, and still called the Chaldani or Chaldee. In its written form, it bears a close resemblance to the Chaldee of the book of Daniel. The dialect spoken by the mountain tribes varies slightly from that used in the villages of the plains; and the differences arise chiefly from local circumstances. It is an interesting fact that the Chaldean spoken in Assyria is almost identical with the language of the Sabæans, or Christians of St. John, as they are vulgarly called,—a remarkable tribe who reside in the province of Khuzistan or Suisana and in the districts near the mouth of the Euphrates, and who are probably the descendants of the ancient inhabitants of Babylonia and Chaldea.

receiving it among the rest. They were disposed to feel hurt
at my declining to join them, until I explained that I did not refuse from any religious prejudice. When the service was ended
the congregation embraced one another, as a symbol of brotherly
love and concord,* and left the church.   I could not but contrast
these simple and primitive rites with the senseless mummery,
and degrading forms, adopted by the converted Chaldeans of the
plains—the unadorned and imageless walls, with the hideous
pictures, and monstrous deformities which encumber the churches
of Mosul.

It may not be here out of place to remind the reader of the
peculiar doctrine which has earned for the Chaldeans the title
of Nestorians, a name probably given to them by the Roman
Catholic missionaries.   The Mussulmans term them simply
" Nasara," or " the Christians," while they call themselves
" Caldani" and " Souraiyah," or in the mountains by the name
of the tribe to which they belong.   Although they undoubtedly
profess the doctrine taught by Nestorius, who is looked upon as
one of the great fathers of their church, they deny having im-
bibed it from him, asserting that such as it is they received it
from the Apostles.   It is certain that the opinions preached
by Nestorius had already spread widely in the East, and were
particularly inculcated in the schools of the Chaldeans.   The
most important point of difference between the Chaldean and
other Christian churches is the assertion on the part of the
former of the divisibility and separation of the two persons, as
well as of the two natures, in Christ.   This of course involves
the refusal of the title of " Mother of God" to the Virgin, which
renders them particularly odious to the church of Rome, and is
probably the cause of their being accused of more heresies than
they really admit.   The profession of faith adopted by their
church, and still repeated twice a day, differs in few respects
from the Nicene creed, and it is evident, not only from it,

---

* This custom, it will be remembered, prevailed generally among the
primitive Christians.   The Roman Catholic church has retained the
remembrance of it in the " Pax."

but from the writings of Nestorius himself, and of the earliest
fathers of the Eastern church, that there is nothing to authorize
the violent charge of heresy made against the Chaldeans by
their enemies. It is admitted, on the other hand, that they have
retained in all their purity many of the doctrines and forms of
primitive Christianity.

Mosheim, whose impartiality can scarcely be doubted, thus
speaks of them :—" It is to the lasting honor of the Nestorian
sect, that of all the Christian societies established in the East,
they have preserved themselves the most free from the numberless superstitions which have found their way into the Greek
and Latin churches." * A Protestant may, therefore, wish to
ascertain in what respects they differ, otherwise than in the
doctrine already alluded to, from other Christian sects, and what
their belief and observances really are. The most important
points of difference may be summed up in a few words. They
refuse to the Virgin those titles, and that exaggerated veneration, which were the origin of most of the superstitions and
corruptions of the Romish and Eastern churches. They deny
the doctrine of purgatory, and are most averse, not only to the
worship of images, but even to their exhibition. The figure
of the cross is found in their churches, and they are accustomed to make the sign in common with other Christians of
the East ; not, however, considering this ceremony essential,
but rather as a badge of Christianity and a sign of brother-
hood among themselves, scattered as they are amid men of a
hostile faith. They agree with the reformed church in the
rejection of the doctrine of transubstantiation, and in the dis-
tribution of the bread and wine among the communicants.
There appear to be considerable doubts as to the number and
nature of their sacraments ; they are generally stated to amount
to seven, and to include baptism, marriage, and ordination.
The five lower grades of the clergy, under the rank of bishop,
are allowed to marry. In the early ages of the church the same
privilege was extended to the bishop and archbishop, and even

* Mosheim, Cent. XVI. Sect. iii. Part i.

to the patriarch. The fasts of the Chaldeans are numerous and very strictly observed, even fish not being eaten. There are 152 days in the year on which abstinence from animal food is enjoined. On the Sabbath no Nestorian performs a journey or does any work.

The vestibule of the church of Birijai was occupied by a misshapen and decrepit nun. Her bed was a mat in the corner of the building, and she was cooking her garas on a small fire near the door. She inquired, with many tears, after Mar Sha-moun, and hung round the neck of my companion when she learned that he had been living with him. Vows of chastity are very rarely taken among the Nestorian Chaldeans; and this woman, whose deformity might have precluded the hope of marriage, was the sole instance we met with in the mountains. Convents for either sex are unknown.

Birijai contained, at the time of my visit, nearly one hundred houses, and Ghissa forty. The inhabitants were comparatively rich, possessing numerous flocks, and cultivating a large extent of land. There were priests, schools, and churches in both villages.

One of the meleks of the tribe came early from Tkhoma Gowaia,* the principal village in the district, to welcome me to his mountains, and to conduct me to his house. He explained that as it was Sunday the Chaldeans did not travel, and conse-quently the other meleks and the principal inhabitants had not been able to meet me. We took leave of the good'people of Birijai, who had treated us with great hospitality, and followed Melek Putros up the valley.

To our left was the small Kurdish hamlet of Hayshat, high up in a sheltered ravine. An uninterrupted line of gardens brought us to the church of Tkhoma Gowaia, standing in the midst of scattered houses, this village being built like those of Tiyari. Here we found almost the whole tribe assembled, and in deep consultation on the state of affairs. We sat in a loft

* i. e. Middle or Center Tkhoma.

above the church during the greater part of the day, engaged
in discussion on the course to be pursued to meet the present
difficulties, and to defend the valley against the expected
attack of Beder Khan Bey. The men, who were all well
armed, declared that they were ready to die in the defense of
their villages; and that, unless they were overcome by numbers,
they would hold the passes against the forces of the Kurdish
chief. The Kurds, who inhabited two or three hamlets in
Tkhoma, had also assembled. They expressed sympathy for
the Christians, and offered to arm in their behalf. After much
debate it was resolved to send at once a deputation to the pashaw
of Mosul, to beseech his protection and assistance. Two priests,
two persons from the families of the meleks, and two of the
principal inhabitants, were chosen; and a letter was written by
Kasha Bodaca, one of the most learned and respectable priests in
the mountains. It was a touching appeal, setting forth that they
were faithful subjects of the sultan, had been guilty of no offense,
and were ready to pay any money, or submit to any terms that
the pashaw might think fit to exact. The letter, after having
been approved by all present, and sealed with the seals of the
chiefs, was delivered to the six deputies, who started at once on
foot for Mosul. At the same time no precaution was to be
omitted to place the valley in a state of defense, and to prepare
for the approach of the Kurds.

There were in Tkhoma three meleks, each chosen from a
different family by the tribe. The principal was Melek Putros,
—a stout, jovial fellow, gayly dressed, and well armed. His
colleagues were of a more sober and more warlike appearance.
There were no signs of poverty among the people; most of the
men had serviceable weapons, and the women wore gold and
silver ornaments. All the young men carried cross-bows, and
were skillful in their use, killing the small birds as they rested
on the trees. A well-armed and formidable body of men might
have been collected from the villages; which, properly directed,
could, I have little doubt, have effectually resisted the invasion
of Beder Khan Bey.

We passed the night on the roof of the church, and rose early to continue our journey to Baz. The valley and pass, separating Tkhoma from this district, being at this time of the year uninhabited, is considered insecure, and we were accompanied by a party of armed men, furnished by the meleks. The chiefs themselves walked with us to the village of Mezrai, whose gardens adjoin those of Tkhoma Gowaia. The whole valley, indeed, up to the rocky barrier, closing it toward the east, is an uninterrupted line of cultivation. Above the level of the artificial water-courses, derived from the torrent near its source, and irrigating all the lands of the district, are forests of oaks, clothing the mountains to within a short distance of their summits. Galls are not so plentiful here as in Tiyari; they form, however, an article of commerce with Persia, where they find a better market than in Mosul. Rice and flax are very generally cultivated, and fruit-trees abound.

We stopped for a few minutes at Gunduktha, the last village in Tkhoma, to see Kasha Bodaka, whom we found preparing, at the request of his congregation, to join the deputation to the Pashaw of Mosul. We took leave of him, and he started on his journey. He was an amiable, and, for the mountains, a learned man, greatly esteemed by the Chaldean tribes. Being one of the most skillful penmen of the day, his manuscripts were much sought after for the churches. He was mild and simple in his manners; and his appearance was marked by that gentleness, and unassuming dignity, which I had found in more than one of the Nestorian priests.*

The torrent enters the valley of Tkhoma by a very narrow gorge, through which a road, partly constructed of rough stones, piled up in the bed of the stream, is with difficulty carried. In the winter, when the rain has swollen the waters, this entrance must be impracticable; and even at this time, we could scarcely drag our mules and horses over the rocks, and through the deep

* Mr. Ainsworth, writing of Kasha Kana of Lizan, observes that he resembled in his manners and appearance an English clergyman. Kasha Bodaka was murdered by the chief of Chal shortly after our visit.

pools in which the torrent abqunds. All signs of cultivation
now ceased. Mountains rose on all sides, barren and treeless.
Huge rocks hung over the road, or towered above us. On their
pinnacles, or in their crevices, a few goats sought a scanty
herbage. The savage nature of the place was heightened by
its solitude.

Soon after entering the ravine, we met a shepherd boy,
dragging after him a sheep killed by the bears; and a little
beyond we found the reeking carcass of a bullock, which had
also fallen a victim to these formidable animals, of whose depredations we heard continual complaints. I observed on the
mountain sides several flocks of ibex, and some of our party
endeavored to get within gun-shot; but after sunrise their
watchfulness can not be deceived, and they bounded off to the
highest peaks, long before the most wary of our marksmen
could approach them.

We were steadily making our way over the loose stones and
slippery rocks, when a party of horsemen were seen coming
toward us. They were Kurds, and I ordered my party to keep
close together, that we might be ready to meet them in case of
necessity. As they were picking their way over the rough
ground, like ourselves, to the evident risk of their horses' necks
as well as of their own, I had time to examine them fully as
they drew near. In front, on a small, lean, and jaded horse,
rode a tall, gaunt figure, dressed in all the tawdry garments
sanctioned by Kurdish taste. A turban of wonderful capacity,
and almost taking within its dimensions horse and rider, buried
his head, which seemed to escape by a miracle being driven in
between his shoulders by the enormous pressure. From the
center of this mass of many-colored rags rose a high conical
cap of white felt. This load appeared to give an unsteady,
rolling gait to the thin carcass below, which could with difficulty support it. A most capacious pair of claret-colored
trowsers bulged out from the sides of the horse, and well nigh
stretched from side to side of the ravine. Every shade of red
and yellow was displayed in his embroidered jacket and cloak;

and in his girdle were weapons of extraordinary size, and most fanciful workmanship. His eyes were dark and piercing, and overshadowed by shaggy eyebrows; his nose aquiline, his cheeks hollow, his face long, and his beard black and bushy. Notwithstanding the ferocity of his countenance, and its unmistakable expression of villainy, it would have been difficult to repress a smile at the absurdity of the figure, and the disparity between it and the miserable animal concealed beneath. This was a Kurdish dignitary of the first rank; a man well known for deeds of oppression and blood; the mutesellim, or lieutenant-governor under Nur-Ullah Bey, the chief of Hakkiari. He was followed by a small body of well-armed men, resembling their master in the motley character of their dress; which, however, was somewhat reduced in the proportions, as became an inferiority of rank. The cavalcade was brought up by an individual, differing considerably from those who had preceded. His smooth and shining chin, and the rich glow of raki* upon his cheeks, were undoubted evidences of Christianity. He had the accumulated obesity of all his companions; and rode, as became him, upon a diminutive donkey, which he urged over the loose stones with the point of a claspknife. His dress did not differ much from that of the Kurds, except that, instead of warlike weapons, he carried an ink-horn in his girdle. This was Bircham, the "goulama d'Mira,"† as he was commonly called,—a half-renegade Christian, who was the steward, banker, and secretary of the Hakkiari chief.

I saluted the mutesellim, as we elbowed each other in the narrow pass; but he did not seem inclined to return my salutation, otherwise than by a curl of the lip, and an indistinct grunt, which he left me to interpret in any way I thought proper. It was no use quarreling with him, so I passed on. We had not proceeded far, when one of his horsemen returned to us, and called away Yakoub Rais, Ionunco, and one of the men of Tkhoma. Looking back, I observed them all in deep

---

* Ardent spirits. extracted from raisins or dates.
† The servant of the Mir or Prince.

consultation with the Kurdish chief, who had dismounted to wait for them. I rode on, and it was nearly an hour before the three Chaldeans rejoined us. Ionunco's eyes were starting out of his head with fright, and the expression of his face was one of amusing horror. Even Yakoub's usual grin had given way to a look of alarm. The man of Tkhoma was less disturbed. Yakoub began by entreating me to return at once to Tkhoma and Tiyari. The mutesellim, he said, had used violent threats; declaring that as Nur-Ullah Bey had served one infidel, who had come to spy out the country, and teach the Turks its mines, alluding to Schultz,* so he would serve me; and had sent off a man to the Hakkiari chief to apprise him of my presence in the mountains. "We must turn back at once," exclaimed Yakoub, seizing the bridle of my horse, "or, Wallah! that Kurdish dog will murder us all." I had formed a different plan; and, calming the fears of my party as well as I was able, I continued my journey toward Baz. Ionunco, however, racked his brain for every murder that had been attributed to Nur-Ullah Bey; and at each new tale of horror Yakoub turned his mule, and vowed he would go back to Asheetha.

We rode for nearly four hours through this wild, solitary valley. My people were almost afraid to speak, and huddled together as if the Kurds were coming down upon us. Two or three of the armed men scaled the rocks, and ran on before us as scouts; but the solitude was only broken by an eagle soaring above our heads, or by a wild goat which occasionally dashed across our path. In the spring, and early summer, these now desolate tracts are covered with the tents of the people of Tkhoma, and of the Kurds, who find on the slopes a rich pasture for their flocks.

It was mid-day before we reached the foot of the mountain dividing us from the district of Baz. The pass we had to cross is one of the highest in the Chaldean country, and at this season there was snow upon it. The ascent was long, steep,

---

* It will be remembered that this traveler was murdered by Nur-Ullah Bey.

and toilsome. We were compelled to walk, and even without
our weight, the mules could scarcely climb the acclivity. But
we were well rewarded for our labor when we gained the
summit. A scene of extraordinary grandeur opened upon us.
At our feet stretched the valley of Baz,—its villages and gardens but specks in the distance. Beyond the valley, and on all
sides of us, was a sea of mountains—peaks of every form and
height, some snow-capped, others bleak and naked; the further-
most rising in the distant regions of Persia. I counted nine
distinct mountain ranges. Two vast rocks formed a kind of
gateway on the crest of the pass, and I sat between them for
some minutes, gazing upon the sublime prospect before us.

The descent was rapid and dangerous, and so precipitous
that a stone might almost have been dropped on the church of
Ergub, first visible like a white spot beneath us. We passed a
rock, called the "Rock of Butter," from a custom, perhaps, of
pagan origin, existing among the Chaldean shepherds, of placing
upon it, as an offering, a piece of the first butter made in early
spring. As we approached the village, we found several of the
inhabitants laboring in the fields. They left their work, and
followed us. The church stands at some distance from the
houses; and when we reached it, the villagers compelled all
my servants to dismount, including Ibrahim Agha, who mut-
tered a curse upon the infidels, as he took his foot out of the
stirrup. The Christians raised their turbans,—a mark of reverence always shown on these occasions.

The houses of Ergub are built in a group. We stopped in
a small open place in the center of them, and I ordered my
carpet to be spread near a fountain, shaded by a cluster of
trees. We were soon surrounded by the inhabitants of the
village. The melek and the priest seated themselves with me;
the rest stood round in a circle. The men were well dressed
and armed; and, like those of Tkhoma, they could scarcely be
distinguished from the Kurds. Many of the women were pretty
enough to be entitled to the front places they had taken in the
crowd. They wore silver ornaments and beads on their

foreheads, and were dressed in jackets and trowsers of gay
colors.

After the letter of the patriarch had been read, and the
inquiries concerning him fully satisfied, the conversation turned
upon the expected expedition of Beder Khan Bey against
Tkhoma, and the movements of Nur-Ullah Bey, events causing
great anxiety to the people of Baz.   Although this district had
been long under the chief of Hakkiari, paying an annual tribute
to him, and having been even subjected to many vexatious
exactions, and to acts of oppression and violence, yet it had
never been disarmed, nor exposed to a massacre such as had
taken place in Tiyari.   There was now cause to fear that
the fanatical fury of Beder Khan Bey might be turned upon it
as well as upon Tkhoma; and the only hope of the inhabitants
was in the friendly interference of Nur-Ullah Bey, whose subjects they now professed themselves to be.   They had, however,
begun to conceal their church books and property, in anticipa-
tion of a disaster.

Both the melek and the priest pressed me to accept their
hospitality.   I preferred the house of the latter, to which we
moved in the afternoon.   My host was suffering much from the
ague, and was moreover old and infirm.   I gave him a few
medicines to stop his fever, for which he was very grateful.
He accompanied me to the church; but the bare walls alone
were standing.   The books and furniture had been partly carried away by the Kurds, and partly removed for security by the
people of the village.

After the events of the morning, I had made up my mind to
proceed at once to Nur-Ullah Bey, whose residence was only a
short day's journey distant; but on communicating my intention
to Mr. Hormuzd Rassam, he became so alarmed, and so resolutely declared that he would return alone rather than trust himself in the hands of the Mir of Hakkiari, that I was forced to give
up my plan.   In the present state of the mountains, there were
only two courses open to me: either to visit the chief, who
would probably, after learning the object of my journey, receive

and assist me as he had done Dr. Grant, or to retrace my steps
without delay. I decided upon the latter with regret, as I was
thus unable to visit Jelu and Diz, the two remaining Christian
districts. Without communicating my plans to any one, I sent
for two of Nur-Ullah Bey's attendants who happened to be in
the village, and induced them, by a small present, to take a note
to their master. They were led to believe that it was my intention to visit him on the following day, and I sent a Christian
to see that they took the road to Julamerik. The treachery
and daring of Nur-Ullah Bey were so well known, that I
thought it most prudent to deceive him, in case he might wish
to waylay me on my return to Tkhoma. I started therefore
before daybreak without any one in the village being aware of
my departure, and took the road by which we had reached Baz
the day before.

We crossed the pass as quickly as we were able, hurried
through the long barren valley, and reached Gunduktha, without meeting any one during our journey: to the no small comfort of my companions, who could not conceal their alarm
during the whole of our morning's ride.

We stopped to breakfast at Gunduktha, and saw the meleks
at Tkhoma Gowaia. The people of this village had felt much
anxiety on our account, as the mutesellim had passed the night
there, and had used violent threats against us. I learned that he
was going to Chal, to settle some differences which had arisen
between the Kurds of that district and of Hakkiari, and that
Bircham had been sent to Tkhoma by Nur-Ullah Bey to withdraw his family and friends; "for, this time," said the chief,
"Beder Khan Bey intends to finish with the Christians, and
will not make slaves for consuls and Turks to liberate."

As I was desirous of leaving Tkhoma as soon as possible, I
refused the proffered hospitality of Melek Putros, and rode on
to Birijai.

Being unwilling to return to Asheetha by Raola and the villages we had already visited, I determined—notwithstanding
the account given by the people of Tkhoma of the great diffi-

culty of the passes between us and the Zab—to cross the
mountain of Khouara, which rises at the back of Birijai. Their
descriptions had not been exaggerated. After dragging ourselves for two hours over loose stones, and along narrow ledges,
we reached the summit, weary and breathless. From the
crest we overlooked the whole valley of Tkhoma, with its
smiling villages, bounded to the east by the lofty range of
Kareetha; to the west I recognized the peaks of Asheetha, the
valley of the Zab, Chal, and the heights inhabited by the
Apenshai Kurds.

The mountain of Khouara is the Zoma—or summer pasture-
grounds—of the inhabitants of Ghissa and Birijai. As we
ascended we passed many rude sheds and caverns, half-blocked
up at the entrance with loose stones—places in which the
flocks are kept during the night, to preserve them from wild
animals. There is a fountain at a short distance from the top
of the pass, and a few trees near it; but the mountain is otherwise naked, and, at this time of the year, without verdure of
any kind.

An hour's rapid descent brought us to the Tiyari village of
Be-Alatha,—a heap of ruins on the two sides of a valley.
The few surviving inhabitants were in extreme poverty, and
the small-pox was raging among them. The water-courses
destroyed by the Kurds had not been repaired, and the fields
were mostly uncultivated. Even the church had not yet been
rebuilt; and as the trees which had been cut down were still
lying across the road, and the charred timber still encumbered
the gardens, the place had a most desolate appearance. We
were hospitably received by a shamasha, or deacon; whose
children, suffering from the prevailing disease, and covered with
discolored blains, crowded into the wretched cottage. Women
and children, disfigured by the malignant fever, came to me
for medicines; but it was beyond my power to relieve them.
Our host, as well as the rest of the inhabitants, was in extreme poverty. Even a little garas, and rancid butter, could
with difficulty be collected by contributions from all the houses,

and I was at a loss to discover how the people of Be-Alatha
lived. Yet the deacon was cheerful and contented, dwelling
with resignation upon the misfortunes that had befallen his village, and the misery of his family.

On leaving the village, now containing only ten families, I
was accosted by an old priest, who had been waiting until we
passed, and who entreated me to eat bread under his roof. As
his cottage was distant, I was compelled to decline his hospitality, though much touched by his simple kindness, and mild
and gentle manners. Finding that I would not go with him,
he insisted upon accompanying us to the next village, and took
with him three or four sturdy mountaineers, to assist us on our
journey; for the roads, he said, were nearly impassable.

Without the assistance of the good priest our attempt to reach
Marth d' Kasra would certainly have been hopeless. More
than once we turned back in despair, before the slippery rocks
and precipitous ascents. Ibrahim Agha, embarrassed by his
capacious boots, which, made after the fashion of the Turks,
could have contained the extremities of a whole family, was
more beset with difficulties than all the party. When he attempted to ride a mule, unused to a pack-saddle, he invariably
slid over the tail of the animal, and lay sprawling on the ground,
to the great amusement of Yakoub Rais, with whom his adventures were a never-failing source of anecdote in the village
assemblies. If he walked, either his boots became wedged into
the crevices of the rocks, or filled with gravel, to his no small
discomfort. At length, in attempting to cross a bed of loose
stones, he lost all presence of mind, and remained fixed in the
middle, fearful to advance or retreat. The rubbish yielded to
his grasp, and he looked down into a black abyss, toward which
he found himself gradually sinking with the avalanche he had
put in motion. There was certainly enough to frighten any
Turk, and Ibrahim Agha clung to the face of the declivity—
the picture of despair. "What's the Kurd doing?" cried a
Tiyari, with whom all Mussulmans were Kurds, and who was
waiting to pass on; "is there any thing here to turn a man's

face pale ? This is dashta, dashta" (a plain, a plain). Ibrahim
Agha, who guessed from the words Kurd and dashta, the meaning
of which he had learned, the purport of the Christian's address,
almost forgot his danger in his rage and indignation. " Gehan-
nem with your dashta !" cried he, still clinging to the moving
stones, " and dishonor upon your wife and mother. Oh ! that
I could only get one way or the other to show this infidel what
it is to laugh at the beard of an Osmanli, and to call him a Kurd
in the bargain !" With the assistance of the mountaineers he
was at length rescued from his perilous position, but not restored
to good-humor. By main force the mules were dragged over
this and similar places; the Tiyaris seizing them by the halter
and tail, and throwing them on their sides.

We were two hours struggling through these difficulties before reaching Marth d' Kasra, formerly a large village, but now
containing only forty houses.* Its appearance, however, was
more flourishing than that of Be-Alatha ; and the vineyards,
and gardens surrounding it, had been carefully trimmed and
irrigated. Above Marth d' Kasra, on a lofty overhanging rock,
is the village of Lagippa, reduced to ten houses. It is not accessible to beasts of burden. I rode to the house of a priest,
and sat there while the mules were resting.

The road between Marth d' Kasra and Chonba was no less
difficult and dangerous than that we had taken in the morning.
The gardens of the former village extend to the Zab, and we
might have followed the valley ; but the men who were with
us preferred the shorter road over the mountain, that we might
reach Chonba before nightfall.

The villages in the valley of the Zab suffered more from
the Kurds than any other part of Tiyari. Chonba was almost
deserted, its houses and churches a mass of ruins, and its gardens and orchards uncultivated and neglected. There was no
roof, under which we could pass the night ; and we were obliged to spread our carpets under a cluster of walnut-trees, near

* In the village are two churches and two priests.

a clear and most abundant spring. Beneath these trees was pitched the tent of Beder Khan Bey, after the great massacre; and here he received Melek Ismail, when delivered a prisoner into his hands. Yakoub Rais, who had been present at the murder of the unfortunate chief of the Tiyari, thus described the event. After heading his people in their defense of the pass which led into the upper districts, and performing prodigies of valor, Melek Ismail, his thigh broken by a musket-ball, was carried by a few followers to a cavern in a secluded ravine; where he might have escaped the search of his enemies, had not a woman, to save her life, betrayed his retreat. He was dragged down the mountain with savage exultation, and brought before Beder Khan Bey. Here he fell upon the ground. "Wherefore does the infidel sit before me?" exclaimed the ferocious chief, who had seen his broken limb, "and what dog is this that has dared to shed the blood of true believers?" "O Mir," replied Melek Ismail, still undaunted, and partly raising himself, "this arm has taken the lives of twenty Kurds; and, had God spared me, as many more would have fallen by it." Beder Khan Bey rose and walked to the Zab, making a sign to his attendants to bring the melek to him. By his directions they held the Christian chief over the river, and, severing his head from his body with a dagger, cast them into the stream.

All the family of the melek had distinguished themselves, at the time of the invasion, by their courage. His sister, standing by his side, slew four men before she fell mortally wounded.

Over the spring, where we had alighted, formerly grew a cluster of gigantic walnut-trees, celebrated in Tiyari for their size and beauty. They had been cut down by the Kurds, and their massive trunks were still stretched on the ground. A few smaller trees had been left standing, and afforded us shelter. The water, gushing from the foot of an overhanging rock, was pure and refreshing; but the conduits, which had once carried it into the fields, having been destroyed, a small marsh had been formed around the spring. The place conse-

quently abounded in mosquitoes, and we were compelled to keep
up large fires during the night, to escape their attacks.

On the following morning we ascended the valley of the Zab,
for about three miles, to cross the river. The road led into
the district of upper Tiyari, its villages being visible from
the valley, perched on the summits of isolated rocks, or half
concealed in sheltered ravines. The scenery is sublime. The
river forces itself through a deep and narrow gorge, the mountains rising one above the other in wild confusion, naked and
barren—except where the mountaineers have collected the
scanty soil, and surrounded their cottages with gardens and
vineyards.

A bridge of wicker-work at this part of the river was in better
repair than that of Lizan, and we crossed our mules without
difficulty. Descending along the banks of the Zab for a short
distance, we struck into the mountains; and passing through
Kona Zavvi and Bitti, two Kurdish villages buried in orchards,
reached Serspeetho about mid-day. We sat for two hours in
the house of the priest, who received us very hospitably. Out
of eighty families, thirty have alone survived; the rest had been
utterly destroyed. The two churches were still in ruins, and
but a few cottages had as yet been rebuilt. In the afternoon we
resumed our journey, and crossing a high and barren mountain,
descended into the valley of Asheetha.

As I was desirous of visiting some copper mines, described
to me by the people of the district, I engaged Kasha Hormuzd,
and one Daoud, who had been a workman at Nimroud, to
accompany me. We left Asheetha, followed by Yakoub Rais, the
priests and principal inhabitants, who took leave of us at some
distance from the village. We chose a different road from that
we had followed on entering the mountain, and thus avoided a
most precipitous ascent. Descending into the valley, leading
from Berwari to Asheetha, we came upon a large party of travelers, whom we at first took for Kurds. As they discharged
their guns, and stopped in the middle of a thicket of rushes
growing in the bed of the torrent, we approached them. They

proved to be Nestorian Chaldeans returning from Mosul to the
mountains. Among them, I found Kasha Oraho,* a learned
and worthy priest, who had fled from Asheetha at the time of
the massacre.   On account of his erudition, intimate knowledge of the political condition of the tribes, and acquaintance
with the tenets and ceremonies of the Chaldean church, he
had acted as secretary to Mar Shamoun during his exile.
Nearly three years had elapsed since he had quitted his mountains, and he pined for his native air.   Against the advice of
his friends he had determined to leave the plains, and he was
now on his return, with his wife and son, to Tiyari.   I sat with
him for a few minutes, and we parted never to meet again.   A
few days afterward, Beder Khan Bey and his hordes descended
into Asheetha.   Fresh deeds of violence recalled the scenes of
bloodshed to which the poor priest had formerly been a witness;
and he died of grief bewailing the miserable condition of the
Christian tribes.

Leaving the valley we had ascended on our approach to Tiyari, we entered the mountains to the right, and, after a rapid
ascent, found ourselves in a forest of oaks.   Our guides were
some time in discovering the mouth of the mine, which was only
known to a few of the mountaineers.   At a distance from the
entrance, copper ores were scattered in abundance among the
loose stones.   I descended with some difficulty, and saw many
passages running in various directions, all more or less blocked
up with rubbish and earth, much of which we had to remove
before I could explore the interior of the mine.

Leaving the district of Holamoun and Geramoun to our
right, we entered a deep valley, and rode for five hours through
a thick forest of oak, beech, and other mountain trees.   We
passed a few encampments of Kurds, who had chosen some
lawn in a secluded dell to pitch their black tents; but we saw
no villages until we reached Challek.   By the roadside, as we
descended to this place, I observed an extensive ruin, of sub-

* A corruption of Auraham, Abraham.

stantial masonry of square stones. I was unable to learn that
any tradition attached to the remains; nor could I ascertain
their name, or determine the nature of the building. It was
evidently a very ancient work, and may have been an Assyrian
fort to command the entrance into the mountains. The pass is
called Kesta, from a Kurdish village of that name.

Challek is a large village, inhabited partly by Chaldeans and
partly by Kurds. There are about fifteen families of Christians,
who have a church and a priest. The gardens are very extensive, and well irrigated, and the houses are almost concealed in
a forest of fruit-trees. We passed the night in the residence of
the kiayah, and were hospitably entertained.

In the morning we rode for some time along the banks of
the Khabour, and about five hours and a half from Challek
forded the Supna, one of its confluents. We stopped at the
Kurdish village of Ourmeli during the middle of the day, and
found there a su-bashi—a kind of superintendent tax-gatherer
—from Mosul, who received me in a manner worthy the dignity of both. He was dressed in an extraordinary assortment
of Osmanlu and Kurdish garments, the greater part of which
had been, of course, robbed from the inhabitants of the district
placed under his care. He treated me with sumptuous hospitality, at the expense of the Kurds, to whom he proclaimed me
a particular friend of the vizier, and a person of very exalted
worth. He brought, himself, the first dish of pillau, which was
followed by soups, chicken-kibaubs, honey, yaghort, cream,
fruit, and a variety of Kurdish luxuries. He refused to be
seated, and waited upon me during the repast. As it was
evident that all this respectful attention, on the part of so great
a personage, was not intended to be thrown away, when he
retired I collected a few of the Kurds, and, obtaining their
confidence by paying for my breakfast, soon learned from them
that the host had dealt so hardly with the villages in his jurisdiction, that the inhabitants, driven to despair, had sent a
deputation to lay their grievances before the pashaw. This
explained the fashion of my reception, which I could scarcely

attribute to my own merits. As I anticipated, my host came
to me before I left, and commenced a discourse on the character ·of Kurds in general, and on the way of governing
them. "Wallah, Billah, O Bey!" said. he, "these Kurds are
no Mussulmans; they are worse than unbelievers; they are
nothing but thieves and murderers; they will cut a man's
throat for a para. You will know what to tell his highness
when he asks you about them. They are beasts that must be
driven by the bit and the spur; give them too much barley,"
continuing the simile, "and they will get fat and vicious, and
dangerous. No, no, you must take away the barley, and leave
them only the straw." "You have, ·no doubt," I observed,
eying his many-colored Kurdish cloak, "taken care that as
little be left them to fatten upon as possible." "I am the lowest
of his highness's servants," he replied, scarcely suppressing a
broad grin; "but nevertheless, God knows that I am not the
least zealous in his service." It was at any rate satisfactory to
find that, in the su-bashi's system of government, the Kurds and·
Christians were placed on·an equal footing, and that the Mussulmans themselves now tasted of the miseries they had so long
inflicted with impunity upon others.

, We soon crossed the valley of Amadiyah, and meeting the
high-road between Daoudiyah and Mosul, entered some low
hills thickly set with Kurdish villages. In Kuremi, through
which we passed, there dwells a very holy sheikh, who enjoys
a great reputation for sanctity and miracles throughout Kurdistan. He was seated in the iwan, or open chamber, of a very
neat house, built, kept in repair, and continually whitewashed
by the inhabitants of the place. A beard, white as snow, fell
almost to his waist; and he wore a turban and long gown of
spotless white linen. He is almost blind, and sat rocking himself to and fro, fingering his rosary. He keeps a perpetual
Ramazan, never eating between dawn and sunset. On a slab,
near him, was a row of water-jugs of every form, ready for use
when the sun went down. Ibrahim Agha, who was not more
friendly to the Kurds than the su-bashi, treated the sheikh to

a most undignified epithet as he passed; which, had it been overheard by the people of the village, might have led to hostilities. Although I might not have expressed myself so forcibly as the cawass, I could not but concur generally in his opinion when reflecting that this man, and some others of the same class, had been the chief cause of the massacres of the unfortunate Christians; and that, at that moment, his son, Sheikh Tahar,* was urging Beder Khan Bey to prove his religious zeal by shedding anew the blood of the Nestorians. We stopped for the night in the large Catholic Chaldean village of Mungayshi, containing above forty Christian houses, a new church, and two priests.

A pass, over a richly wooded range of hills, leads from Mungayshi into a fertile plain, watered by several streams, and occupied by many Kurdish villages. Beyond, the mountains are naked and most barren. We wandered for some hours among pinnacles, through narrow ravines, and over broken rocks of sandstone, all scattered about in the wildest confusion. Not a blade of vegetation was to be seen; the ground was parched by the sun, and was here and there blackened by volcanic action. We came to several hot sulphurous springs, bubbling up in the valley, and forming large pools. In the spring the Kurds and the inhabitants of the surrounding villages congregate near these reservoirs, and pitch their tents for nearly a month to bathe in the waters, which have a great reputation for medicinal qualities.

A long defile brought us to the town of Dohuk, formerly a place of some importance, but now nearly in ruins. It is built on an island formed by a small stream, and probably occupies an ancient site. Its castle, a mud building with turrets, was held for some time by the hereditary Kurdish chief of the place, against Injeh Bairakdar Mohammed Pashaw; but was re-

* This fanatic, who was one of Beder Khan Bey's principal advisers, when entering Mosul, was accustomed to throw a vail over his face, that his sight might not be polluted by Christians, and other impurities in the place. He exercises an immense influence over the Kurdish population, who look upon him as a saint and worker of miracles.

duced, and has since been inhabited by a Turkish governor. Ismail Bey, the mutesellim, received me very civilly, and I breakfasted with him. The son of a neighboring Kurdish chief was visiting the bey. He was dressed in most elaborately embroidered garments, had ponderous jeweled rings in his ears, carried enormous weapons in his girdle, and had stuck in his turban a profusion of marigolds and other flowers. He was a handsome, intelligent boy; but, young as he might be, he was already a precocious pupil of Sheikh Tahar; and when I put him upon a religious topic, he entered most gravely into an argument to prove the obligation imposed upon Mussulmans to exterminate the unbelievers, supporting his theological views by very apt quotations from the Koran.

My horses, which had been sent from Amadiyah, were waiting for me here; and leaving our jaded mules, we proceeded to the Christian village of Malthaiyah, about one hour beyond, and in the same valley as Dohuk. Being anxious to visit the rock-sculptures near this place, I took a peasant with me and rode to the foot of a neighboring hill. A short walk up a very difficult ascent brought me to the monuments.

Four tablets have been cut in the rock; each occupied by nine figures. The subjects represented in the four bas-reliefs are similar, and appear to be an adoration of the gods by two kings. The first god wears the square horned cap, surmounted by a point, or fleur-de-lys; holds a ring in one hand, and a thong or snake in the other, and stands on two animals, a bull and a kind of gryphon, or lion with the head of an eagle, but without wings. The second divinity is beardless, also carries a ring, and is seated on a chair, the arms and lower parts of which are supported by human figures with tails, and by birds with human heads. The whole rests on two animals, a lion and a bull. The third divinity resembles the first, and stands on a winged bull. The four following have stars with six rays on the horned cap. The first of them has a ring in one hand, and stands on a gryphon without wings; the second also holds a ring, and is raised on a horse caparisoned as in the sculptures of Khorsabad; the third wields an object precisely

similar to the conventional thunderbolt of the Greek Jove, and is supported by a winged lion; the fourth is beardless, carries a ring, and stands on a lion without wings.

The two kings who are facing the divinities, have one hand elevated, and bear an object resembling a mace, always represented as carried by the monarch when engaged in religious ceremonies.

All the tablets have suffered much from exposure to the atmosphere, and one has been almost destroyed by the entrance into a tomb, which was probably cut in the rock at a long period subsequent to the Assyrian empire.

Assyrian Deity. On a rock tablet at Malthaiyah.

The details in the bas-reliefs are similar in character to those on the later Assyrian monuments, and are interesting in many respects. The thrones or arm-chairs, supported by animals and human figures, resemble those of the ancient Egyptians, and of the monuments of Kouyunjik, Khorsabad, and Persepolis. They also remind us of the throne of Solomon, which had "stays (or arms) on either side on the place of the seat, and *two lions stood beside the stays*. And twelve lions stood there, on the one side and on the other upon the six steps."[*]

I returned to the village after sunset. My cawass and servants had established themselves for the night on the roof of the church; and the kiayah had prepared a very substantial repast. The inhabitants of Malthaiyah are Catholic Chaldeans; their conversion not dating many years. The greater part joined us in the evening.

* 1 Kings x. 19, 20.

Next morning we rode over a dreary plain to Alkosh. In a defile, through the hills behind the village, I observed several

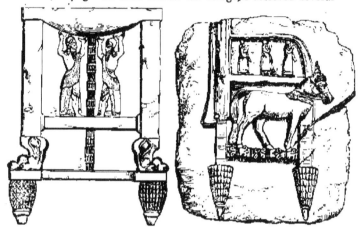

Assyrian Chairs.

rock-tombs,—excavations similar to those of Malthaiyah ; some having rude ornaments above the entrance, the door-ways of others being simply square holes in the rock.

Alkosh is a large Christian village. The inhabitants, who were formerly pure Chaldeans, have been converted to Roman Catholicism. It contains, according to a very general tradition, the tomb of Nahum, the prophet—the Alkoshite, as he is called in the introduction to his prophecies. It is a place held in great reverence by Mohammedans and Christians, but especially by Jews, who keep the building in repair, and flock here in great numbers at certain seasons of the year. The tomb is a simple plaster box, covered with green cloth, and standing at the upper end of a large chamber. On the walls of the room are pasted slips of paper, upon which are written, in distorted Hebrew characters, religious exhortations, and the dates and particulars of the visits of various Jewish families. The house

containing the tomb is a modern building. There are no inscriptions, nor fragments of any antiquity about the place; and
I am not aware in what the tradition originated, or how long
it has attached to the village of Alkosh.*

After visiting the tomb, I rode to the convent of Rabban
Hormuzd, built on the almost perpendicular sides of lofty rocks,
inclosing a small recess or basin, out of which there is only
one outlet,—a narrow and precipitous ravine, leading abruptly
into the plains. The spot is well suited to solitude and devotion. Half buried in barren crags, the building can scarcely
be distinguished from the natural pinnacles by which it is surrounded. There is scarcely a blade of vegetation to be seen,
except a few olive-trees, encouraged, by the tender solicitude of
the monks, to struggle with the barren soil. Around the convent, in almost every accessible part of the mountain, are a
multitude of artificial chambers in the rock, said to have once
served as a retreat for a legion of hermits, and from which most
probably were ejected the dead, to make room for the living;
for they appear to have been, at a very remote period, places
of burial. The number of these recesses must at one time
have been very considerable. They are now rapidly disappearing, and have been so doing for centuries. Still the sides
of the ravine are in some places honey-combed by them.

The hermits, who may once have inhabited the place, have
left no successors. A lonely monk from the convent may occasionally be seen clambering over the rocks; but otherwise the
solitude is seldom disturbed by the presence of a human being.

The ascent to the convent, from the entrance of the ravine,
is partly up a flight of steps rudely constructed of loose stones,
and partly by a narrow pathway cut in the rock. We were,
therefore, obliged to dismount, and to leave our horses in a
cavern at the foot of the mountain.

* According to St. Jerome, El Kosh or El Kosha, the birth-place of the
prophet, was a village in Galilee; and his tomb was shown at Bethogabra
near Emmaus. As his prophecies were written after the captivity of the
ten tribes, and apply exclusively to Nineveh, the tradition which points to
the village in Assyria as the place of his death, is not without weight.

Rabban Hormuzd was formerly in the possession of the Nestorian Chaldeans; but has been appropriated by the Catholics since the conversion of the inhabitants of Alkosh, Tel Kef, and other large villages of the plain. It is said to have been founded by one of the early Chaldean patriarchs, in the latter part of the fourth century. The saint, after whom the convent is called, is much venerated by the Nestorians, and was, according to some traditions, a Christian martyr, and the son of a king of Persia. The convent is partly excavated in the rocks, and partly constructed of well-cut stone. Since it was plundered by the Kurds, under the Bey of Rowandiz, no attempt has been made to restore the rich ornaments which once decorated the chapel, and principal halls. The walls are now naked and bare, except where hung with a few hideous pictures of saints and holy families, presented or stuck up by the Italian monks who occasionally visit the place. In the chapel are the tombs of several patriarchs of the Chaldean church, buried here long before its division, and whose titles, carved upon the monuments, are always " Patriarch of the Chaldeans of the East."* Six or eight half-famished monks reside in the building. They depend for supplies, which are scanty enough, upon the faithful of the surrounding country.

It was night before we reached the large Catholic village of Tel Kef. I had sent a horseman in the morning, to apprise the people of my intended visit; and Gouriel, the kiayah, with several of the principal inhabitants, had assembled to receive me. As we approached they emerged from a dark recess, where they had probably been waiting for some time. They carried a few wax lights, which served as an illumination, and whose motion, as the bearers advanced, was so unsteady, that there could be no doubt of the condition of the bearers.

Gouriel and his friends reeled forward toward my cawass,

---

* The seal used by Mar Shamoun bears the same title; and the patriarch so styles himself in all public documents. It is only lately that he has been induced, on some occasions, *when addressing Europeans.* to call himself " Patriarch of the Nestorians," the name never having been used by the Chaldeans themselves.

who chanced to be the first of the party ; and believing him to be
me, they fell upon him, kissing his hands and feet, and clinging
to his dress. Ibrahim Agha struggled hard to extricate himself, but in vain. "The Bey is behind," roared he. "Allah!
Allah! will no one deliver me from these drunken infidels ?"
Rejoicing in the mistake, I concealed myself among the horsemen. Gouriel, seizing the bridle of Ibrahim Agha's horse, and
unmindful of the blows which the cawass dealt about him, led
him in triumph to his residence. It was not before the wife of
the kiayah and some women, who had assembled to cook our
dinner, brought torches, that the deputation discovered their
error. I had alighted in the meanwhile unseen, and had found
my way to the roof of the house, where all the cushions that
could be found in the village were piled up in front of a
small table covered with bottles of raki and an assortment of
raisins and parched peas, prepared in my honor. I hid myself
among the pillows, and it was some time before the kiayah
discovered my retreat. He hiccuped out excuses till he was
breathless, and endeavoring to kiss my feet, asked forgiveness
for the unfortunate blunder. "Wallah! O Bey," exclaimed
Ibrahim Agha, who had been searching for a stable, "the
whole village is drunk. It is always thus with these unbelievers. They have now a good pashaw, who neither takes
jerums nor extra salian,* nor quarters hytas upon them.
What dirt do they then eat ? Instead of repairing their houses,
and sowing their fields, they spend every para in raki, and sit
eating and drinking, like hogs, night and day." I was forced
to agree with Ibrahim Agha in his conclusions, and would have
remonstrated with my hosts; but there was no one in a fit state
to hear advice ; and I was not sorry to see them at midnight
scattered over the roof, buried in profound sleep. I ordered the
horses to be loaded, and reached Mosul as the gates opened at
daybreak.

The reader may desire to learn the fate of Tkhoma. A few

---

* At Mosul jerums mean fines ; salian, the property tax, or taxes levied
on corporations under the old system.·

days after my return to Mosul, notwithstanding the attempts of
Tahyar Pashaw to avert the calamity, Beder Khan Bey marched
through the Tiyari mountains, levying contributions on the
tribes and plundering the villages, on his way to the devoted
district.   The inhabitants, headed by their meleks, made some
resistance, but were soon overpowered by numbers.   An indiscriminate massacre took place.   The women were brought
before the chief, and murdered in cold blood.   Those who attempted to escape were cut off.   Three hundred women and
children, who were flying into Baz, were killed in the pass I have
described.   The principal villages with their gardens were
destroyed, and the churches pulled down.   Nearly half the
population fell victims to the fanatical fury of the Kurdish
chief; among them were one of the meleks, and Kasha Bodaca.
With this good priest, and Kasha Auraham, perished the most
learned of the Nestorian clergy; and Kasha Kana is the last
who has inherited any part of the knowledge, and zeal, which
once so eminently distinguished the Chaldean priesthood.

The Porte was prevailed upon to punish this atrocious massacre, and to crush a rebellious subject who had long resisted
its authority.   An expedition was fitted out under Osman
Pashaw; and after two engagements, in which the Kurds were
signally defeated by the Turkish troops headed by Omar Pashaw,
Beder Khan Bey took refuge in a mountain-castle.   The position
had been nearly carried, when the chief, finding defense hopeless, succeeded in obtaining from the Turkish commander
the same terms which had been offered to him before the
commencement of hostilities.   He was to be banished from
Kurdistan; but his family and attendants were to accompany
him, and he was guaranteed the enjoyment of his property.
Although the Turkish ministers more than suspected that Osman
Pashaw had reasons of his own for granting these terms, they
honorably fulfilled the conditions upon which the chief, although
a rebel, had surrendered.   He was brought to Constantinople,
and subsequently sent to the Island of Candia—a punishment
totally inadequate to his numerous crimes.

H

After Beder Khan Bey had retired from Tkhoma, a few of the surviving inhabitants returned to their ruined villages; but Nur-Ullah Bey, suspecting that they knew of concealed property, fell suddenly upon them. Many died under the tortures to which they were exposed ; and the rest, as soon as they were released, fled into Persia. This flourishing district was thus destroyed; and it will be long ere its cottages again rise from their ruins, and the fruits of patient toil again clothe the sides of its valleys.

CHAPTER VIII.

A FEW days after my return to Mosul from the Tiyari mountains, a priest of the Yezidis, or, as they are commonly called,
"Worshipers of the Devil," was sent by Sheikh Nasr, the
religious chief of that remarkable sect, to invite Mr. Rassam and
myself to their great periodical feast. The vice-consul was
unable to accept the invitation; but I seized with eagerness the
opportunity of being present at ceremonies not before witnessed
by an European.

The origin of my invitation proves that the Yezidis may lay
claim to a virtue which is, unfortunately, not of frequent
occurrence in the East,—I mean gratitude. When Keritli
Oglu, Mohammed Pashaw, first came to Mosul, this sect was
among the objects of his cupidity and tyranny. He seized by
treachery, as he supposed, their high-priest; but Sheikh Nasr
had time to escape the plot against him, and to substitute in
his place the second in authority, who was carried a prisoner to
the town. Such is the attachment shown by the Yezidis to their
chief, that the deceit was not revealed, and the substitute bore
with resignation the tortures and imprisonment inflicted upon
him. Mr. Rassam having been applied to, obtained his release

from the pashaw, on the advance of a considerable sum of money, which the inhabitants of the district of Sheikhan undertook to repay, in course of time, out of the produce of their fields. They punctually fulfilled the engagement thus entered into, and looked to the British vice-consul as their protector.

Owing to the disturbed state of the country, and the misconduct of the late pashaws, some years had elapsed since the Yezidis had assembled at Sheikh Adi. The short rule of Ismail Pashaw, and the conciliatory measures of the new governor, had so far restored confidence among persons of all sects, that the Worshipers of the Devil had determined to celebrate their great festival with more than ordinary solemnity and rejoicings.

I quitted Mosul, accompanied by Hodja Toma (the dragoman of the vice-consulate), and the cawal, or priest, sent by Sheikh Nasr. We were joined on the road by several Yezidis, who were, like ourselves, on their way to the place of meeting. We passed the night in a small hamlet near Khorsabad, and reached Baadri early next day. This village, the residence of Hussein Bey, the political chief of the Yezidis, is built at the foot of the line of hills crossed in my previous journey to the Chaldean Mountains, and about five miles to the north of Ain Sifni. We traveled over the same dreary plain, leaving the mound of Jerrahiyah to our right.

On approaching the village I was met by Hussein Bey, followed by the priests and principal inhabitants on foot. The chief was about eighteen years of age, and one of the handsomest young men I ever saw. His features were regular and delicate, his eye lustrous, and the long curls, which fell from under his variegated turban, of the deepest black. An ample white cloak of fine texture was thrown over his rich jacket and robes. I dismounted as he drew near, and he endeavored to kiss my hand; but to this ceremony I decidedly objected; and we compromised matters by embracing each other after the fashion of the country. He then insisted upon leading my horse, which he wished me to remount, and it was with difficulty that I at length prevailed

upon him to walk with me into the village. He led me to his
salamlik, or reception room, in which carpets and cushions had
been spread. Through the center ran a stream of fresh water,
derived from a neighboring spring. The people of the place
stood at the lower end of the room, and listened in respectful
silence to the conversation between their chief and myself.

Breakfast was brought to us from the harem of Hussein Bey;
and the crowd having retired after we had eaten, I was left
during the heat of the day to enjoy the cool temperature of the
salamlik.

I was awakened in the afternoon by that shrill cry of the
women, which generally announces some happy event. The
youthful chief entered soon afterward, followed by a long
retinue. It was evident, from the smile upon his features, that
he had joyful news to communicate. He seated himself on my
carpet, and thus addressed me:—" O Bey, your presence has
brought happiness on our house. At your hands we receive
nothing but good. We are all your servants; and, praise be
to the Highest, in this house another servant has been born to
you. The child is yours: he is our first-born, and he will grow
up under your shadow. Let him receive his name from you,
and be hereafter under your protection." The assembly joined
in the request, and protested that this event, so interesting to
all the tribe, was solely to be attributed to my fortunate visit.
I was not quite aware of the nature of the ceremony, if any, in
which I might be expected to join on naming the new-born
chief. Notwithstanding my respect and esteem for the Yezidis,
I could not but admit that there were some doubts as to the
propriety of their tenets and form of worship; and I was
naturally anxious to ascertain the amount of responsibility
which I might incur, in standing godfather to a devil-worship-
ing baby. However, as I was assured that no other form was
necessary than the mere selection of a name (the rite of baptism
being reserved for a future day, when the child could be carried
to the tomb of Sheikh Adi, and could bear immersion in its sacred
waters), I thus answered Hussein Bey:—" O Bey, I rejoice in

this happy event, for which we must return thanks to God. May this son be but the first of many who will preserve, as their forefathers have done, the fame and honor of your house. As you ask of me a name for this child, I could give you many, which, in my language and country, are well-sounding and honorable; but your tongue could not utter them, and they would moreover be without meaning. Were it usual I would call him after his father, whose virtues he will no doubt imitate; but such is not the custom. I have not forgotten the name of his grandfather,—a name which is dear to the Yezidis, and still brings to their memory the days of their prosperity and happiness. Let him therefore be known as Ali Bey; and may he live to see the Yezidis as they were in the time of him after whom he is called." This oration, which was accompanied by a few gold coins to be sewn to the cap of the infant, was received with great applause; and the name of Ali Bey was unanimously adopted; one of the chief's relations hastening to the harem, to communicate it to the ladies. He returned with a carpet and some embroidery, as presents from the mother, and with an invitation to the harem to see the females of the family. I found there the chief's mother and his second wife; for he had already taken two. They assured me that the lady, who had just brought joy to the house, was even more thankful than her husband; and that her gratitude to me, as the author of her happiness, was unbounded. They brought me honey and strings of dried figs from the Sinjar, and entertained me with domestic histories until I thought it time to return to the salamlik.

The Yezidis were some years ago a very powerful tribe. Their principal strongholds were in the district which I was now visiting, and in the Jebel Sinjar, a solitary mountain rising in the center of the Mesopotamian desert to the west of Mosul. The last independent chief of the Yezidis of Sheikhan was Ali Bey, the father of Hussein Bey. He was beloved by his tribe, and sufficiently brave and skillful in war to defend them, for many years, against the attacks of the Kurds and Mussulmans of the plain.   The powerful Bey of Rowandiz, who had united most of the Kurdish tribes of the surrounding mountains under his banner, and long defied both Turks and Persians, resolved to crush the hateful sect of the Yezidis.   Ali Bey's forces were greatly inferior in numbers to those of his persecutor.   He was defeated, and fell into the hands of the Rowandiz chief, who put him to death.   The inhabitants of Sheikan fled to Mosul.   It was spring ; the river had overflowed its banks, and the bridge of boats had been removed.   A few succeeded in crossing the stream ; but a vast crowd of men, women, and children were left upon the opposite side, and congregated on the great mound of Kouyunjik.   The Bey of Rowandiz followed them.   An indiscriminate slaughter ensued ; and the people of Mosul beheld, from their terraces, the murder of these unfortunate fugitives, who cried to them in vain for help—for both Christians and Mussulmans rejoiced in the extermination of an odious and infidel sect, and no arm was lifted in their defense. Hussein Bey, having been carried by his mother to the mountains, escaped the general slaughter.   He was carefully brought up by the Yezidis, and from his infancy had been regarded as their chief.

The inhabitants of the Sinjar were soon after subdued by Mehemet Reshid Pashaw, and a second time by Hafiz Pashaw. On both occasions there was a massacre, and the population was reduced by three fourths.   The Yezidis took refuge in caves, where they were either suffocated by fires lighted at the mouth, or destroyed by discharges of cannon.

It will be remembered that Mohammedans, in their dealings with men of other creeds, make a distinction between such as are believers in the sacred books, and such as have no recognized inspired works.   To the first category belong Christians of all denominations, as receiving the two testaments ; and the Jews, as followers of the old.   With Christians and Jews, therefore, they may treat, make peace, and live ; but with such as are included in the second class, the good Mussulman can have no intercourse.   No treaty nor oath, when they are concerned, is binding. They have the choice between conversion and the sword, and it is unlawful even to take tribute from them. The Yezidis, not being looked upon as "Masters of a Book," have been exposed for centuries to the persecution of the Mohammedans. The harems of the south of Turkey have been recruited from them. Yearly expeditions have been made by the governors of provinces into their districts; and, while the men and women were slaughtered without mercy, the children of both sexes were carried off, and exposed for sale in the principal towns. These annual hunts were one of the sources of revenue of Beder Khan Bey; and it was the custom of the Pashaws of Baghdad and Mosul to let loose the irregular troops upon the ill-fated Yezidis, as an easy method of satisfying their demands for arrears of pay. This system was still practiced to a certain extent within a very few months of my visit; and gave rise to atrocities scarcely equaled in the better known slave-trade.

It was not unnatural that the Yezidis should revenge themselves, whenever an opportunity might offer, upon their oppressors. They formed themselves into bands, and were long the terror of the country. No Mussulman that fell into their hands was spared. Caravans were plundered, and merchants murdered without mercy. Christians, however, were not molested; for the Yezidis looked upon them as fellow-sufferers for religion's sake.

These acts of retaliation furnished an excuse for the invasion of the Sinjar by Mehemet Reshid and Hafiz Pashaws. Since the great massacres which then took place, the Yezidis have been completely subdued, and have patiently suffered under their misfortunes. Their devotion to their religion is no less remarkable than that of the Jews; and I remember no instance of a person of full age renouncing his faith. They invariably prefer death, and submit with resignation to the tortures inflicted upon them.

Sheikh Nasr, the chief priest of the sect, had already left Baadri, and was preparing for the religious ceremonies at the

tomb of Sheikh Adi.   I visited his wife, and was gratified by
the unaffected hospitality of my reception, and by the cleanliness
of the house and its scanty furniture.   All the dwellings which
I entered appeared equally neat, and well built.   Some stood in
small gardens filled with flowers, and near them were streams
of running water, brought from the abundant springs which issue
from the hill above the village.

Next morning at dawn, Hussein Bey issued from his harem,
armed and dressed in his gayest robes, ready to proceed to the
tomb of the saint.   The principal people of the village were soon
collected, and we all started together, forming a long procession,
preceded by musicians with the tamborine and pipe.   The
women were busily employed in loading their donkeys with carpets and domestic utensils.   They were to follow leisurely.
Hussein Bey and I rode together, and as long as the ground permitted, the horsemen and footmen who accompanied us, engaged
in mimic fight, discharging their fire-arms into the air, and singing their war-cry.   We soon reached the foot of a very precipitous ascent, up which ran a steep and difficult pathway.   The
horsemen now rode on in single file, and we were frequently
compelled to dismount and drag our horses over the rocks.   We
gained the summit of the pass in about an hour, and looked
down into the richly wooded valley of Sheikh Adi.   As soon as
the white spire of the tomb appeared above the trees, all our
party discharged their guns.   The echoes had scarcely died
away, when our signal was answered by similar discharges from
below.   As we descended through the thick wood of oaks, we
passed many pilgrims on their way, like ourselves, to the tomb ;
the women seated under the trees, relieving themselves awhile
from their infant burdens ; the men re-adjusting the loads which
the rapid descent had displaced.   As each new body of travelers
caught sight of the object of their journey, they fired their guns,
and shouted the cry of the tribe to those below.

At some distance from the tomb we were met by Sheikh
Nasr and a crowd of priests and armed men.   The sheikh was
dressed in the purest white linen, as were the principal members

N*

of the priesthood. His age could scarcely have exceeded forty ;
his manners were most mild and pleasing ; he welcomed me
with warmth ; and it was evident that my visit had made a very
favorable impression upon all present. After I had embraced
the chief, and exchanged salutations with his followers, we
walked together toward the sacred precincts. The outer court,
as well as the avenue which led to it, was filled with people ; but
they made way for us as we approached, and every one eagerly
endeavored to kiss my hand.

The Yezidis always enter the inner court of the tomb bare-
footed. I followed the custom, and leaving my shoes at the
entrance, seated myself, with Sheikh Nasr and Hussein Bey,
upon carpets spread under an arbor, formed by a wide-spreading
vine. The sheikhs and cawals, two of the principal orders of
the priesthood, alone entered with us, and squatted around-the
yard against the walls. The trees, which grew among and
around the buildings, threw an agreeable shade over the whole
assembly.

The tomb of Sheikh Adi is in a narrow valley, or rather ravine, which has only one outlet, as the rocks rise precipitously
on all sides, except where a small stream forces its way into a
larger valley beyond. It stands in a court-yard, and is surrounded by a few buildings, inhabited by the guardians and
servants of the sanctuary. The interior is divided into a large
hall partitioned in the center by a row of columns and arches,
and having at the upper end a reservoir filled by an abundant
spring issuing from the rock ; and two smaller apartments, in
which are the tombs of the saint, and of some inferior personage. The water of the reservoir is regarded with peculiar
veneration, and is believed to be derived from the holy well of
Zemzem. In it children are baptized, and it is used for other
sacred purposes. The tomb is covered by a large square case,
made of clay and plastered, over which is thrown an embroidered green cloth. It is in the inner room, which is dimly
lighted by a small lamp. On it is written the chapter of the
Koran, called the Ayat el Courci. It is thus made to resemble

as nearly as possible the tomb of a Mussulman saint, to preserve it from profanation by the Kurds.

In the principal hall a few lamps are generally burning, and at sunset lights are placed in niches scattered over the walls.

Two white spires, rising above the building, form a pleasing contrast with the rich foliage by which they are surrounded. They are topped by gilt ornaments, and their sides are fashioned into many angles, causing an agreeable variety of light and shade. On the wall near the doorway are rudely carved a lion, a snake, a hatchet, a man, and a comb. The snake, painted black, is particularly conspicuous. Although it might be suspected that these figures were emblematical, I could obtain no other explanation from Sheikh Nasr, than that they had been cut by the Christian mason who repaired the tomb some years ago, as ornaments suggested by his mere fancy. I observed the hatchet, comb, and a hooked stick, such as is generally carried in the country, carved on many stones in the building, but was assured that they were only marks placed upon them at the request of those who had furnished money toward the restoration of the building, or had assisted in the work.

In the center of the inner court, and under the vine, is a square plaster case, in which is a small recess filled with balls of clay taken from the tomb of the saint. These are sold or distributed to pilgrims, and regarded as very sacred relics—useful against diseases and evil spirits, and to be buried with the dead. Certain members of the priesthood and their families alone inhabit the surrounding buildings. They are chosen to watch over the sacred precincts, and are supported and supplied with provisions by the tribe.

The outer court is inclosed by low buildings, with recesses similar to those in an Eastern bazar. They are intended for the accommodation of pilgrims, and for the stalls of pedlers, during the celebration of the festival. Several gigantic trees throw their shade over the open space, and streams of fresh water are led round the buildings.

Around the tomb, and beneath the trees which grow on the

sides of the mountain, are numerous rudely constructed edifices, each belonging to a Yezidi district or tribe. The pilgrims, according to the place from which they come, reside in them during the time of the feast ; so that each portion of the valley is known by the name of the country, or tribe, of those who resort there.

I sat till nearly mid-day with the assembly, at the door of the tomb. Sheikh Nasr then rose, and I followed him into the outer court, which was filled by a busy crowd of pilgrims. In the recesses and on the ground were spread the stores of the pedlers, who, on such occasions, repair to the valley. Many-colored handkerchiefs, and cotton stuffs, hung from the branches of the trees ; dried figs from the Sinjar, raisins from Amadiyah, dates from Busrah, and walnuts from the mountains, were displayed in heaps upon the pavement. Around these tempting treasures were gathered groups of boys and young girls. Men and women were engaged on all sides in animated conversation, and the hum of human voices was heard through the valley. All respectfully saluted the sheikh, and made way for us as we approached. We issued from the precincts of the principal building, and seated ourselves on the edge of a fountain built by the road-side, and at the end of the avenue of trees leading to the tombs. The slabs surrounding the basin are to some extent looked upon as sacred ; and at this time only Hussein Bey, Sheikh Nasr, and myself were permitted to place ourselves upon them. Even on other occasions the Yezidis are unwilling to see them polluted by Mussulmans, who usually choose this spot, well adapted for repose, to spread their carpets. The water of the fountain is carefully preserved from impurities, and is drank by those who congregate in the valley. Women were now hastening to and fro with their pitchers, and making merry as they waited their turn to dip them into the reservoir. The principal sheikhs and cawals sat in a circle round the spring, and listened to the music of pipes and tamborines.

I never beheld a more picturesque or animated scene. Long

lines of pilgrims toiled up the avenue. There was the swarthy
inhabitant of the Sinjar, with his long black looks, his piercing
eye and regular features—his white robe floating in the wind,
and his unwieldy matchlock thrown over his shoulder. Then
followed the more wealthy families of the Kochers,—the wandering tribes who live in tents in the plains, and among the hills
of ancient Adiabene ; the men in gay jackets and variegated
turbans, with fantastic arms in their girdles ; the women richly
clad in silk antaris ; their hair, braided in many tresses, falling
down their backs, and adorned with wild flowers ; their foreheads almost concealed by gold and silver coins ; and huge
strings of glass beads, coins, and engraved stones hanging round
their necks. Next would appear a poverty-stricken family from
a village of the Mosul district ; the women clad in white, pale
and care-worn, bending under the weight of their children ; the
men urging on the heavily-laden donkey. Similar groups descended from the hills. Repeated discharges of fire-arms, and a
well-known signal, announced to those below the arrival of every
new party.

All turned to the fountain before proceeding to their allotted
stations, and laying their arms on the ground, kissed the hands
of Hussein Bey, Sheikh Nasr, and myself. After saluting the
assembled priests they continued their way up the sides of the
mountains, and chose a wide-spreading oak, or the roof of a
building, for a resting-place during their sojourn in the valley.
They then spread their carpets, and, lighting fires with dry
branches and twigs, busied themselves in preparing their food.
Such groups were scattered in every direction. There was
scarcely a tree without its colony.

All, before entering the sacred valley, washed themselves and
their clothes in the stream issuing from it. They came thus
purified to the feast. I never before saw so much assembled
cleanliness in the East. Their garments, generally white, were
spotless.

During the afternoon, dances were performed before the bey
and myself. They resembled the Arab Debké and the Kurdish

Tchopee. As many young men as could crowd into the small open space in front of the fountain joined in them. Others sang in chorus with the music. Every place, from which a sight could be obtained of the dancers, was occupied by curious spectators. Even the branches above our heads were bending under the clusters of boys who had discovered that, from them, they could get a full view of what was going on below. The manœuvers of one of these urchins gave rise to a somewhat amusing incident, which illustrates the singular superstitions of this sect. He had forced himself to the very end of a weak bough, which was immediately above me, and threatened every moment to break under the weight. As I looked up I saw the impending danger, and made an effort, by an appeal to the chief, to avert it. "If that young Sheit——" I exclaimed, about to use an epithet generally given in the East to such adventurous youths :* I checked myself immediately; but it was already too late; half the dreaded word had escaped. The effect was instantaneous: a look of horror seized those who were near enough to overhear me; it was quickly communicated to those beyond. The pleasant smile, which usually played upon the fine features of the young bey, gave way to a serious and angry ex-pression. I lamented that I had thus unwillingly wounded the feelings of my hosts, and was at a loss to know how I could make atonement for my indiscretion——doubting whether an apology to the Evil principle or to the chief was expected. I endeavored, however, to make them understand, without venturing upon any observations which might have brought me into greater difficul-ties, that I regretted what had passed; but it was some time ere the group resumed their composure, and indulged in their pre-vious merriment.

My carpets had been spread on the roof of a building of some size, belonging to the people of Semil. Around me, but at a convenient distance, were scattered groups of pilgrims from that district. Men, women, and children were congre-

* The term Sheitan (equivalent to Satan) is usually applied in the East to a clever, cunning, or daring fellow.

gated round their caldrons, preparing their evening meal;
or were stretched upon their coarse carpets, resting after the
long march of the day. Near me was the chief, whose mud
castle crowns the mound of the village of Semil. He was a
stern-looking man, gayly dressed, and well armed. He received
me with every demonstration of civility, and I sat for some
time with him and his wives; one of whom was young and
pretty, and had been recently selected from the Kochers, or
wanderers. Her hair was profusely adorned with flowers and
gold coins. They had sacrificed a sheep, and all (including the
chief, whose arms, bare to the shoulder, were reeking with
blood) gathered round the carcass; and, tearing the limbs, distributed morsels to the poor who had been collected to receive
them.

At some distance from the people of Semil were the wife and
family of Sheikh Nasr, who had also slain a sheep. The
sheikh himself resided in the sacred building, and was occupied
during the day in receiving the pilgrims, and performing
various duties imposed upon him on the occasion. I visited
his harem; his wife spread fruit and honey before me, and
entertained me with a long account of her domestic employ-
ments.

Below the cluster of buildings assigned—to the people of
Semil is a small white spire, springing from a low edifice,
neatly constructed, and, like all the sacred places of the Yezidis, kept as pure as repeated coats of whitewash can make it.
It is called the sanctuary of Sheikh Shems, or the Sun; and
is so placed, that the first rays of that luminary should as frequently as possible fall upon it. Near the door an invocation
to Sheikh Shems is carved on a slab; and one or two votive
tablets, raised by the father of Hussein Bey, and other chiefs
of the Yezidis, are built into the walls. The interior, which is
a very holy place, is lighted by a few small lamps. At sunset,
as I sat in the alcove in front of the entrance, a herdsman led
into a pen, attached to the building, a drove of white oxen. I
asked a cawal, who was near me, to whom the beasts belonged.

"They are dedicated," he said, "to Sheikh Shems, and are never slain except on great festivals, when their flesh is distributed among the poor."* This unexpected answer gave rise to an agreeable musing; and I sat, almost unconscious of the scene around me, until darkness stole over the valley.

As the twilight faded, the fakirs, or lower order of priests, dressed in brown garments of coarse cloth, closely fitting to their bodies, and wearing black turbans on their heads, issued from the tomb, each bearing a light in one hand, and a pot of oil, with a bundle of cotton wicks, in the other. They filled and trimmed lamps placed in niches in the walls of the court-yard, and scattered over the buildings on the sides of the valley, and even on isolated rocks and in the hollow trunks of trees. Innumerable stars appeared to glitter on the black sides of the mountain, and in the dark recesses of the forest. As the priests made their way through the crowd, to perform their task, men and women passed their right hands through the flame, and then devoutly carried them to their lips, after rubbing the right eyebrow with the part which had been puri-fied by the sacred element. Some, who bore children in their arms, anointed them in like manner, while others held out their hands to be touched by those who, less fortunate than themselves, could not reach the flame.

The lamps are votive offerings from pilgrims, or from those who have appealed to Sheikh Adi in times of danger or disease, and a yearly sum is given to the guardians of the tomb for oil, and for the support of the priests. They are lighted every evening as long as the supplies last. In the daytime the smoked walls mark where they are placed; and I have ob-served the Yezidis devoutly kissing the blackened stones.

About an hour after sunset the fakirs, who are the servants of the tomb, appeared with platters of boiled rice, roast meat, and fruit. They had been sent to me from the kitchen of the

* The dedication of the bull to the sun, so generally recognized in the religious systems of the ancients, probably originated in Assyria, and the Yezidis may have unconsciously preserved a myth of their ancestors.

holy edifice.   The wife of Sheikh Nasr also contributed some
dishes toward the repast.

As night advanced, those who had assembled—they must
now have amounted to nearly five thousand persons—lighted
torches, which they carried with them as they wandered
through the forest.   The effect was magical ; the varied groups
could be faintly distinguished through the darkness ; men hurrying to and fro ; women, with their children, seated on the
house-tops ; and crowds gathering round the pedlers who
exposed their wares for sale in the court-yard.   Thousands of
lights were reflected in the fountains and streams, glimmered
among the foliage of the trees, and danced in the distance.
As I was gazing on this extraordinary scene, the hum of human
voices was suddenly hushed, and a strain, solemn and melancholy, arose from the valley.   It resembled some majestic chant
which years before I had listened to in the cathedral of a distant
land.   Music so pathetic and so sweet I had never before heard
in the East.   The voices of men and women were blended in
harmony with the soft notes of many flutes.   At measured intervals the song was broken by the loud clash of cymbals and
tambourines ; and those who were without the precincts of the
tomb then joined in the melody.

I hastened to the sanctuary, and found Sheikh Nasr, surrounded by the priests, seated in the inner court.   The place
was illuminated by torches and lamps, which threw a soft light
over the white walls of the tomb and green foliage of the
arbor.   The sheikhs, in their white turbans and robes, all
venerable men with long gray beards, were ranged on one side ;
on the opposite, seated on the stones, were about thirty cawals
in their motley dresses of black and white—each performing on
a tamborine or a flute.   Around stood the fakirs in their dark
garments, and the women of the orders of the priesthood arrayed
in pure white.   No others were admitted within the walls of
the court.

The same slow and solemn strain, occasionally varied in the
melody, lasted for nearly an hour ; a part of it was called

" Makam Azerat Esau," or the song of the Lord Jesus. It was
sung by the sheikhs, the cawals, and the women ; and occasionally by those without. I could not catch the words ; nor
could I prevail upon any of those present to repeat them to me.
They were in Arabic ; and as few of the Yezidis can speak or
pronounce that language, they were not intelligible, even to the
experienced ear of Hodja Toma, who accompanied me. The
tamborines only interrupted at intervals the song of the
priests. As the time quickened they broke in more frequently. The chant gradually gave way to a lively melody,
which, increasing in measure, was finally lost in a confusion
of sounds. The tamborines were beaten with extraordinary
energy ; the flutes poured forth a rapid flood of notes ; the
voices were raised to their highest pitch ; the men outside
joined in the cry ; while the women made the rocks resound
with the shrill *tahlehl.* The musicians, giving way to the
excitement, threw their instruments into the air, and strained
their limbs into every contortion, until they fell exhausted to
the ground. I never heard a more frightful yell than that
which rose in the valley. It was midnight. The time and
place were well suited to the occasion ; and I gazed with
wonder upon the extraordinary scene around me. I did not
marvel that such wild ceremonies had given rise to those stories
of unhallowed rites, and obscene mysteries, which have rendered
the name of Yezidi an abomination in the East. Notwithstanding the uncontrollable excitement which appeared to prevail among all present, there were no indecent gestures nor
unseemly ceremonies. When the musicians and singers were
exhausted, the noise suddenly died away ; the various groups
resumed their previous cheerfulness, and again wandered
through the valley, or seated themselves under the trees.

Some ceremony took place before I joined the assembly at
the tomb, at which no stranger can be present, nor could I
learn its nature from the cawals. Sheikh Nasr gave me to
understand that their holy symbol, the Melek Taous, was then
exhibited to the priests, and he declared that, as far as he was

concerned, he had no objection to my witnessing the whole of their rites; but that many of the sheikhs were averse to it, and he did not wish to create any ill-feeling in the tribe.   Indeed, I found him frank and communicative on all subjects.

After the ceremonies in the inner yard had ceased, I returned with the sheikh and Hussein Bey to the fountain in the avenue.   Around it were grouped men and women with torches, which flung their red gleams upon the water.   Several of the cawals accompanied us to the spot, and sang and played on their flutes and tamborines until nearly dawn.

Daylight had begun to appear before the pilgrims sought repose.   Silence reigned through the valley until mid-day, when new parties of travelers reached the tomb and again awakened the echoes by their cries and the discharge of fire-arms. Toward the evening about seven thousand persons must have assembled.   The festival was more numerously attended than it had been for many years, and Sheikh Nasr rejoiced in the prospect of times of prosperity for his people.   At night the ceremonies of the previous evening were repeated.   New melodies were introduced; but the singing ended in the same rapid measure and violent excitement that I have described.   During the three days I remained at Sheikh Adi, I wandered over the valley and surrounding mountains; visiting the various groups of pilgrims, talking with them of their dwelling-place, and listening to their tales of oppression and bloodshed.   From all I received the same simple courtesy and kindness; nor had I any cause to change the good opinion I had already formed of the Yezidis.   There were no Mohammedans present, nor any Christians, except those who were with me, and a poor woman who had lived long with the sect, and was a privileged guest at their festivals.   Unrestrained by the presence of strangers, the women forgot their usual timidity, and roved unvailed over the mountains.   As I sat beneath the trees, laughing girls gathered round me, examined my dress, or asked me questions.   Some, more bold than the rest, would bring me the strings of beads and engraved stones hanging round their necks, and permit me to examine the Assyrian relics thus collected together; while others, more fearful, though not ignorant of the impression which their charms would create, stood at a distance, and weaved wild flowers into their hair.

The men assembled in groups round the fountains and about the tomb. They talked and made merry; but no dissension or angry words disturbed the general good-humor. The sound of music and of song rose from all sides above the hum of voices. The priests and sheikhs walked among the people, or sat with the families assembled under nearly every tree.

The Yezidis recognize one Supreme Being; but, as far as I could learn, they do not offer up any direct prayer or sacrifice to him. Sheikh Nasr endeavored to evade my questions on this subject; and appeared to shun, with superstitious awe, every topic connected with the existence and attributes of the Deity. The common Mohammedan forms of expression—half oath, half ejaculation—are nevertheless frequently in the mouths of the people, but probably from mere habit. The name of the Evil spirit is, however, never mentioned; and any allusion to it by others so vexes and irritates them, that it is said they have put to death persons who have wantonly outraged their feelings by its use. So far is their dread of offending the Evil principle carried, that they carefully avoid every expression which may resemble in sound the name of Satan, or the Arabic word for "accursed."

When they speak of the Devil, they do so with reverence, as *Melek el Kout,* the mighty angel. Sheikh Nasr distinctly admitted that they possessed a bronze or copper figure of a bird, which, however, he was careful in explaining was only looked upon as a symbol, and not as an idol. There are several of these figures—one always remains with the great sheikh, and is carried with him wherever he may journey. When deputies are sent to any distance to collect money for the support of the tomb and the priests, they are furnished with one of these images, which is shown to those among whom they go, as an authority for their mission. This symbol is called the Melek Taous, and is held in great reverence. Much doubt has prevailed among travelers as to its existence; but Sheikh Nasr, when I had an opportunity of speaking to him in private, so frankly admitted it, that I consider the question as completely set at rest. The admission of the sheikh is moreover confirmed, by the answer of the guardian of the tomb, to a question which I put to him on my first visit, when he was completely off his guard.*

They believe Satan to be the chief of the Angelic host, now suffering punishment for his rebellion against the divine will; but still all-powerful, and to be restored hereafter to his high estate in the celestial hierarchy. He must be conciliated and reverenced, they say; for as he now has the means of doing evil to mankind, so will he hereafter have the power of rewarding them. Next to Satan, but inferior to him in might and wisdom, are seven archangels † who exercise a great influence over the world;—they are Gabrail, Michail, Raphail, Azrail, Dedrail, Azrapheel, and Shemkeel. Christ, according to them, was also a great angel, who had taken the form of man. He did not die on the cross, but ascended to heaven.

They hold the Old Testament in great reverence, and believe in the cosmogony of Genesis, the Deluge, and other events recorded in the Bible. They do not reject the New Testament, nor the Koran; but consider them less entitled to their veneration. Still they always select passages from the latter for their tombs, and holy places. Mohammed they look upon as a prophet; as they do Abraham, and the patriarchs.

They expect the second coming of Christ, as well as the re-

---

* I had afterward an opportunity of seeing the Melek Taous. It is the fanciful image of a bird supported by a stand resembling a candlestick, the whole being of bronze.

† It will be remembered that in the book of Tobit (xii. 15) Raphael is made to say: " I am Raphael, one of the seven holy angels, which present the prayers of the saints, and which go in and out before the glory of the Holy One." " The seven spirits before the throne of God" are mentioned in Revelations i. 4; iv. 5. This number seven, in the hierarchy of the Celestial Host, and in many sacred things, appears to have been connected with Chaldean traditions, and celestial observations.

appearance of Imaum Mehdi, giving credence to the Mussulman fables relating to him.

Sheikh Adi is their great saint; but I could not learn any particulars relating to him; indeed the epoch of his existence seemed doubtful; and on one occasion Sheikh Nasr asserted that he lived before Mohammed.

As to the origin of their name, it is well known that the Mussulmans trace it to the celebrated Ommiade caliph, Yezid, who figures as the persecutor of the family of Ali in their own religious history; but there is reason to believe that it must be sought for elsewhere, as it was used long before the introduction of Mohammedanism, and is not without connection with the early Persian appellation of the Supreme Being.* It is difficult to trace their ceremonies to any particular source. They baptize in water, like the Christians; if possible, within seven days after birth. They circumcise at the same age, and in the same manner as the Mohammedans; and reverence the sun, and have many customs in common with the Sabæans. All these ceremonies and observances may indeed have had a common origin, or may have been grafted at different times on their original creed. They may have adopted circumcision to avoid detection by their Mussulman oppressors; and may have selected passages from the Koran, to carve upon their tombs and sacred places, because, as suggested to me by Sheikh Nasr, they corresponded with their opinions, and were best suited to a country in which Arabic was the spoken language. They have more in common with the Sabæans than with any other sect. I have already alluded to their reverence for the sun, and have described the temple and the oxen dedicated to that luminary.† They are accustomed to kiss the object on

---

* Theophanes (Chronographia, p. 492 ed. Bon), mentions a settlement of Iesdem, on the lesser Zab, near which the Emperor Heracleus encamped,— καὶ ἠπίλκευσεν εἰς τοὺς οἴκους τοῦ Ἰεσδίᾳ. They may have been Yezidis, and of the ancestors of the present sect. Major Rawlinson has pointed out the name as occurring in Adiabene.

† I must observe that although the inscriptions, in the sanctuary described, were all addressed to Sheikh Shems, and that both Sheikh Nasr and the

which its first beams fall; and I have frequently when traveling in their company at sunrise, observed them perform this
ceremony. For fire, as symbolical, they have nearly the same
reverence; they never spit into it, but frequently pass their
hands through the flame, kiss them, and rub them over their
right eyebrow, or sometimes over the whole face.* The color
blue, to them, as to the Sabæans, is an abomination; and never
to be worn in dress, or to be used in their houses. Their
Kubleh, or the place to which they look while performing their
holy ceremonies, is that part of the heavens in which the sun
rises, and toward it they turn the faces of their dead.† In their
fondness for white linen, in their cleanliness of habits, and in
their frequent ablutions, they also resemble the Sabæans.

The lettuce, the bamiyah, ‡ and some other vegetables, are
never eaten by them. Pork is unlawful; but not wine, which
is drunk by all. Although they assert that meat should not be
eaten, unless the animal has been slain according to the Mosaic
and Mohammedan law, they do not object to partake of the food
of Christians.

I could not learn that there were any religious observances
on marriage. I was informed by the cawals that the men
and women merely presented themselves to a sheikh, who
ascertains that there is mutual consent. A ring is then given
to the bride, or sometimes money instead. A day is fixed for
rejoicings, on which they drink sherbet, and dance, but have no

cawals assured me that it was dedicated to the sun, it is just possible that,
under the title of Sheikh Shems, some other object than the sun or some
particular person is designated, and that my informants were unwilling to
enter into any explanation.

* Some travelers have asserted that they will not blow out a candle;
but such is not the case; nor is it an insult to spit in their presence.

† All Eastern sects appear to have had some Kubleh, or holy point, to
which the face was to be turned during prayer. The Jews, it will be remembered, looked toward Jerusalem. The Sabæans, according to some,
to the north star, or, according to others, toward that part of the heavens
in which the sun rises. The early Christians chose the East; Mohammed,
who recognized the general custom, and found it necessary to adhere to it,
appointed the holy Kaaba of Mecca to be the Kubleh of his disciples.

‡ Hibiscus Esculentus.

religious ceremonies. The number of wives is limited to one, but the chief has the power to transgress the law.

Their year begins with that of the Eastern Christians, whom they follow also in the order and names of their months. Some fast three days at the commencement of the year; but this is not considered necessary. They do not observe the Mohammedan Ramazan. Wednesday is their holyday, and although some always fast on that day, yet they do not abstain from work on it, as the Christians do on the Sabbath.

Sheikh Nasr informed me that they had a date of their own, and that he believed we were then, according to their account, in the year 1550. This suggested some connection with Manes; but neither by direct nor indirect questions could I ascertain that they were acquainted with his name, or recognized him in anywise as the originator of their peculiar doctrines with regard to the Evil principle.

Their names, both male and female, are generally those used by Mohammedans and Christians, or such as are common among the Kurds, and not strictly of Mussulman origin. The name of *Goorgis* (George) is, however, objectionable; and is never, I believe, given to a Yezidi.

They have four orders of priesthood, the Pirs, the Sheikhs, the Cawals, and the Fakirs; and, what is very remarkable, and, I believe, unexampled in the East, these offices are hereditary, and descend to females, who, when enjoying them, are treated with the same respect and consideration as the men.

The *Pirs,** or saints, are most reverenced after the great sheikh, or religious head of the sect. They are believed to have the power, not only of interceding for the people, but of curing disease and insanity. They are expected to lead a life of great sanctity and honesty; and are looked up to with great reverence. They are not confined, I believe, to any particular fashion of dress. The only pir I knew was one Sino, who was recognized as the deputy of Sheikh Nasr, and had suffered imprisonment in his stead.

* This is a Kurdish (Persian) title,—it means, literally, an old man.

The *Sheikhs* are next in rank.   They are acquainted with
the hymns, and are expected to know something of Arabic, the
language in which the hymns are written.   Their dress should
be entirely white, except the skull-cap beneath the turban,
which is black.   As servants of Sheikh Adi, they are the
guardians of his tomb, keep up the holy fires, and bring provisions and fuel to those who dwell within its precincts, and to
pilgrims of distinction.   They always wear round their bodies a
band of red and black, or red and orange plaid, as the mark of
their office; with it they bind together the wood, and other
supplies which they bring to the sacred edifice.   The women
carry the same badge, and are employed in the same services.
There are always several sheikhs residing in the valley of
Sheikh Adi.   They watch over the tomb, and receive pilgrims;
taking charge in rotation of the offerings that may be brought,
or selling the clay balls and other relics.

The *Cawals*, or preachers, appear to be the most active
members of the priesthood.   They are sent by Hussein Bey
and Sheikh Nasr on missions, going from village to village with
the symbol of the bird as teachers of the doctrines of the sect.
They alone are the performers on the flute and tamborine;
both instruments being looked upon, to a certain extent, as
sacred.   I observed that before, and after, using the tamborine
they frequently kissed it, and then held it to those near them,
to be similarly saluted.   They are taught singing at a very early
age, are skillful musicians, and dance occasionally at festivals.
They usually know a little Arabic, but barely more than
necessary to get through their chants and hymns.   Their robes
are generally white, although colored stuffs are not forbidden;
but their turbans, unlike those of the sheikhs, are black, as are
also their skull-caps.

The *Fakirs* are the lowest in the priesthood.   They wear
coarse dresses of black, or dark brown cloth, or canvas,
descending to the knee and fitting tightly to the person; and
a black turban, across which is generally tied a red kerchief.

I

They perform all menial offices connected with the tomb, trim and light the votive lamps, and keep clean the sacred buildings.

While each tribe and district of Yezidis has its own chief, and Hussein Bey is really both political and religious head of the whole sect, Sheikh Nasr is looked up to as the high-priest, and is treated with great reverence and respect. His office is hereditary; but the Yezidis frequently chose, without reference to priority of claim, the one among the descendants of the last sheikh most qualified, by his knowledge and character, to succeed him. The father of Sheikh Nasr held the office for some years; and no one better suited to it than the son could have been chosen to fill his place.

The language in general use among all the Yezidis is a Kurdish dialect, and very few, except the sheikhs and cawals, are acquainted with Arabic. The chants and hymns,—the only form of prayer, which, as far as I could ascertain, they possess,—are, as I have already stated, in Arabic. They have, I believe, a sacred volume, containing their traditions, their hymns, directions for the performance of their rites, and other matters connected with their religion. It is preserved either at Baazini or Baasheikha, and is regarded with so much superstitious reverence that I failed in every endeavor to obtain a copy, or even to see it. This I much regretted, as its contents would probably throw new light upon the origin and history of this remarkable sect, and would clear up many doubts which still hang over their tenets. It is considered unlawful to know how to read and write. There are only one or two persons among the Yezidis who can do either: even Sheikh Nasr is unacquainted with the alphabet. Those who know how to read have only been taught in order that they may preserve the sacred book, and may refer to it for the doctrines and ceremonies of the sect.

The Yezidis have a tradition that they originally came from Busrah, and from the country watered by the lower part of the Euphrates; and that, after their emigration, they first settled in Syria, and subsequently took possession of the Sinjar hill, and the districts they now inhabit in Kurdistan.   This tradition, with the peculiar nature of their tenets and ceremonies, points to a Sabæan or Chaldean origin.   With the scanty materials which we possess regarding their history, and owing to the ignorance prevailing among the people themselves,—for I believe that even the priests, including Sheikh Nasr, have but a very vague idea of what they profess, and of the meaning of their religious forms,—it is difficult to come to any conclusion as to the source of their peculiar opinions and observances. There is in them a strange mixture of Sabæanism, Christianity, and Mohammedanism, with a tincture of the doctrines of the Gnostics and Manicheans.   Sabeanism, however, appears to be the prevailing feature; and it is not improbable that the sect may be a remnant of the ancient Chaldees, who have, at various times, outwardly adopted the forms and tenets of the ruling people, to save themselves from persecution and oppression: and have gradually, through ignorance, confounded them with their own belief and mode of worship.   Such has been the case with a no less remarkable sect than the Sabæans or Mendai (the Christians of St. John, as they are commonly called), who still inhabit the banks of the Euphrates, and the districts of ancient Susiana.

The Yezidis are known among themselves by the name of the district or tribe to which they respectively belong.   Those who inhabit the country near the foot of the Kurdish Hills, are called Dasni or Daseni, most probably from the ancient name of a province.*   Tribes of Yezidis are found in the north of Syria, in Northern Kurdistan, Georgia (where they have migrated), Gebel Tour, Bohtan, Sheikhan, and Missouri.   In the plains, their principal settlements are in the villages of Baazani, Baasheikha, and Semil.

Having spent three days at Sheikh Adi, and witnessed all the ceremonies at which a stranger could be present, I prepared to return to Mosul.   Hussein Bey, Sheikh Nasr, and the principal

* There is a tribe of Kurds of this name, living in the mountains near Suleimaniyah.

sheikhs and cawals, insisted upon accompanying me about three miles down the valley; as I preferred this road to the precipitous pathway over the mountains. After parting with me, the chiefs returned to the tomb to finish their festival. I made my way to the village of Ain Sifni, and reached Mosul early in the afternoon.

Tahyar Pashaw had for some time been planning an expedition to the Sinjar, not with any hostile intention, but for the purpose of examining the state of the country; which had been ruined by the vexatious extortions, and cruelty of the late governor of Mosul. He had previously sent an agent to inquire into the condition of the villages; and a deputation of the inhabitants had returned with him to petition for a diminution of taxes, which, from the destitute state of the district, they were unable to pay.

His excellency had invited me to accompany him on this expedition, the arrangements for which, after numerous delays, were completed on the 8th of October. Three o'clock of that day was declared to be the fortunate hour for leaving the town. The principal inhabitants, with the cadi and mufti at their head, were collected in the large square opposite the palace and without the walls, ready to accompany the pashaw, as a mark of respect, some distance from the gates. It was with difficulty that I made my way to the apartments of the governor, through the crowd of irregular troops, and servants which thronged the court-yard of the serai. The attendants of his Excellency were hurrying to and fro, laden with every variety of utensil and instrument; some carrying gigantic telescopes, or huge bowls in leathern cases; others laboring under bundles of pipe-sticks, or bending under the weight of calico bags crammed with state documents. The gray-headed kiayah had inserted his boots into a pair of capacious boots, leaving room enough for almost any number of intruders. Round his fez, and the lower part of his face, were wound endless folds of white linen, which gave him the appearance of a patient emerging from a hospital; and he carried furs and cloaks enough to keep out the

cold of the frigid zone.   The Divan Effendesi, although a man
of the pen, strutted about with sword and spurs, followed by
clerks and inkstand-bearers.   At the door of the harem waited
a bevy of aghas; among them the lord of the towel, the lord
of the washing-basin, the lord of the cloak, the chief of the
coffee-makers, and the chief of the pipe-bearers, the treasurer,
and the seal-bearer.*   At length the pashaw approached; the
cawasses forced the crowd out of the way; and his excellency placed his foot in the stirrup, the trumpet sounded as
a signal for the procession to move onward.   First came a
regiment of infantry, followed by a company of artillerymen
with their guns.   The trumpeters, and the pashaw's own standard, a mass of green silk drapery, embroided with gold, with
verses from the Koran, succeeded; behind were six led Arab
horses, richly caparisoned in colored saddle-cloths, glittering with
gold embroidery.   The pashaw himself then appeared, surrounded
by the chiefs of the town and the officers of his household.   The
procession was finished by the irregular cavalry, divided into
companies, each headed by its respective commander, and by the
wild Suiters, with their small kettle-drums fastened in front of
their saddles.

I was accompanied by my cawass and my own servants, and
rode as it best suited, and amused me, in different parts of the
procession.   We reached Hamaydat, a ruined village on the
banks of the Tigris, three caravan hours from Mosul, about sunset.   Here we had the first proofs of the commissariat arrangements; for there was neither food for ourselves nor the horses,
and we all went supperless to bed.

On the following day, after a ride of six hours through a
barren and uninhabited plain, bounded to the east and west
by ranges of low limestone hills, we reached a ruined village,
built on the summit of an ancient artificial mound, called Abou
Maria.   The Aneyza Arabs were known to be out on this side
of the Euphrates, and during our march we observed several

---

* These are all offices in the household of a Turkish pashaw.

of their scouts watching our movements. The irregular
cavalry frequently rushed off in pursuit; but the Arabs, turning their fleet mares toward the desert, were soon lost in the
distance.

We passed the ruins of three villages. The plain, once
thickly inhabited, is now deserted; and the wells, formerly
abundant, are filled up. In spring, the Arab tribe of Jehesh
frequently encamp near the pools of water supplied by the rains.
The remains of buildings, and the traces of former cultivation,
prove that at some period, not very remote, others than the roving Bedouins dwelt on these lands; while the artificial mounds,
scattered over the face of the country, show that long ere the
Mussulman invasion, this was one of the flourishing districts of
ancient Assyria.

A most abundant spring issues from the foot of the mound of
Abou Maria. The water is collected in large, well-built reservoirs. Near them is a mill, now in ruins, but formerly turned
by the stream, within a few yards of its source. Such an ample
supply of water, although brackish to the taste, must always
have attracted a population in a country where it is scarce. The
village, which was deserted during the oppressive government
of Mohammed Pashaw, belonged to the Jehesh.

Three hours' ride, still over the desert, brought us to Tel
Afer, which we reached suddenly on emerging from a range of
low hills. The place had a much more important and flourishing appearance than I could have expected. A very considerable eminence, partly artificial, is crowned by a castle, whose
walls are flanked by numerous towers of various shapes. The
town, containing some well-built houses, lies at the foot of the
mound, and is partly surrounded by gardens wooded with
olive, fig, and other fruit trees; beyond this cultivated plot is the
broad expanse of the desert. A spring, as abundant as that of
Abou Maria, gushes out of a rock beneath the castle, supplies
the inhabitants with water, irrigates their gardens, and turns
their mills.

Tel Afer was once a town of some importance; it is mentioned by the early Arab geographers, and may perhaps be identified with the Telassar of Isaiah, referred to, as it is, in connection with Gozan and Haran.* It has been three times besieged, within a few years, by Ali Pashaw of Baghdad, Hafiz Pashaw, and Injeh Bairakdar Mohammed Pashaw. On each occasion the inhabitants offered a vigorous resistance. Moham-

TEL AFER.

med Pashaw took the place by assault. More than two thirds of the inhabitants were put to the sword, and the property of the

* Isaiah xxxvii. 12. The name does not occur elsewhere in the Bible; and we have consequently no means of determining its locality.

remainder was confiscated. Great wealth is said to have been discovered in the place, on its pillage by Mohammed Pashaw, who took all the gold and silver, and distributed the remainder of the spoil among his soldiers.

The inhabitants of Tel Afer are of Turcoman origin, and speak the Turkish language. They occasionally intermarry, however, with the Arabs, and generally understand Arabic.

Toward evening I ascended the mound, and visited the castle, in which was quartered a small body of irregular troops. The houses, formerly inhabited by families whose habitations are now built at the foot of the artificial hill, are in ruins, except that occupied by the commander of the garrison. From the walls I had an uninterrupted view over a vast plain, stretching westward toward the Euphrates, and losing itself in the hazy distance. The ruins of ancient towns and villages rose on all sides; and, as the sun went down, I counted above one hundred mounds, throwing their dark and lengthening shadows across the plain. These were the remains of Assyrian civilization and prosperity. Centuries have elapsed since a settled population dwelt in this district of Mesopotamia. Now, not even the tent of the Bedouin could be seen. The whole was a barren, deserted waste.

We remained two days at Tel Afer. The commissariat was replenished, as far as possible, from the scanty stores of the inhabitants. The pashaw recommended forbearance and justice; but his advice was not followed; nor were his orders obeyed. The houses were broken into, and a general pillage ensued. At length, on the 13th, we resumed our march.

The Sinjar is about thirty miles distant from Tel Afer. A very low range of hills diverges from its southern spur, and unites with that behind the town. The pashaw, with his troops, took the road across the plain.

We passed the first night on the banks of a small salt stream, near the ruins of a village, called, by the people of the Sinjar and Tel Afer, Zabardok; and by the Arabs simply Kharba, or the ruins. We had seen, during the day, several other ruins, and water-courses. The second day we encamped in the plain, near the southern end of the Sinjar mountain, and under the village of Mirkan, the white houses of which, rising one above the other on the declivity, were visible from below. Here the pashaw was met by all the chiefs of the mountain, except those of the small district in which we had halted.

Mirkan is one of the principal Yezidi settlements in the Sinjar. Its inhabitants had been exposed to great extortions, and many were put to death by Mohammed Pashaw. They expected similar treatment at our hands. No promises could remove their fears, and they declared their intention of resolutely defending their village. The pashaw sent up an officer of his household, with a few irregular troops, to re-assure them, and to restore obedience. I accompanied him. As we entered the village we were received by a general discharge of fire-arms. Two horsemen, who had accidentally, —and as I thought at the time somewhat disrespectfully,— pushed forward before the officer and myself, fell dead at our feet, and several of our party were wounded. The pashaw, exasperated at this unprovoked and wanton attack, ordered an advance of the hytas and Arab irregulars; who, long thirsting for plunder, hastened toward the village. The Yezidis had already deserted it, and had taken refuge in a narrow gorge; abounding in caverns and isolated rocks,—their usual place of refuge on such occasions.

The village was soon occupied; the houses were entered, and plundered of the little property that had been left behind. A few aged women and decrepit old men, too infirm to leave with the rest, and found hiding in the small dark rooms, were murdered, and their heads severed from their bodies. Blazing fires were made in the neat dwellings, and the whole village was delivered to the flames. Even the old pashaw, with his gray hair and tottering step, hurried to and fro among the smoking ruins, and helped to add the torch where the fire was not doing its work.

The old Turkish spirit of murder and plunder was roused;

I*

the houses were soon burnt to the ground; but the inhabitants were still safe. When the irregulars had secured all the property they could discover, they rushed toward the gorge, scarcely believing that the Yezidis would venture to oppose them. But they were received by a steady and well-directed fire. The foremost fell, almost to a man. The caverns were high•up among the rocks, and all attempts to reach them completely failed. The contest was carried on till night; when the troops, dispirited and beaten, were called back to their tents.

In the evening the heads of the miserable old men and women, taken in the village, were paraded about the camp; and those who were fortunate enough to possess such trophies wandered from tent to tent, claiming a present as a reward for their prowess. I appealed to the pashaw, who had been persuaded that every head brought to him was that of a powerful chief, and after some difficulty prevailed upon him to have them buried; but the troops were not willing to obey his orders, and it was late in the night before they were induced to resign their bloody spoil, which they had arranged in grim array, and lighted up with torches.

On the following morning the contest was renewed; but the Yezidis defended themselves with undiminished courage. The loss of the hytas was very considerable; not a cavern had been carried; nor a Yezidis, as far as the assailants could tell, killed, or even wounded.

The next day the pashaw ordered a fresh attack. To encourage his men he advanced himself into the gorge, and directed his carpet to be spread on a rock. Here he sat, with the greatest apathy, smoking his pipe, and carrying on a frivolous conversation with me, although he was the object of the aim of the Yezidis; several persons within a few feet of us falling dead, and the balls frequently throwing up the dirt into our faces. Coffee was brought to him occasionally as usual, and his pipe was filled when the tobacco was exhausted; yet he was not a soldier, but what is termed "a man of the pen." I have frequently seen similar instances of calm indifference in the midst of danger among Turks, when such displays were scarcely called for, and would be very unwillingly made by an European. Notwithstanding the example set by his excellency, and the encouragement which his presence gave to the troops, they were not more successful in their attempts to dislodge the Yezidis than they had been the day before. One after another, the men were carried out of the ravine, dead or dying. The wounded were brought to the pashaw, who gave them water, money, or words of encouragement. The "Ordou cadesi," or cadi of the camp, reminded them that it was against the infidels they were fighting; that every one who fell by the enemies of the prophet was rewarded with instant translation to Paradise; while those who killed an unbeliever were entitled to the same inestimable privilege. The dying were comforted, and the combatants animated by the promises and exhortations of the cadi; who, however, kept himself well out of the way of danger behind a rock.

Attempts were made during the day to induce the Yezidis to surrender, and there was some chance of success. However, night drew near, and hostilities still continued. The regular and irregular troops were then posted at all the known places of access to the gorge. The morning came, and the attack was recommenced. No signs of defense issued from the valley. The hytas rushed in, but were no longer met by the steady fire of the previous day. They paused, fearing some trick or ambuscade; they advanced cautiously, but still unnoticed. They reached the mouths of the caves;—no one opposed them. It was some time, however, before they ventured to look into them. They were empty. The Yezidis had fled during the night, and had left the ravine by some pathway known only to themselves, and which had escaped the watchfulness of the Turkish soldiery.

While attempts were being made to discover the retreat of the fugitives, the Turkish camp remained near the village of Mirkan. I took this opportunity of visiting other parts of the

Sinjar. The residence of the governor of the district is in the village built among the ruins of the old city—the Singara of the Romans, and the "Belled Sinjar" of the Arabs. A small mud fort, raised a few years ago, stands on a hill in the midst of the remains of walls and foundations; but the principal part of the ancient city appears to have occupied the plain below. Around this fort, at the time of my visit, were congregated about two hundred families. The Yezidi inhabitants of the village, unlike those of the other districts, are mixed with Mussulmans. The latter, however, are so lax in their religious observances, and in dress so like the Yezidis, that it is difficult to distinguish them from the unbelievers. I was continually falling into mistakes, and eliciting a very indignant exclamation of "God forbid!"

It would be difficult to point out, with any degree of certainty, ruins at Belled Sinjar more ancient than the Mohammedan conquest. It became a place of some importance in the early ages of Islam, and had its own semi-independent rulers. There are the remains of several fine buildings; and the lower part of a minaret, constructed, like that of the great mosque of Mosul, of colored tiles and bricks, is a conspicuous object from all parts of the plain. There are very abundant springs within the circuit of the old walls; the air is declared to be salubrious, and the soil rich and productive.

All the villages of the Sinjar are built upon one plan. The houses rise on the hill-sides, and are surrounded by terraces, formed of rough stones piled one above the other as walls, to confine the scanty earth. These terraces are planted with olive and fig-trees; a few vineyards are found near some villages. The houses, which are flat-roofed, are exceedingly clean and neat, and frequently contain several apartments. The walls of the interior are full of small recesses, like pigeon-holes, which are partly ornamental, and partly used to keep the domestic utensils and property of the owner. They give a very singular and original appearance to the rooms; and the oddity of the effect is considerably increased by masses of red and black paint daubed in patches on the white wall.

The principal, and indeed now the only, trade carried on by the inhabitants of the Sinjar, is in dried figs, which are celebrated in this part of Turkey, and supply all the markets in the neighboring provinces. The soil is fertile, and, as the means of irrigation are abundant, corn and various useful articles of produce might be raised in great plenty from the extensive tracts of arable land belonging to the villages. But the people have been almost ruined by misgovernment; they can now scarcely cultivate corn enough for their own immediate wants.

The pashaw still lingered at Mirkan; and as I was anxious to return to Mosul, to renew the excavations, I took my leave of him, and rode through the desert to Tel Afer. I was accompanied by a small body of irregular cavalry,—a necessary escort, as the Aneyza Arabs were hanging about the camp, and plundering stragglers and caravans of supplies. As evening approached, we saw, congregated near a small stream, what appeared to be a large company of dismounted Arabs, their horses standing by them. As we were already near them, and could not have escaped the watchful eye of the Bedouin, we prepared for an encounter. I placed the baggage in the center of my small party, and spread out the horsemen as widely as possible to exaggerate our numbers. We approached cautiously, and were surprised to see that the horses still remained without their riders: we drew still nearer, when they all galloped off toward the desert. They were wild asses. We attempted to follow them. After running a little distance they stopped to gaze at us, and I got sufficiently near to see them well; but as soon as they found that we were in pursuit, they hastened their speed, and were soon lost in the distance.*

* The reader will remember that Xenophon mentions these beautiful animals which he must have seen during his march in these very plains. He faithfully describes the country, and the animals and birds which inhabit it, as they are to this day, except that the ostrich is not now to be found so far north. "The country," says he, "was a plain throughout, as even as the sea, and full of wormwood; if any other kinds of shrubs or reeds grew

I reached Mosul in two days, taking the road by Kessi Kupri, and avoiding the desert beyond Abou-Maria, which we had crossed on our march to the Sinjar.

there, they had all an aromatic smell; but no trees appeared. Of wild creatures, the most numerous were wild asses, and not a few ostriches, besides bustards and roe deer (gazelles), which our horsemen sometimes chased. The asses, when they were pursued, having gained ground of the horses, stood still (for they exceeded them much in speed); and when these came up with them, they did the same thing again; so that our horsemen could take them by no other means but by dividing themselves into relays, and succeeding one another in the chase. The flesh of those that were taken was like that of red deer, but more tender." (Anab. lib. i. c. 5.) In fleetness they equal the gazelle: and to overtake them is a feat which only one or two of the most celebrated mares have been known to accomplish. The Arabs sometimes catch the foals during the spring, and bring them up with milk in their tents. I endeavored in vain to rear a pair. They are of a light fawn-color—almost pink. The Arabs still eat their flesh. The "wild asses of the desert" are mentioned in Job xxxiv. 5, xxxix. 5.

CHAPTER IX.

On my return to Mosul, I received letters from England, in-
forming me that Sir Stratford Canning had made over his share
in the discoveries in Assyria to the British nation; and that the
British Museum had received a grant of funds for the continuation of the researches commenced at Nimroud, and elsewhere.
The grant was small, and scarcely adequate to the objects in view.
There were many difficulties to contend with, and I was doubtful
whether, with the means placed at my disposal, I should be able
to fulfill the expectations which appeared to have been formed as
to the results of the undertaking.   The sum given to M. Botta
for the excavations at Khorsabad alone, greatly exceeded the
whole grant to the Museum, which was to include private ex-
penses, those of carriage, and many extraordinary outlays in-
evitable in the East, when works of this nature are to be carried
on.   I determined, however, to accept the charge of superintending the excavations, to make every exertion, and to economize as
far as it was in my power—that the nation might possess as
extensive and complete a collection of Assyrian antiquities as,
considering the smallness of the means, it was possible to collect.

It was, in the first place, necessary to organize a band of workmen best fit to carry on the work. A general scarcity of corn had

driven the Arab tribes to the neighborhood of the town, where
they sought to gain a livelihood by engaging in labors not very
palatable to a Bedouin.   I had no difficulty in finding workmen
among them.   There was, at the same time, this advantage
in employing these wandering Arabs—they brought their tents
and families with them, and, encamping round the ruins and
the village, formed a very efficient guard against their brethren
of the Desert, who looked to plunder, rather than to work, to
supply their wants.   To increase my numbers I chose only one
man from each family ; and, as his male relations accompanied
him, I had the use of their services, as far as regarded the protection of my sculptures.   Being well acquainted with the
sheikhs of the Jebours, I selected my workmen chiefly from
that tribe.   The chiefs promised every protection ; and I knew
enough of the Arab character not to despair of bringing the
men under proper control.   The Arabs were selected to remove
the earth—they were unable to dig ; this part of the labor
required stronger and more active men ; and I chose for it
about fifty Nestorian Chaldeans, who had sought work for the
winter in Mosul, and many of whom, having already been employed, had acquired some experience in excavating.   They
went to Nimroud with their wives and families.   I engaged at
the same time one Bainan, a Jacobite or Syrian Christian, who
was a skillful marble-cutter, and a very intelligent man.   I also
made a valuable addition to my establishment in a standard-
bearer of the irregular troops, of whose courage I had seen such
convincing proofs during the expedition to the Sinjar, that I
induced his commander to place him in my service.   His name
was Mohammed Agha ; but he was generally called, from the
office he held in his troop, the " Bairakdar, or standard-bearer."
He was a native of Scio, and had been carried off at the time
of the massacre, when a child, by an irregular, who had brought
him up as a Mussulman.   In his religious opinions and observances, however, he was as lax, as men of his profession
usually are.   He served me faithfully and honestly, and was of
great use during the excavations.   Awad still continued in

my employ; my cawass, Ibrahim Agha, returned with me to
Nimroud; and I hired a carpenter and two or three men of
Mosul as superintendents.

I was again among the ruins by the end of October. The
winter season was fast approaching, and it was necessary to
build a proper house for the shelter of myself and servants. I
marked out a plan on the ground, in the village of Nimroud,
and in a few days our habitations were complete. My workmen formed the walls of mud bricks dried in the sun, and
roofed the rooms with beams and branches of trees. A thick
coat of mud was laid over the whole, to exclude the rain. Two
rooms for my own accommodation were divided by an iwan, or
open apartment, the whole being surrounded by a wall. In a
second court-yard were huts for my cawass, Arab guests, and
servants, and stables for my horses. Ibrahim Agha displayed
his ingenuity by making equidistant loopholes, of a most warlike
appearance, in the outer walls; which I immediately ordered to
be filled up, to avoid any suspicion of being the constructor of
forts and castles, with the intention of making a permanent
Frank settlement in the country. We did not neglect precau-
tions, however, in case of an attack from the Bedouins, of whom
Ibrahim Agha was in constant dread. Unfortunately the only
shower of rain, that I saw during the remainder of my residence
in Assyria, fell before my walls were covered in, and so satu-
rated the bricks that they did not dry again before the following
spring. The consequence was that the only verdure, on which
my eyes were permitted to feast before my return to Europe,
was furnished by my own property—the walls in the interior
of the rooms being continually clothed with a crop of grass.

On the mound itself, and immediately above the great winged
lions first discovered, were built a house for my Nestorian workmen and their families, and a hut to which any small objects
discovered among the ruins could at once be removed for safety.
I divided my Arabs into three parties, according to the branches
of the tribe to which they belonged. About forty tents were
pitched on different parts of the mound, at the entrances to the

principal trenches. Forty more were placed round my dwelling, and the rest on the bank of the river, where the sculptures
were deposited previous to their embarkation on the rafts. The
men were all armed. I thus provided for the defense of my
establishment.

Mr. Hormuzd Rassam lived with me ; and to him I confided
the payment of the wages, and the accounts. He soon obtained
an extraordinary influence among the Arabs, and his fame
spread through the desert.

The workmen were divided into bands. In each set were
generally eight or ten Arabs, who carried away the earth in
baskets ; and two, or four, Nestorian diggers, according to the
nature of the soil and rubbish which had to be excavated. They
were overlooked by a superintendent, whose duty it was to keep
them to their work, and to give me notice when the diggers
approached any slab, or exposed any small object to view, that
I might myself assist in its uncovering or removal. I scattered
a few Arabs of a hostile tribe among the rest, and by that
means I was always made acquainted with what was going on,
could easily learn if there were plots brewing, and could detect
those who might attempt to appropriate any relics discovered
during the excavations. The smallness of the sum placed at
my disposal, compelled me to follow the same plan in the excavations that I had hitherto adopted,—digging trenches along
the walls of the chambers, and exposing the whole of the slabs,
without removing the earth from the center. Thus, few chambers were fully explored ; and many small objects of great
interest may have been left undiscovered. As I was directed
to bury the buildings with earth after they had been examined,
I filled up the trenches, to avoid unnecessary expense, with the
rubbish taken from those subsequently opened, having first copied
the inscriptions, and drawn the sculptures.

The excavations were recommenced, on a large scale, by
the 1st of November. My working parties were distributed
over the mound — in the ruins of the N. W. and S. W.
palaces ; near the gigantic bulls in the center ; and in the south-

east corner, where no traces of buildings had as yet been discovered.

It will be remembered that the greater number of slabs forming the southern side of the large hall in the N.W. palace had fallen with their faces to the ground. I was, in the first place, anxious to raise these bas-reliefs, and to pack them for transport to Busrah. To accomplish this, it was necessary to remove a large accumulation of earth and rubbish—to empty, indeed, nearly the whole chamber, for the fallen slabs extended almost half-way across it. The sculptures on nine slabs were found to be in admirable preservation, although broken by the fall. The slabs were divided, as those already described, into two compartments, by inscriptions which were precisely similar.

The sculptures were of the highest interest. They represented the wars of the king, and his victories over foreign nations. The upper bas-reliefs, on the first two slabs, formed one subject—the king, with his warriors, in battle under the walls of a hostile castle. He stood, gorgeously attired, in a chariot drawn by three horses richly caparisoned, and was discharging an arrow either against those who defended the walls; or against a warrior, who, already wounded, was falling from his chariot. An attendant protected the person of the king with a shield, and a charioteer held the reins, and urged on the horses. Above the king was the emblem of the supreme Deity, represented as at Persepolis by a winged figure within a circle, wearing a horned cap resembling that of the human-headed lions. Like the king, he was shooting

Emblem of the Deity. (N.W. Palace, Nimroud.)

an arrow, the head of which was in the form of a trident.

Behind the king were three chariots; the first drawn by three horses—one of which was rearing and another falling—

and occupied by a wounded warrior demanding quarter of his pursuers. In the others were two warriors, one discharging an arrow, the other guiding the horses, which were at full speed. In each Assyrian chariot was a standard—the devices, which were inclosed in a circle ornamented with tassels and streamers, being an archer, with the horned cap but without wings, standing on a bull ; and two bulls, back to back. At the bottom of the first bas-relief were wavy lines, to indicate water or a river; and trees were scattered over both. Assyrian footmen, fighting or slaying the enemy, were introduced in several places ; and three headless bodies above the principal figures in the second bas-relief represented the dead in the background.*

On the upper part of the two slabs following the battle-scene was the triumphal return after victory. In front of the procession were warriors throwing the heads of the slain at the feet of the conquerors. Two musicians, playing on stringed instruments, preceded the charioteers, who were represented unarmed, and bearing their standards ; above them was an eagle with a human head in its talons. The king came next in his chariot, carrying in one hand his bow, and in the other two arrows—the attitude in which he is so frequently represented on Assyrian monuments, and probably denoting triumph over his enemies. Above the horses was the presiding divinity ; also holding a bow. The attendant, who in war bore the shield, was now replaced by an eunuch, raising the open parasol — the Eastern emblem of royalty. The horses were led by grooms,

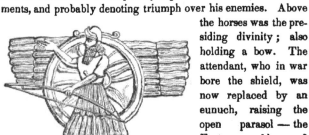

Emblem of the Deity. (N.W. Palace, Nimroud.)

although the charioteer still held the reins. Behind the king's chariot was a horseman leading a second horse, gayly caparisoned.

* These bas-reliefs are in the British Museum.

After the procession, was the castle and pavilion of the victorious king—the former represented by a circle, divided into four equal compartments, and surrounded by towers and battlements. In each compartment were figures evidently engaged in preparing the feast : one was slaying a sheep ; another appeared to be baking bread ; and others stood before bowls and utensils placed on tables. The pavilion was supported by three columns ; one surmounted by a fir-cone—the emblem so fre-

A Table.
(N. W. Palace, Nimroud.)

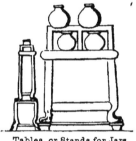

Tables, or Stands for Jars.
(N. W. Palace, Nimroud.)

quently seen in the Assyrian sculptures ; the others by figures of the ibex or mountain goat. It was probably of silk or woolen stuff, richly ornamented and edged with a fringe of fir-cones and tulip-shaped ornaments. Beneath the canopy was a groom cleaning one horse ; while others, picketed by their halters, were feeding at a trough. An eunuch stood at the entrance of the tent, to receive four prisoners, who, with their hands bound behind, were brought to him by an Assyrian warrior. Above this group were two singular lion-headed figures, one holding a whip or thong in the right hand, and grasping his under jaw with the left, the other raising his hands. They were clothed in tunics descending to the knees, and skins falling from the head, over the shoulders, to the ankles, and were accompanied by a man raising a stick.

The four following bas-reliefs recorded a battle, in which were represented the king, two warriors with their standards,

JUNIOR WARRIOR IN BATTLE. (N. W. Palace, Nimroud.)

and an eunuch in chariots, and four warriors, among whom was also an eunuch, on horses. The enemy were on foot, and discharged their arrows against the pursuers. Eagles hovered above the victors, and were feeding on the slain. The winged divinity in the circle was again seen above the king.

These bas-reliefs in many respects illustrate the manners and civilization of the Assyrians. We here find the eunuch commanding in war and engaging with the enemy in combat, as we have before seen him ministering to the king during religious ceremonies, or waiting upon him as his arms-bearer during peace. That eunuchs rose to the highest rank among the Assyrians, and were even generals over their armies, we learn from Scripture, where the rabsaris, or chief of the eunuchs, is mentioned as one of the three principal officers of Sennacherib, and as one of the princes of Nebuchadrezzar.* They appear, indeed, to have held the same important posts, and to have exercised the same influence in the Assyrian court, as they have since enjoyed in Turkey and Persia, where they have frequently attained to the post of vizier or prime minister.

The horses of the archers were led by mounted warriors, wearing circular skull caps, probably of iron. Horsemen are frequently mentioned in the Bible as forming an important part of the Assyrian armies. Ezekiel (xxiii. 6) describes " the Assyrians clothed in blue, captains and rulers, all of them desirable young men, horsemen riding upon horses ;" and Holofernes had no less than 12,000 archers on horseback. The rider is seated on the naked back of the horse, which is only adorned with a cloth when led behind the chariot of the king, probably for his use in case of accident to the chariot.

The horses represented in the sculptures appear to be of noble breed. Assyria, and particularly that part of the empire which was watered by the Tigris and Euphrates, was celebrated at the earliest period for its horses, as the same plains are to

---

* 2 Kings xviii. 17 ; Jeremiah xxxix. 3.

this day for the noblest races of Arabia. The Jews probably obtained horses for their cavalry from this country; and horses

Horsemen—one drawing the Bow, the other holding the Reins
of both Horses.   (N.W. Palace, Nimroud.)

were offered to them by the general of the Assyrian king, as an acceptable present.* On Egyptian monuments horses from Mesopotamia are continually mentioned among the spoil or tribute. The horse of the Assyrian bas-reliefs was evidently drawn from the finest model. The head is small and well-shaped, the nostrils large and high, the neck arched, the body long, and the legs slender and sinewy. The prophet exclaims of the horses of the Chaldeans, "They are swifter than the leopards, and more fierce than the evening wolves;"† and the

---

* "Now, therefore, I pray thee, give pledges to my lord the king of Assyria, and I will deliver thee two thousand horses, if thou be able on thy part to set riders upon them."—2 Kings xviii. 23.
† Habakkuk i. 8.

magnificent description of the war-horse in the book of Job is familiar to every reader.* At a later period the plains of Babylonia furnished horses to the Persians, both for the private use of the king and for his troops. The rich pasture-grounds of Mesopotamia must have always afforded them ample sustenance, while those vast plains, exposed to the heats of summer and cold of winter, inured them to hardships and fatigue.

The lower series of bas-reliefs contained three subjects—the siege of a castle, the king receiving prisoners, and the king, with his army, crossing a river. The first occupied the under compartments of three slabs. The castle had three towers, and apparently several walls, one behind the other, all surmounted by angular battlements. The besiegers having brought a battering ram to the outer wall, one of the besieged was endeavoring to catch the engine, and to break the blows, by a chain lowered from the walls; while two warriors of the assailing party were holding the ram in its place by hooks. This part of the bas-relief illustrates the account in Chronicles and Josephus, of the *machines for battering walls, instruments to cast stones, and grappling irons* made by Uzziah.† Another warrior was throwing fire (traces of the red paint being still visible in the sculpture) from above upon the battering-ram: while the besiegers endeavored to quench the flames, by pouring water upon them from the movable tower. Two figures, in full armor, were undermining the walls with instruments like blunt spears; while two others appeared to have found a secret passage into the castle. Wounded men were falling from the walls; and upon one of the towers were women tearing their hair and extending their hands to ask for quarter. The enemy were mounting to the assault, by scaling ladders placed against the walls. The king, discharging an arrow, and protected by a shield held by a warrior in complete armor, stood on one side of the castle. He was attended by two eunuchs, one holding the open umbrella, the other his quiver and mace.

* Ch. xxxix. 19.   † 2 Chron. xxvi. 15, and Josephus lib. ix. c. 10.

Behind them was an Assyrian warrior leading three women and a child, and driving three bullocks, as part of the spoil. It was thus that the Assyrians carried away captive the people of Samaria, replacing the population of the conquered country by colonies of their own.* The women were represented as tearing their hair and throwing dust upon their heads, the usual signs of grief in the East.

On the other side of the castle were two kneeling figures, one discharging an arrow, the other holding a shield for his companion's defense. Behind them was the vizier, also shooting an arrow, and protected by the shield of a second warrior. He was followed by three warriors, the first an archer kneeling, the others an archer and his shield-bearer in complete armor, erect. They had left their chariot, in which the charioteer was still standing, the horses being held by a groom. Behind the chariot were two warriors, each carrying a bow and a mace. The shields represented in this bas-relief were probably of wicker-work, and were chiefly used during a siege. They covered the whole person of the archer, who was thus able to discharge his arrows in comparative security. Such were probably the bucklers which Herodotus describes as forming a complete fence before the Persian archers at the battle of Platea.†

The three following bas-reliefs represented the king receiving captives, apparently of the same nation as those portrayed in the upper part of the hall, and already described. Behind the chariot of the king were two other chariots, each containing a charioteer alone ; passing under the wall of a castle, on which were women, apparently viewing the procession, and discussing the results of the expedition.

In these bas-reliefs the harness and trappings of the horses and chariots are remarkable for their richness and elegance. Above the heads of the horses rise gracefully plumed and fanciful crests, ornamented with long ribbons or streamers, which were probably of many colors. Like the Arabs and Persians of the present day, the Assyrians appear to have been lavish of tassels

* 2 Kings xvii. 6.   † Lib. ix. c. 61.

of silk and wool, which were attached to all parts of the harness. The bridle consisted of a headstall, a strap divided into three parts joining the bit, and straps over the forehead, under the cheeks, and behind the ears. We find sacred emblems used as ornaments in the trappings of horses, as on the robes of figures; the winged bull, the sun, moon, stars, and horned cap being frequently introduced.

Three richly embroidered straps, passing round the body of the horse, kept the harness and chariot-pole in their places, and were attached to a highly decorated breast-band. To the yoke was suspended an elegant ornament, formed by the head of an animal and a circle, into which was generally introduced a winged bull, a star, or some other sacred device.

Embroidered trappings, such as are described by Ezekiel* as *the precious clothes for chariots*, coming from Dedan, covered the backs of the horses. Their bits, as well as the metal used in the harness, may have been of gold and other precious materials, like those of the ancient Persians.† Their manes were either allowed to fall loosely on the neck or were plaited, and their tails were bound in the center with ribbons adorned with tassels.

In the Bible frequent mention is made of the use of chariots and horsemen both in sieges and battles. "The choicest valleys shall be full of chariots, and the horsemen shall *set themselves in array against the gate*."‡ Among the tributaries of the Assyrians, the Elamites were celebrated for their *chariots carrying archers*.§ The Jewish kings appear to have granted certain privileges to cities equipping chariots, hence called "chariot cities," which in the time of Solomon supplied no less than one thousand four hundred chariots and twelve thousand horsemen.|| Chariots of iron were used in Palestine from the earliest period, and appear to have been so formidable in war, that the Israelites were long unable to contend with them.¶

* xxvii. 20.   † 1 Esdras iii. 6; Xenophon, Cyrop. lib. i. c. 3.
‡ Isaiah xxii. 7.   § Isaiah xxii. 6. || 2 Chron. i. 14; Isaiah xxii.
¶ Judges i. 19., and iv. 8.

The three remaining bas-reliefs—the passage of the river—
were highly interesting and curious. In the first was a boat
containing a chariot, in which stood the king. In one hand he
held two arrows, in the other a bow. An eunuch, standing in
front of the chariot, appeared to point to some object in the
distance, perhaps the stronghold of the enemy. Behind the
chariot was a second eunuch, holding a bow and mace. The
boat was towed by two naked men; four men sat at the oars,
and one oar with a broad flat end, attached to a thick wooden
pin at the stern, served both for steering and propelling. It is
singular that this is precisely the kind of vessel used by the
natives of Mosul to this day; and such probably were the Babylonian boats described by Herodotus, constructed of willow-
boughs and covered with skins. A man, standing in the vessel, held the halters of four horses, swimming over the
stream, in which was a naked figure on an inflated skin. This
bas-relief, with the exception of the king and the chariot,
might represent a scene daily witnessed on the banks of the
Tigris—probably the river here represented. On the next
slab were two smaller boats; one carrying the couch of the king
and a jar or large vessel; the other an empty chariot: they
were impelled by two rowers, seated face to face. Five men,
two leading horses by their halters, were swimming on skins.

A Boat carrying a Chariot, and Men swimming on inflated Skins.
(N. W. Palace, Nimroud.)

On the third slab was represented men embarking the chariots
and preparing to cross the river. The proceedings were su-

perintended by officers, one of whom, an eunuch, held a whip, which was probably used—as in the army of Xerxes—to keep the soldiers to their duty, and prevent them flying from the enemy.*

On the opposite side of the hall, between the entrances, only one slab was discovered in its original position. The upper

Flying Warrior turning back to discharge an Arrow.   (N. W. Palace, Nimroud.)

compartment was almost completely defaced; in the lower was represented a battle between Assyrian warriors, in chariots, and

* Herod. lib. vii. ch. 56, in which Xerxes is described as seeing his troops driven by blows over the bridge across the Hellespont; it was also the custom for the officers to carry whips to urge the soldiers to the combat: lib. vii. ch. 223.

the cavalry of the enemy. The conquered people wore high boots, turned up at the toes, and conical caps, probably of felt or linen. One of the horsemen turned back, while his horse was at full speed, to discharge an arrow against his pursuers. This mode of fighting is described by ancient authors as peculiar to the Parthian and Persian tribes, and is still practiced by the irregular cavalry of Persia.*

The Arabs employed in removing the rubbish from the chamber with the kneeling winged figures,† discovered a quantity of iron, in which I soon recognized the scales of the armor represented on the sculptures. These scales were from two to three inches in length, rounded at one end, and square at the other, with a raised or embossed line in the center, and had probably been fastened to a vest of linen or felt. The iron was so eaten by rust, that I had much difficulty in detaching it from the soil. Two or three baskets were filled with these relics.

As the earth was removed, other portions of armor were found. At length a perfect helmet of iron inlaid with copper bands, resembling in shape and in the ornaments the pointed helmet represented in the bas-reliefs, was discovered.

Several helmets of other shapes, some with the arched crest, were also dug out ; but they fell to pieces as soon as exposed to the air ; and I was only able to collect a few of the fragments.

Several slabs in this chamber had fallen from their places, and were broken. Beneath them were the fragments of a number of alabaster vases, and of several vessels of baked clay. The name and title of the Khorsabad king, accompanied by the figure of a lion, were still preserved on some of the fragments. Upon the pottery were painted characters re-

---

* Anab. lib. iii. ch. 8.
        " Fidentemque fugâ Parthum, versisque sagittis."
                                        Virg. Georg. 3.
and Hor. Carm. lib. i. ode xix.
        † Chamber I, plan 3.

sembling the rounded letters of Babylonia and Phœnicia, probably a cursive writing in common use, while the cuneiform was

reserved for monuments. The earthen vases were of a light'
yellow color, ornamented with bars, zigzag lines, and simple
designs in black.

While I was collecting and examining these curious relics, a
workman found a perfect vase; but unfortunately broke the
upper part by striking it with his pick. I took the instrument,
and, working cautiously myself, was rewarded by the discovery
of two perfect vases, one in alabaster, the other in glass. Each
bore the name and title of the Khorsabad king, in cuneiform
characters, with the figure of a lion.

A kind of exfoliation had taken place on the surface of the
glass vase, which was incrusted with thin, semi-transparent lam-
irfa, glowing with the brilliant colors of the opal. This beautiful appearance is a well-known result of age, and is found on
glass from Egyptian, Greek, and other early tombs. It is remarkable that this vase has been turned from a block and not
blown, the marks left by the instrument being perfectly preserved in the interior. Both these interesting relics are now in
the British Museum.

In the lower compartment of a slab in the same chamber,
were two beardless figures, which from a certain feminine character in the features, and from a cluster of long curls falling
down their backs, appeared to be women. They wore the usual
horned cap and had wings. They faced one another, and between them was the sacred tree. In one hand they held a garland or chaplet; and wore round their necks a necklace, with
seven stars.*

* This bas-relief is in the British Museum.

The adjoining chamber was paneled with unsculptured slabs, and contained no object of particular interest.

One of the most remarkable discoveries was made in the center of the mound, where, as I have already mentioned,* a pair of gigantic winged bulls appeared to form the entrance to a building. The inscriptions upon them contained a name, differing from that of the king of the N. W. palace. On digging further I found a brick, on which was a genealogy, the new name occurring first, as that of the son of the founder of the earlier edifice.

I dug round these sculptures, expecting to find the remains of walls, but there were no other traces of building. As the backs of the slabs were completely covered with inscriptions, in large and well-formed characters, it was possible that these bulls might originally have stood alone. Suspecting that there must have been other sculptures near them, I directed a deep trench to be opened, at right angles, behind the northern bull. After digging about ten feet, the workmen came upon a colossal winged figure in low relief, lying flat on the brick pavement. Beyond was a similar figure, still more gigantic in its proportions, being about fourteen feet high. The beard and part of the legs of a winged bull, in yellow limestone, were next found. The trench was carried in the same direction to the distance of fifty feet, but without any other result. I had business in Mosul, and was giving directions to the workmen to guide them during my absence. Standing on the edge of the hitherto unprofitable trench, I doubted whether I should carry it any further; but made up my mind at last not to abandon it until my return, which would be on the following day. I mounted my horse; but had scarcely left the mound when the corner of a monument in black marble was uncovered, which proved to be an obelisk, about six feet six inches in height, lying on its side, ten feet below the surface.

An Arab was sent after me without delay, to announce the discovery; and on my return I found, completely exposed to

* P. 32.

view, an obelisk terminated by three steps or gradines and flat at the top. I descended eagerly into the trench, and was immediately struck by the singular appearance, and evident antiquity, of the remarkable monument before me. We raised it

THE OBELISK.

and speedily dragged it out of the ruins. On each side were five small bas-reliefs, and above, below, and between them was carved an inscription 210 lines in length. The whole was in the best preservation. The king was twice represented followed

K*

by his attendants; a prisoner was at his feet, and his vizier and eunuchs were introducing captives and tributaries carrying

Elephant and Monkeys. (Obelisk, Nimroud.)

vases, shawls, bundles of rare wood, elephant's tusks, and other objects of tribute, and leading various animals, among which were the elephant, the rhinoceros, the Bactrian or two-humped camel, the wild bull, and several kinds of monkeys. In one

Bactrian or Two-humped Camels. (Obelisk, Nimroud.)

bas-relief were two lions hunting a stag in a wood, probably to denote the nature of one of the countries conquered by the king. From the animals portrayed, particularly the double-humped

camel,* and the elephant, which is of the Indian and not of the
African species, it is natural to conjecture that the obelisk was

The Bull, the Rhinoceros, and an Antelope.   (Obelisk, Nimroud.)

sculptured to commemorate the conquest of nations far to the
east of Assyria, on the confines of the Indian peninsula.   The

Large Monkey and Ape.   (Obelisk, Nimroud.)

name of the king, whose deeds it records, was the same as that
on the center bulls.

* This animal is a native of the great steppes inhabited by the Tatar
tribes.   It is almost unknown to the Arabs, and is rarely seen to the west
of Persia, except among a few isolated families of Turcomans who now
pitch their tents in the north of Syria, and probably brought this camel
with them on their first migration.

In the S. W. corner, discoveries of scarcely less interest and importance were made almost at the same time. The southern entrance to the palace was formed by a pair of winged lions, of which the upper part, including the head, had been almost entirely destroyed.* They differed in many respects from those in the N.W. palace. They had but four legs; the material in which they were sculptured was a coarse limestone, and not alabaster; and behind the body of the lion, and in front above the wings, were several figures, which were unfortunately greatly injured, and could with difficulty be traced. The figures behind were a dragon with the head of an

Figures on Lions.   (S.W. Palace, Nimroud.)

eagle and the claws of a bird, followed by a man carrying the usual square vessel, standing above a priest bearing a pole surmounted by a fir-cone, and a human figure, the upper part of which was destroyed in all the sculptures; those in front were

* This monument is now in the British Museum.

a human figure, and a monster with the head of a lion, the body of a man, and the feet of a bird, raising a sword.

Figures on Lions.   (S.W. Palace, Nimroud.)

Between the two lions, forming this entrance, were a pair of crouching sphinxes, not in relief, but entire. The human head was beardless; and the horned cap square, and highly orna-mented at the top, like that of the winged bulls of Khorsabad. The body was that of a winged lion. These sphinxes may have been altars for sacrifice or offerings.

The whole entrance was buried in charcoal, and the sphinxes were almost reduced to lime. One had been nearly destroyed ; but the other, although cracked into a thousand pieces, was still standing when uncovered. I endeavored to secure it with rods of iron and wooden planks; but the alabaster was too much calcined to resist exposure to the atmosphere. I had scarcely time to make a careful drawing, before the whole fell into fragments, too small to admit of their being collected with

a view to future restoration.   The sphinxes, when entire, were
about five feet in height, and the same in length.

Sphinx from S.W. Palace.   (Nimroud.)

Buried in the charcoal, was found a small head in alabaster,
with the high-horned cap, precisely similar to that of the large
sphinx ; and subsequently the body was dug out, giving thus
a complete model of the larger sculptures.*   In the same place
I discovered the bodies of two lions, united and forming a platform or pedestal, like the one crouching sphinx ; but the human
heads were wanting, and the rest of the sculpture had been so
much injured by fire, that I was unable to preserve it.

The plan of the edifice in which these discoveries were made
could not yet be determined.   All the slabs uncovered had
evidently been brought from another building ; chiefly from
the N. W. palace.   The entrance I have just described,
proved this beyond a doubt ; as it enabled me to distinguish between the back and front of the walls.   I was now
convinced that the sculptures hitherto found, were not meant to
be exposed to view ; but had been placed *against* the wall of

* Now in the British Museum.

sun-dried bricks; the backs of the slabs, smoothed preparatory to being re-sculptured, having been turned toward the interior of the chambers.

There were no inscriptions between the legs of the lions just described, as in other buildings at Nimroud and Khorsabad. I had not before found sculptures unaccompanied by the name and genealogy of the founder of the edifice in which they had been placed. When no inscription was on the face, it was invariably on the back of the slab. I dug, therefore, at the back of the lions, and was not disappointed in my search; a few lines in the cuneiform character were discovered, containing the names of three kings in genealogical series. The name of the first king nearly resembled that of the builder of the N. W. palace; that of his father was identical with the name on the bricks found in the ruins opposite Mosul; and that of his grandfather with the name of the founder of Khorsabad. This fortunate discovery served to connect the latest palace at Nimroud with two other Assyrian edifices.

While excavations were thus successfully carried on among the center ruins, and those of the two palaces first opened, discoveries of a different nature were made in the S. E. corner, which was much higher than any other part of the mound. I dug to a considerable depth, without meeting with any other remains than fragments of inscribed bricks and pottery, and a few entire earthen vessels. At length an imperfect slab bearing a royal name similar to that on the bull in the center of the mound, was found at some depth beneath the surface. On raising it to copy the inscription, I found to my surprise that it had been used as a lid to an earthen sarcophagus, which, with its contents, was still entire beneath. The sarcophagus was about five feet in length, and very narrow. The skeleton was well preserved, but fell to pieces almost immediately when exposed to the air; by its sides were two jars in baked clay of a red color, and a small alabaster bottle, precisely resembling in shape similar vessels discovered in Egyptian tombs. There was no other clew to the date, or origin of the sepulcher.

The sarcophagus was too small to contain a man of ordinary size if stretched at full length; and it was evident, from the position of the skeleton, that the body had been doubled up. A second earthen case was soon found, resembling a dish-cover in shape, and scarcely four feet long. In it were also vases of baked clay, and it was closed by an inscribed slab like the sarcophagus first discovered. Although the skulls were entire when first exposed to view, they crumbled into dust as soon as an attempt was made to move them.

The six weeks following the commencement of excavations upon a large scale were among the most prosperous, and fruitful in events, during my researches in Assyria. Every day produced some new discovery. The Arabs entered with zeal into the work, and felt almost as much interested in its results as I did myself. They were now well organized, and I had no difficulty in managing them. Even their private disputes and domestic quarrels were referred to me. They found this a cheaper fashion of settling their differences than litigation; and I have reason to hope that they received an ampler measure of justice than they could have expected at the hands of his reverence the cadi. The tents had greatly increased in numbers, as the relatives of those who were engaged in the excavations came to Nimroud and swelled the encampment; for although they received no pay, they managed to live upon the gains of their friends. They were, moreover, preparing to glean,—in the event of there being any crops in the spring,— and to take possession of little strips of land along the banks of the river, for the cultivation of millet during the summer. They already began to prepare water-courses, and machines for irrigation. The mode of raising water in Mesopotamia is very simple. In the first place a high bank, which is never completely deserted by the river, is chosen, and a broad recess is cut in it down to the water's edge. Over this recess are fixed three or four upright poles, according to the number of oxen to be employed, united at the top by rollers running on a swivel, and supporting a large framework of boughs and grass, which extends to some distance behind, and is intended as a shelter from the sun. Over each roller are passed two ropes, one fastened to the mouth, and the other to the opposite end, of a sack, formed out of an entire bullock skin. These ropes are attached to oxen, who throw all their weight upon them by descending an inclined plane. A trough formed of wood, and lined with bitumen, or shallow trench coated with matting, is constructed at the bottom of the poles, and leads to a canal running into the fields. When the sack is drawn up to the roller, the ox turns round at the bottom of the inclined plane. The rope attached to the lower part of the bucket being fastened to the back part of the animal, he raises, in turning, the bottom of the sack, and the contents are poured into the trough. As the ox ascends, the bucket is again lowered into the stream. Although this mode of irrigation is very toilsome, and requires the constant labor of several men and animals, it is generally adopted on the banks of the Tigris and Euphrates. In this way all the gardens of Baghdad and Busrah are watered; and by such means the wandering Arabs, who condescend to cultivate—when famine is staring them in the face—raise a little millet to supply their immediate wants.

The principal public quarrels, over which my jurisdiction extended, related to property abstracted, by the Arabs, from one another's tents. These I disposed of in a summary manner, as I had provided myself with handcuffs; and Ibrahim Agha and the bairakdar were always ready to act with energy and decision, to show how much they were devoted to my service. But the domestic dissensions were of a more serious nature, and their adjustment offered far greater difficulties. They related, of course, always to the women. As soon as the workmen saved a few piastres, their thoughts were turned to the purchase of a new wife, a striped cloak, and a spear. To accomplish this, their ingenuity was taxed to the utmost extent. The old wife naturally enough raised objections, and picked a quarrel with the intended bride, which generally ended in an appeal to physical force. Then the fathers and brothers were dragged

into the affair; from them it extended to the various branches
of the tribe, always anxious to fight for their own honor, and
for the honor of their women. At other times, a man repented
himself of his bargain, and refused to fulfill it; or a father,
finding his future son-in-law increasing in wealth, demanded a
higher price for his daughter—a breach of faith which would
naturally lead to violent measures on the part of the disappointed lover. Then a workman, who had returned hungry
from his work, and found his bread unbaked, or the water-skin
still lying empty at the entrance of his tent, or the bundle of
fagots for his evening fire yet ungathered, would, in a moment
of passion, pronounce three times the awful sentence, and divorce
his wife ; or, avoiding such extremities, would content himself
with inflicting summary punishment with a tent-pole. In the
first case he probably repented himself of the act an hour or
two afterward, and wished to be remarried ; or endeavored
to prove that, being an ignorant man, he had mispronounced
the formula, or omitted some words—both being good grounds
to invalidate the divorce, and to obviate the necessity of any
fresh ceremonies. But the mullah had to be summoned, wit-
nesses called, and evidence produced. The beating was generally
the most expeditious, and really, to the wife, the most satisfactory way of adjusting the quarrel. I had almost nightly to settle
such questions as these: Mr. Hormuzd Rassam, who had obtained an immense influence over the Arabs, and was known
among all the tribes, was directed to ascertain the merits of
the story, and to collect the evidence. When this process had
been completed, I summoned the elders, and gave judgment in
their presence. The culprit was punished summarily, or, in
case of a disputed bargain, was made to pay more, or to refund,
as the case required.

When I first employed the Arabs, the women were sorely ill-
treated, and subjected to great hardships. I endeavored to
introduce some reform into their domestic arrangements, and
punished severely those who inflicted corporal chastisement on
their wives. In a short time the number of domestic quarrels

was greatly reduced; and the women, who were at first afraid
to complain of their husbands, now boldly appealed to me for
protection. They had, however, some misgivings as to the
future, which were thus expressed by a deputation sent to
return thanks after an entertainment:—" O Bey! we are your
sacrifice. May God reward you! Have we not eaten wheaten
bread, and even meat and butter, since we have been under your
shadow? Is there one of us that has not now a colored kerchief
for her head, bracelets, and ankle-rings, and a striped cloak!
But what shall we do when you leave us, which God forbid you
ever should do? Our husbands will then have their turn, and
there will be nobody to help us."

These poor creatures, like all Arab women, were exposed to
constant hardships. They were obliged to look after the children, to make the bread, to fetch water, and to cut wood, which
they brought home from afar on their heads. Moreover they
were intrusted with all the domestic duties, wove their wool
and goats' hair into clothes, carpets, and tent-canvas; and were
left to strike and raise the tents, and to load and unload the
beasts of burden when they changed their encamping ground.
If their husbands possessed sheep or cows, they had to drive
them to the pastures, and to milk them at night. When moving,
they carried their children at their backs during the march, and
were even troubled with this burden when employed in their
domestic occupations, if the children were too young to be left
alone. The men sat indolently by, smoking their pipes, or
listening to the gossip of some stray Arab of the desert. At first
the women, whose husbands encamped on the mound, brought
water from the river; but I relieved them from this labor by
employing horses and donkeys. The weight of a large sheep or
goat's skin filled with water, is not inconsiderable. It is hung on
the back by cords strapped over the shoulders, and upon it is
frequently seated the child, who can not be left in the tent, or is
unable to follow its mother on foot. The bundles of fire-wood,
brought from a considerable distance, were enormous, completely
concealing the head and shoulders of those who tottered beneath

them. And yet the women worked cheerfully, and it was seldom that their husbands had to complain of their idleness. Some
were more active than others. There was a young girl named
Hadla, who particularly distinguished herself, and was consequently sought in marriage by all the men. Her features were
handsome, and her form erect, and exceedingly graceful. She
carried the largest burdens, was never unemployed, and was
accustomed, when she had finished the work imposed upon her
by her mother, to assist her neighbors in completing theirs.

The dinners or breakfasts (for the meal comprised both) of
the Arab workmen, were brought to them at the mound, about
eleven o'clock, by the younger children. Few had more than a
loaf of millet bread, or millet made into a kind of paste, to satisfy
their hunger ;—wheaten bread was a luxury. Sometimes their
wives had found time to gather a few herbs, which were boiled
in water with a little salt, and sent in wooden bowls ; and in
spring, curds and sour milk occasionally accompanied their
bread. The little children, who carried their father's or brother's
portion, came merrily along, and sat smiling on the edge of the
trenches, or stood gazing in wonder at the sculptures, until they
were sent back with the empty platters and bowls. The working parties eat together in the trenches in which they had been
employed. A little water, drank out of a large jar, was their
only beverage. Yet they were happy and joyous. The joke
went round ; or, during the short time they had to rest, one told
a story, which, if not concluded at a sitting, was resumed on the
following day. Sometimes a pedler from Mosul, driving before
him his donkey, laden with raisins or dried dates, would appear
on the mound. Buying up his store, I would distribute it among
the men. This largess created an immense deal of satisfaction
and enthusiasm, which any one, not acquainted with the character of the Arab, might have thought almost more than equivalent
to the consideration.

The Arabs are naturally hospitable and generous. If one of
the workmen was wealthy enough to buy a handful of raisins,
or a piece of camel's or sheep's flesh, or if he had a cow, which

occasionally yielded him butter or sour milk, he would immediately call his friends together to partake of his feast. I was
frequently invited to such entertainments; the whole dinner,
perhaps, consisting of half a dozen dates or raisins spread out
wide, to make the best show, upon a corn-sack; a pat of butter
upon a corner of a flat loaf; and a few cakes of dough baked
in the ashes. And yet the repast was ushered in with every
solemnity;—the host turned his dirty keffiah, or head-kerchief,
and his cloak, in order to look clean and smart; appearing both
proud of the honor conferred upon him, and of his means to
meet it in a proper fashion.

I frequently feasted the workmen, and sometimes their wives
and daughters were invited to separate entertainments, as they
would not eat in public with the men. Generally of an evening, after the labors of the day were finished, some Kurdish
musicians would stroll to the village with their instruments, and
a dance would be commenced, which lasted through the greater
part of the night. Sheikh Abd-ur-rahman, or some sheikh of
a neighboring tribe, occasionally joined us; or an Arab from
the Khabour, or from the more distant tribes of the desert,
would pass through Nimroud, and entertain a large circle of
curious and excited listeners with stories of recent fights, plundering expeditions, or the murder of a chief. I endeavored, as
far as it was in my power, to create a good feeling among all,
and to obtain their willing co-operation in my work. I believe
that I was to some extent successful.

The Tiyari diggers resided chiefly on the mound, where
I had built a large hut for them. A few only returned at
night to the village. Many of them had brought their wives
from the mountains. The women made bread, and cooked
for all. Two of the men walked to the village of Tel Yakoub,
or to Mosul, on Saturday evening, to fetch flour for the whole
party, and returned before the work of the day began on
Monday morning; for they would not journey on the Sabbath. They kept their holydays and festivals with as much
rigor as they kept the Sunday. On these days they assembled

on the mound or in the trenches; and one of the priests or
deacons (for there were several among the workmen) repeated
prayers, or led a hymn or chant. I often watched these poor
creatures, as they reverentially knelt—their heads uncovered
—under the great bulls, celebrating the praises of Him whose
temples the worshipers of those frowning idols had destroyed,
—whose power they had mocked. It was the triumph of truth
over paganism. Never had triumph been more forcibly illustrated than by those who now bowed down in the crumbling
halls of the Assyrian kings.

I experienced some difficulty in settling disputes between the
Arabs and the Tiyari, which frequently threatened to finish in
bloodshed. The Mussulmans were always ready, on the slightest
provocation, to bestow upon the Chaldeans the abuse usually
reserved in the East for Christians. But the hardy mountaineers
took these things differently from the humble Rayahs of the
plain, and retorted with epithets very harsh to a Mohammedan's
ear. This, of course, led to the drawing of sabers and priming
of matchlocks; and it was not until I had inflicted a few summary punishments, that some check was placed upon these disorders.

On Sunday, sheep were slain for the Tiyari workmen, and
they feasted during the afternoon. When at night there were
music and dances, they would sometimes join the Arabs; but
generally performed a quiet dance with their own women, with
more decorum, and less vehemence, than their more excitable
companions.

As for myself I rose at daybreak, and, after a hasty breakfast, rode to the mound. Until night I was engaged in drawing
the sculptures, copying and molding the inscriptions, and
superintending the excavations, and the removal and packing
of the bas-reliefs. On my return to the village, I was occupied
till past midnight in comparing the inscriptions with the paper
impressions, in finishing drawings, and in preparing for the
work of the following day. Such was our manner of life
during the excavations at Nimroud; and I owe an apology to

the reader for entering into such details. They may, however, be interesting as illustrative of the character of the genuine Arab, with whom the traveler is seldom brought so much into contact as I have been.

Early in December a sufficient number of bas-reliefs were collected for another raft, and I consequently rode into Mosul to make preparations for sending a second cargo to Baghdad. I had soon procured all that was necessary for the purpose ; and loading a small raft with spars and skins for the construction of a larger, and with mats and felts for packing the sculptures; I returned to Nimroud.

The raft-men having left Mosul late in the day, and not reaching the awai until after nightfall, were afraid to cross the dam in the dark; they therefore tied the raft to the shore, and went to sleep. They were attacked during the night, and plundered. I appealed to the authorities, but in vain. The Arabs of the desert, they said, were beyond their reach. If this robbery passed unnoticed, the remainder of my property, and even my person, might run some risk. Besides, I did not relish the reflection, that the mats and felts destined for my sculptures were now furnishing the tents of some Arab sheikh. Three or four days elapsed before I ascertained who were the robbers. They belonged to a small tribe encamped at some distance from Nimroud—notorious in the country for their thieving propensities, and the dread of my Jebours, whose cattle were continually disappearing in a very mysterious fashion. Having learned the position of their tents, I started off one morning at dawn, accompanied by Ibrahim Agha, the bairakdar, and a horseman, who was in my service. We reached the encampment after a long ride, and found the number of the Arabs to be greater than I had expected. The arrival of strangers drew together a crowd, which gathered round the tent of the sheikh, where I seated myself. A slight bustle was apparent in the women's department. I soon perceived that attempts were being made to hide various ropes and felts, the ends of which, protruding from under the canvas, I had little difficulty in recognizing. "Peace be with you!" said I, addressing the sheikh, who showed by his countenance that he was not altogether ignorant of the object of my visit. "Your health and spirits are, please God, good. We have long been friends, although it has never yet been my good fortune to see you. I know the laws of friendship; that which is my property is your property, and the contrary. But there are a few things, such as mats, felts, and ropes, which come from afar, and are very necessary to me, while they can be of little use to you; otherwise God forbid that I should ask for them. You will greatly oblige me by giving these things to me." "As I am your sacrifice, O Bey," answered he, "no such things as mats, felts, or ropes were ever in my tents (I observed a new rope supporting the principal pole). Search, and if such things be found, we give them to you willingly." "Wallah! the sheikh has spoken the truth," exclaimed all the by-standers. "That is exactly what I want to ascertain; and as this is a matter of doubt, the pashaw must decide between us," replied I, making a sign to the bairakdar, who had been duly instructed how to act. In a moment he had handcuffed the sheikh, and, jumping on his horse, dragged the Arab, at an uncomfortable pace, out of the encampment. "Now, my sons," said I, mounting leisurely, "I have found a part of that which I wanted; you must search for the rest." They looked at one another in amazement. One man, more bold than the rest, was about to seize the bridle of my horse; but the weight of Ibrahim Agha's courbatch across his back, drew his attention to another object. Although the Arabs were well armed, they were too much surprised to make any attempt at resistance; or perhaps they feared too much for their sheikh, still jolting away at an uneasy pace in the iron grasp of the bairakdar, who had put his horse to a brisk trot, and held his pistol cocked in one hand. The women, swarming out of the tents, now took part in the matter. Gathering round my horse, they kissed the tails of my coat and my shoes, making the most dolorous supplications. I was not to be moved, however; and extricating myself with difficulty from the crowd, I rejoined the bairakdar, who was hurrying on his prisoner with evident good-will.

The sheikh had already made himself well known to the authorities by his dealings with the villages, and there was scarcely a man in the country who could not bring forward a specious claim against him—either for a donkey, a horse, a sheep, or a copper-kettle. He was consequently most averse to an interview with the pashaw, and looked with evident horror on the prospect of a journey to Mosul. I added considerably to his alarm, by dropping a few friendly hints on the advantage of the dreary subterraneous lock-up house under the governor's palace, and of the pillory and sticks. By the time he reached Nimroud, he was fully alive to his fate, and deemed it prudent to make a full confession. He sent an Arab to his tents; and next morning an ass appeared in my court-yard bearing the missing property, with the addition of a lamb and a kid, by way of a conciliatory offering. I dismissed the sheikh with a lecture, and had afterward no reason to complain of him or of his tribe,—nor indeed of any tribes in the neighborhood; for the story got abroad, and was invested with several horrible facts in addition, which could only be traced to the imagination of the Arabs, but which served to produce the effect I desired— a proper respect for my property.

During the winter Mr. Longworth, and two other English travelers, visited me at Nimroud. They were the only Europeans (except Mr. Ross), who saw the ruins when uncovered.*

I was riding home from the ruins one evening with Mr. Longworth. The Arabs returning from their day's work were following a flock of sheep belonging to the people of the village, shouting their war-cry, flourishing their swords, and indulging in the most extravagant gesticulations. My friend, less acquainted with the excitable temperament of the children of the desert than myself, was somewhat amazed at these vio-

* Mr. Seymour was also with me at Nimroud, but before the excavations were in an advanced stage.

lent proceedings, and desired to learn their cause. I asked one of the most active of the party. " O Bey," they exclaimed almost all together, " God be praised, we have eaten butter and wheaten bread under your shadow, and are content—but an Arab is an Arab. It is not for a man to carry about dirt in baskets, and to use a spade all his life; he should be with his sword and his mare in the desert. We are sad as we think of the days when we plundered the Aneyza, and we must have excitement, or our hearts would break. Let us then believe that these are the sheep we have taken from the enemy, and that we are driving them to our tents !" And off they ran, raising their wild cry and flourishing their swords, to the no small alarm of the shepherd, who, seeing his sheep scampering in all directions, did not seem inclined to enter into the joke.

By the middle of December, a second cargo of sculptures was ready to be sent to Baghdad. I was again obliged to have recourse to the buffalo-carts of the pashaw; and as none of the bas-reliefs and objects to be moved were of great weight, these rotten and unwieldy vehicles could be patched up for the occasion. On Christmas-day I had the satisfaction of seeing a raft, bearing twenty-three cases, in one of which was the obelisk, floating down the river. I watched them until they were out of sight, and then galloped into Mosul to celebrate the festivities of the season, with the few Europeans whom duty or business had collected in this remote corner of the globe.

CHAPTER X.

DEATH OF TAHYAR PASHAW.—DISCOVERIES IN THE NORTHWEST PALACE.
—IVORY ORNAMENTS AND CARTOUCHES WITH HIEROGLYPHICS.—PAINTED
CHAMBERS.—POTTERY.—DISCOVERY OF UPPER CHAMBERS.—PAINTINGS
ON THE WALLS.—PAVEMENT SLABS.—DISCOVERIES IN THE CENTER OF
THE MOUND.—TOMBS CONTAINING VASES AND ORNAMENTS.—SCULP-
TURES.—FURTHER DISCOVERIES IN THE SOUTHWEST EDIFICE.—SCULP-
TURES.—DISCOVERY OF MORE TOMBS IN THE SOUTHEAST CORNER.—
OF CHAMBERS BENEATH THEM.—OF A VAULTED ROOM.

As I was drawing one morning at the mound, Ibrahim Agha
came to me, with his eyes full of tears, and announced the death
of Tahyar Pashaw.   The cawass had followed the fortunes of
the late Governor of Mosul almost since childhood, and was
looked upon as a member of his family.   Like other Turks of
his class, he had been devoted to the service of his patron, and
was treated more like a companion than a servant.   In no
country in the world are ties of this nature more close than in
Turkey ; nowhere does there exist a better feeling between the
master and the servant, and the master and the slave.

I was much grieved at the sudden death of Tahyar; for he
was a man of gentle and kindly manners, just and considerate
in his government, and of considerable information and learning for a Turk.   The cause of his death showed his integrity.
His troop had plundered a friendly tribe, falsely represented
to him as rebellious by his principal officers, who were anxious to have an opportunity of enriching themselves with the
spoil.   When he learned the truth, and that the tribe, so far
from being hostile, were peaceably pasturing their flocks on the
banks of the Khabour, he exclaimed, "You have destroyed my
house" (i.e. its honor); and, without speaking again, died of a
broken heart.   He was buried in the court-yard of the principal
mosque at Mardin.   A simple but elegant tomb, surrounded by

flowers and evergreens, was raised over his remains; and an
Arabic inscription records the virtues and probable reward of
one of the most honest and amiable men that it has been my
lot, in a life of some experience among men of various kinds,
to meet. . I visited his monument during my journey to Constantinople. From the lofty terrace, where it stands, the eye
wanders over the vast plains of Mesopotamia, stretching to the
Euphrates,—in spring one great meadow, covered with the
tents and flocks of innumerable tribes.

The kiayah, or chief secretary, was chosen governor of the
province by the council, until the Porte could name a new
pashaw, or take other steps for the administration of affairs.
Essad Pashaw, who had lately been at Beyrout, was at length
appointed to succeed Tahyar, and soon after reached his
pashawlic. These changes did not affect my proceedings. Armed
with my vizirial letter, I was able to defy the machinations of
the cadi and the ulema, who did not cease their endeavors to
throw obstacles in my way.

After the celebration of Christmas I returned to Nimroud,
and the excavations were again carried on with activity.

The N. W. palace was naturally the most interesting portion of the ruins, and to it were principally directed my researches. I had satisfied myself beyond a doubt that it was
the most ancient building yet explored in Assyria; although,
not having been destroyed by fire, it was in a better state of
preservation than any edifice hitherto discovered.

When the excavations were resumed after Christmas, eight
chambers had been opened. There were now so many outlets and entrances, that I had no trouble in finding new chambers,—one leading into another. By the end of the month of
April I had explored almost the whole building; and had
opened twenty-eight rooms cased with alabaster slabs. Although
many new sculptures of considerable interest were found in
them, still the principal part of the edifice seems to have been
that to the north, where the best artists had evidently been
employed upon the walls of the chambers, and the bas-reliefs

excelled all those that had yet been discovered, in the elegance and finish of the ornaments, and in the spirited delineation of the figures.   In the other chambers were either winged figures, separated by the sacred tree, and resembling one another in every respect, or the standard inscription alone was carved upon the slabs.

THE KING.   (N. W. Palace, Nimroud.)

The colossal figure of a female with four wings, carrying a garland, now in the British Museum, was discovered in a chamber on the south side of the palace,* as was also the fine bas-relief of the king leaning on a wand or staff, one of the best preserved and most highly finished specimens in the national collection.

In the center of the palace was a great hall, nearly square, with entrances on the four sides formed by colossal human-headed lions and bulls. The slabs which paneled the walls were unsculptured, but upon each was the standard inscription.

To the south of this hall, was a cluster of small chambers, opening into each other. At the entrance to one of them were winged figures wearing garlands, and carrying a wild goat and an ear of corn.† In another chamber were discovered the beautiful ivory ornaments now in the British Museum. These interesting relics adhered so tenaciously to the soil, and were so completely decomposed, that it was a task of great difficulty to remove them even in fragments. The ivory separated in flakes, or fell into powder. Consequently many interesting objects were irretrievably lost, notwithstanding the care which was taken to collect the smallest pieces. Those preserved were restored in England by an ingenious process, which, replacing the gelatinous matter, and thus reuniting the decaying particles into one solid body, gave them the appearance and consistency of recent ivory.

The most interesting of these ivories are two small tablets, one nearly entire, the other much injured, on which are carved two sitting figures, holding in one hand the Egyptian scepter or symbol of power. Between the figures is a cartouche, containing a name in hieroglyphics, and surmounted by a feather or plume, such as is found in monuments of the eighteenth, and subsequent dynasties of Egypt. The robes of the figures, the chairs on which they are seated, the hieroglyphics in the cartouche,

* In chamber L (plan 8). In front of this figure was an earthen pipe connecting the floor of the chamber with a drain—the whole cemented with bitumen. It may have been used to carry off the blood of the sacrifice.
† One of these figures is in the British Museum:

and the feather above it, were enameled with a blue sub-
stance let into the ivory; and the uncarved portions of the
tablet, the cartouche, and part of the figures, were originally
gilded,—remains of the gold leaf still adhering to them. The
forms, and style of art, have a purely Egyptian character;
although there are certain peculiarities in the execution, and
mode of treatment, that would seem to mark the work of a
foreign, perhaps an Assyrian, artist. The same peculiarities
characterized all the other objects discovered. Several small
human heads in frames, supported by low pillars, and the heads
of lions and bulls, show not only a considerable acquaintance
with art, but an intimate knowledge of the process of working in
ivory. Found with them were oblong tablets, upon which are
sculptured, with great delicacy, standing figures, with one hand
elevated, and holding in the other a stem or staff, surmounted
by an ornament resembling the Egyptian lotus. Scattered about
were fragments of winged sphinxes, the head of a lion of singular
beauty, which unfortunately fell to pieces, human heads, hands,
legs, and feet, bulls, flowers, and scroll-work. In all the
specimens the spirit of the design and the delicacy of the workmanship are equally to be admired. These ornaments may
have belonged to a throne or chest, or may have decorated the
walls or ceilings of the room. In Scripture we find frequent
allusion to the employment of this beautiful material both in
architecture and in furniture. Ahab had an ivory house, and
ivory palaces are mentioned in the Psalms. Solomon made a
throne of ivory, and ivory beds are spoken of by the prophets.* The hands and feet probably belonged to an entire
human figure, the draped part of which was in wood or metal,
resembling the chryselephantine statues of the Greeks.

On two slabs, forming an entrance to a small chamber in this
part of the building† were inscriptions containing the name
of the king who built the Khorsabad palace. They had been

* Compare 1 Kings x. 18, and xxii. 39; Psalms xlv. 8; Amos iii. 15,
and vi. 4.
† Chamber U.

cut above the usual inscription, to which they are evidently long posterior, a fact which alone proves the greater antiquity of the Nimroud ruins.

In all the chambers to the south of the center hall, were found copper vessels of peculiar shape; but they fell to pieces almost immediately on exposure to the air, and I was unable to preserve one of them entire.

When the chambers paneled with alabaster slabs ceased, I was unable for some time to trace any remains of the building beyond. A brick pavement proved that the ruins did not end here, and on examining the trenches carefully it was found that we had entered chambers, the walls of which were of sun-dried bricks, covered with a coating of plaster, and painted with figures and ornaments. The colors had faded so completely, that scarcely any of the subjects or designs could be traced. It required the greatest care to separate the rubbish from the walls, without removing at the same time the plaster, which fell off in flakes, notwithstanding all my efforts to preserve it. The subject of the paintings, as far as could be judged from the remains, was the king, followed by eunuchs and warriors, receiving prisoners and tribute. The figures appear to have been nearly in black outline upon a blue ground, and I was unable to distinguish any other colors.

As the means at my disposal did not warrant any outlay in making mere experiments, without the certainty of the discovery of removable objects, I felt myself compelled, much against my inclination, to abandon the excavations in this part of the mound, after uncovering portions of two chambers. The doorway, which united them, was paved with one large slab, ornamented with flowers and scroll-work. The flooring was of baked bricks.

On the western face of the great mound, to the south of the N. W. palace, there is a considerable elevation. To examine it, a trench was opened on a level with the platform. It was some time before I ascertained that we were cutting into a kind of tower, or nest of upper chambers, constructed entirely of unbaked bricks; the walls being plastered, and elaborately painted. I explored three rooms, and part of a fourth on the southern side of this building.

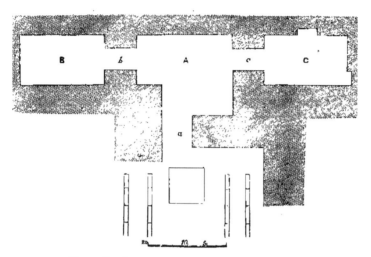

PLAN 4.—Upper Chambers on the west side of the Mound. (Nimroud.)

It is probable that there were four similar groups of chambers, facing the cardinal points. In front of the southern entrance,* was a large square slab with slightly raised edges, similar to those frequently found in the N. W. palace. ·On two sides of it were narrow pieces of alabaster, forming parallel lines, which I can only compare to the rails of a railroad. I can not form any conjecture as to their use. The rooms had been more than once painted, and two distinct coats of plaster were visible on the walls. The outer coating, when carefully detached, left the under, on which the designs were different.

* Entrance *a*, Plan 4.

The painted ornaments were remarkable for their elegance. The Assyrian bull was frequently introduced, sometimes with wings, sometimes without. Above the animals was a border resembling the battlements of castles in the sculptures, and below, forming a kind of cornice, squares and circles, tastefully arranged. The colors were blue, red, white, yellow, and black; and although thus limited in number, were arranged with much taste and skill, the contrasts being carefully preserved, and the combinations generally agreeable to the eye. The pale yellow ground, on which the designs were painted, resembled the tint on the walls of Egyptian monuments; and a strong well-defined black outline is a peculiar feature in Assyrian as in Egyptian painting, in the ornaments described, black frequently combining with white alone, or alternating with other colors.

But the most important discovery, connected with these upper chambers, was that of the pavement slabs at two entrances. The inscriptions upon them contained the names of several kings, most of which were new, and are of the greatest interest, as adding to the list of monarchs of the earliest dynasty.*

I could not ascertain whether there were any chambers, or remains of buildings, beneath this upper edifice; or whether it was a tower constructed on the solid outer wall. A deep trench was opened on the eastern side of it, and, about twenty feet below the surface, a pavement of brick and several square slabs of alabaster were uncovered; but these remains did not throw any light upon the nature of the building above; nor were they sufficient to show that the N. W. palace had been carried under it. To the south of it there were no remains of building, the platform of unbaked bricks being continued up to the level of the flooring of the chambers.

In the center of the mound, I had in vain endeavored to find the walls and other remains of the palace which must at one time have stood there. Except the colossal bulls, the obelisk,

* One of these slabs is in the British Museum.

two winged figures, and a few fragments of yellow limestone, which appeared to have formed part of a gigantic bull or lion, no sculptures had yet been discovered there. Excavations to the south of the bulls disclosed a tomb built of bricks and closed by a slab of alabaster. It was about five feet in length, and scarcely more than eighteen inches in breadth in the interior. On removing the lid, parts of a skeleton were exposed to view; the skull and some of the larger bones were still entire; but soon crumbled into dust. A vase of reddish clay, with a long narrow neck, stood near the body, in a dish of such delicate fabric, that I had great difficulty in moving it entire. Over the mouth of the vase was placed a bowl or cup, also of red clay. In the dust, which had accumulated round the skeleton, were found beads and small ornaments of opaque-colored glass, agate, cornelian, and amethyst. A small crouching lion of lapis lazuli, pierced on the back, had been attached to the end of the necklace. With the beads was a cylinder, on which was represented the king in his chariot, hunting the wild bull, as in the bas-relief from the N. W. palace; a copper ornament resembling a modern seal, two bracelets of silver, and a pin for the hair. These remains show the tomb to be that of a female.

On digging beyond this tomb, I found others, similarly constructed, and of the same size. In them were vases of highly glazed green pottery, elegant in shape, and in perfect preservation, copper mirrors, and copper lustral spoons.*

I was surprised to find, about *five feet beneath these tombs,* the remains of a building. Walls of unbaked bricks could still be traced; but the alabaster slabs, with which they had been paneled, had been removed, and were heaped on the pavement. Slab succeeded to slab; and when I had removed nearly twenty tombs, and had cleared a space about fifty feet square, the ruins presented a very singular appearance. Above

---

* Most of the small objects discovered in the tombs, and described in the text, are now in the British Museum.

one hundred slabs were uncovered, placed in rows, one against the other, like the leaves of a gigantic book. Every slab was sculptured; and as they followed each other according to the subjects upon them, it was evident that they had been moved, in the order in which they stood, from their original positions; and had been left as found, preparatory to their removal elsewhere. That they had not been thus collected prior to their arrangement against the walls, was evident from the fact, proved beyond a doubt by repeated observation, that the Assyrians sculptured the slabs, with the exception of the great bulls and lions, after they had been placed. The slabs had also been *split*, if I may be allowed the expression, in order to reduce their dimensions, and render them more easily transportable. To the south of the center bulls were two colossal figures, similar to those discovered to the north.

The bas-reliefs resembled, in many respects, some of those discovered in the S. W. palace, in which the sculptured faces of the slabs were turned, it will be remembered, toward the walls of unbaked brick. It would appear, therefore, that the one building had been destroyed, to supply materials for the construction of the other. But here were tombs *over* the ruins. The edifice had perished, and in the rubbish accumulating above its remains, a people, whose funereal vases and ornaments were nearly identical with those found in the catacombs of Egypt, had buried their dead. What race, then, occupied the country after the destruction of the Assyrian palaces? At what period were these tombs made? What antiquity did their presence assign to the buildings beneath them? It is difficult to answer these questions. The tombs undoubtedly prove that the Assyrian edifices were overthrown and buried at a very remote period. The Egyptian character of the pottery, beads, and ornaments, is very remarkable, and would seem to indicate that those who were buried at Nimroud came from Egypt, or were closely connected with that country. The mode of sepulture is, however, undoubtedly not Egyptian; it is, on the contrary, that which prevailed throughout Assyria and Babylonia during an epoch yet unfixed. It resembles in some respects that adopted by the early Persians,—Cyrus and Darius having been buried in sarcophagi or troughs. All we can at present assert is, that these tombs prove the remote period of the utter destruction of the palaces.

Pottery found in the Tombs above the Ruins at Nimroud.

The subjects of the sculptures thus found collected together, with the exception of a few colossal figures of the king and his attendant eunuchs, and of the winged priests or divinities, were principally battle-pieces and sieges. Some cities were represented as standing on a river, in the midst of groves of date-trees, and among the conquered people were warriors mounted on camels. It may be inferred, therefore, that one series of these bas-reliefs recorded the conquest of an Arab nation, or perhaps of a part of Babylonia—the inhabitants of the cities being assisted by auxiliaries, from the neighboring desert. The conquered races, as in the bas-reliefs of the N. W. palace,

ASSYRIAN HORSEMEN PURSUING A MAN, PROBABLY AN ARAB, ON A CAMEL. (Center Palace, Nimroud.)

were generally without armor or helmets, their hair falling loosely on their shoulders. Some, however, wore helmets, which varied in shape from those of the conquerors.

Helmets. (Center Palace, Nimroud.)

Battering-rams also differed in form from those represented in the earlier sculptures. The besieged castles, like those of the Assyrians, appear to have been built upon artificial mounds. The battering-ram was rolled up to the walls on an inclined plane constructed of earth, stones, and trees, which appears to have been sometimes paved with bricks or squared stones, to facilitate the ascent of the engine. This mode of besieging a city, as well as the various methods of attack portrayed in the sculptures, are frequently alluded to in Scripture. Ezekiel,* prophesying of Jerusalem, exclaims, " Lay siege against it, and *build a fort against it, and cast a mound against it* ; set the camp also against, and set *battering-rams* against it round about :" and Isaiah, " Thus saith the Lord concerning the King of Assyria : he shall not come into this city, nor shoot an arrow there, nor come before it with shields, *nor cast a bank against it.*"† The shields mentioned by the prophet are probably those of wicker-work, represented in the

* Ch. iv. 2.
† Isaiah xxxvii. 33; compare 2 Kings xix. 32; Jeremiah xxxii. 24, and xxxiii. 4; Ezekiel xvii. 17.

bas-reliefs as covering the whole person and resting on the ground. Some of the battering-rams were not provided with towers for armed men, and some were without wheels; the latter were probably "the forts" which Nebuchadnezzar built round about Jerusalem.* These forts appear to have been mere temporary erections of wood and wicker-work; and the Jews were expressly forbidden to use for the purpose trees affording sustenance to man,—"only the trees which thou knowest that they be not trees for meat, thou shalt destroy and cut them down: and *thou shalt build bulwarks against the city* that maketh war with thee, until it be subdued."† Ezekiel, in prophesying the destruction of Tyre by Nebuchadnezzar, has faithfully recorded the events of an Assyrian siege, and the treatment of the conquered people; his description illustrates in a remarkable manner, the bas-reliefs of Nimroud:—

"Thus saith the Lord God; Behold, I will bring upon Tyrus Nebuchadrezzar king of Babylon, a king of kings, from the north, with horses, and with chariots, and with horsemen, and companies, and much people. He shall slay with the sword thy daughters in the field: and he shall make a fort against thee, and cast a mount against thee, and lift up the buckler against thee. And he shall set engines of war against thy walls, and with his axes he shall break down thy towers. By reason of the abundance of his horses, their dust shall cover thee: thy walls shall shake at the noise of the horsemen, and of the wheels, and of the chariots, when he shall enter into thy gates, as men enter into a city wherein is made a breach. With the hoofs of his horses shall he tread down all thy streets: he shall slay thy people by the sword, and thy strong garrisons shall go down to the ground. And they shall make a spoil of thy riches, and make a prey of thy merchandise: and they shall break down thy walls, and destroy thy pleasant houses: and they shall lay thy stones and thy timber and thy dust in the midst of the water."‡

---

* Jeremiah lii. 4.   † Deut. xx. 19, 20.   ‡ Ezek. xxvi. 7–12.

The battering-ram appears to have been directed by men within the framework, which was frequently covered with drapery or hides, ornamented with fringes and even with devices.

Warriors before a besieged City. A Battering-ram drawn up to the Walls, and Captives impaled. (Center Palace, Nimroud.)

On two slabs was a bas-relief of considerable interest, representing the sack of a city.* The conquerors were seen carrying away the spoil, and two eunuchs, standing near the gates, wrote down with a pen on rolls of some pliable material, probably a kind of paper or leather, the number of sheep and cattle driven away by the soldiers. In the lower part of the bas-relief, were

* Now in the British Museum.

carts drawn by oxen, carrying women and children. Near the
gates were two battering-rams, which, the city having been
taken, were no longer at work.

Assyrian Warriors fighting with the Enemy. An Eagle is carrying
away the Entrails of the Slain. (Center Palace, Nimroud.)

Among other bas-reliefs may be mentioned the king seated
on his throne, receiving prisoners with their arms bound behind
them; eunuchs registering the heads of the enemy, laid at their
feet by the conquerors; idols borne on the shoulders of men;
and a walled city, standing on the sea, or on a river.

The spoil represented in these bas-reliefs as carried away
from the conquered nations, consisted chiefly of cattle, sheep,

and camels.   The cattle were evidently of two kinds, probably the buffalo and common ox, distinguished in the sculptures

Captive Women in a Cart drawn by Oxen. (Center Palace, Nimroud.)

by horns curved toward the back of the head, and horns projecting in front.   The sheep also appear to have been of

Walled City standing on a River or on the Sea. (Center Palace, Nimroud.)

two species; that with the broad tail is still found in the country, and is described by Herodotus as peculiar to Mesopotamia.* The goats have long spiral horns. The camel is faithfully delineated. This valuable animal formed at the remotest period the riches of the inhabitants of Assyria and Arabia, and was no doubt by them, as it still is by the Arab, ranked among the most desirable objects of plunder. It was used even in those days by couriers, and for posts, and flocks of them were possessed by Abraham and Jacob.†

To the east of the center bulls several slabs were discovered, still standing in their original position. The lower part of the bas-reliefs alone remained, the upper having been completely destroyed. They represented colossal winged figures, carrying the usual square vessel, and sacred flowers of various forms.

The only part of the S. W. palace sufficiently well preserved to give any idea of its original form, was one large hall curiously constructed. It had two entrances, formed by human-headed bulls and lions sculptured in a coarse gray limestone ; and, in the center, was a portal (also formed by winged bulls), in a kind of partition, which divides the hall into four distinct parts, but appears to have been merely intended to support beams for the roof. Between the bulls forming the center portal were a pair of sphinxes.

The whole of this hall was paneled with slabs brought from other buildings. Some, and by far the greater number, were from the N. W., others from the center, palace. But there were many bas-reliefs which differed greatly, in the style of art, from the sculptures discovered in both these ruins. From whence they were obtained I am unable to determine ; whether from a palace of another period once existing at Nimroud, and still concealed in a part of the mound not explored, or from some edifice in the neighborhood.

All the walls had been exposed to fire, and, the slabs nearly reduced to lime, were too much injured to bear removal. They

---

* Lib. iii. c. 118. This broad tail is mentioned in Leviticus iii. 9, vii. 3, where it is rendered "rump."
† Esther viii. 10, 14 ; Genesis xii. 16, xxx. 43 ; and compare Genesis xxiv. 19, xxxi. 34 ; 1 Samuel xxx. 17.

were not all sculptured ; the bas-reliefs being scattered here and there, and always turned toward the wall of sun-dried brick.

Among the most interesting bas-reliefs discovered were the following :—A king seated on his throne, receiving his vizier, and surrounded by his attendants, within the walls of a castle ; a warrior wearing a crested helmet on a rearing horse, asking

Enemy asking quarter of Assyrian horsemen. (S.W. Palace, Nimroud.)

quarter of Assyrian horsemen ; a spearman on horseback hunting the wild bull ; the king of the N.W. palace in his chariot fighting

with the enemy; the siege of a castle, in which was represented
a bucket attached to a pulley; a pair of human-headed bulls in
low relief; and a king placing his foot on the neck of a captive,
and raising a spur in his right hand, the only instance in which
he is represented with this weapon—a bas-relief illustrating

Part of a bas-relief, showing a Pulley, and a Warrior cutting a Bucket
from a Rope.

the passage of Scripture which describes the captains of Israel
placing their feet upon the necks of the captive kings: "And
it came to pass, when they brought out those kings unto Joshua,
that Joshua called for all the men of Israel, and said unto the
captains of the men of war which went with him, Come near,
and put your feet upon the necks of these kings. And they

To face page 253

came near, and put their feet upon the necks of them."* To
make "a footstool of mine enemies" is a common biblical expression of triumph. A procession of warriors carrying away
the idols of a conquered nation, was highly interesting on account of the figures of the gods. The first was that of a female
seated on a high-backed chair, holding a ring in one hand, and
a kind of fan in the other. Her face was in full, and she wore
the horned cap surmounted by a star, The next figure was also
that of a seated female, wearing a similar cap, and holding a
ring in one hand. The third was partly concealed by a screen
placed on a chair; and the fourth was that of a man walking,
raising an ax in one hand, and grasping an object resembling
the conventional thunderbolt of the Greek Jove in the other. The
female figures may be those of Hera and Rhea, who were wor-
shiped in the temple of Babylon; while the god may be identified with Baal or Belus, the supreme deity of the Semitic races,
who, according to Diodorus Siculus, was represented in the act
of walking. This bas-relief illustrates more than one passage
in the Bible. Hosea prophesied that the idol of Samaria *should
be carried away* by the Assyrians;† and Jeremiah declares that
the Babylonians should burn the gods of the Egyptians, and *carry
them away captive*.‡ In the epistle supposed to have been
written by the prophet Jeremiah to the captive Jews, to warn
them against the idolatries of the Babylonians, we find the following remarkable description of the gods represented in the
Assyrian sculptures. "Now shall ye see, in Babylon, gods of
silver, and of gold, and of wood, *borne upon shoulders*. And
he that can not put to death one that offendeth him, holdeth a
scepter, as though he were a judge of the country. He *hath
also in his right hand a dagger and an ax*."§ We learn from
the same epistle that these idols were of wood laid over with
gold, and that parts of them were polished by the workmen,
that crowns were placed on their heads, that they were decked

* Joshua x. 24.   † Chapter x. 6.   ‡ Chapter xliii. 12.
§ That the Jews looked upon this Epistle as genuine, may be inferred
from the reference to it in 2 Maccab. xi. 2, 3.

out in garments and purple raiment, and that fires or lamps
were kept burning before them. Jeremiah describes the gods
of the heathen as cut out of a tree of the forest, decked with
silver and gold, fastened with nails, and with blue and purple
garments.* The star above the horned-cap of the figures in the
bas-relief appears to point to an astral system personified in the
idols ; and it is to this custom of placing the star above the head
of the god to which the prophet Amos probably alludes, when he
condemns the house of Israel for having " borne the tabernacle
of Moloch and Chiun, their images and *the star* of their god,
which they had made for themselves."†

Some of the sculptures had been carefully erased, and only
a few traces of the figures remained. Several of the bas-reliefs
were accompanied by descriptive inscriptions ; and on the
pavement was discovered a tablet recording the conquests of
a king whose name occurs in no other ruins yet discovered,
and to whom no place can yet be assigned in the Assyrian
royal lists.

The three entrances to the south of the palace appear to have
led into a magnificent hall, about 220 feet in length, the northern
entrance to which was also formed by a pair of human-headed
bulls. The side walls had in some places completely disappeared, and the sculptures which were still standing had all suffered
more or less from the conflagration and subsequent long exposure to the atmosphere.

As the level of the S. W. palace was considerably above
that of the N. W., and as the site of many sculptures in it
had not been discovered, it appeared to me possible that it had
been built over the ruins of some more ancient building. By
way of experiment, therefore, I directed long and very deep
trenches to be opened in three different directions: nothing,
however, was found, but a box or square hole, twenty feet beneath the surface, formed by bricks carefully fitted together,
and containing several small idols in unbaked clay. They

* Chapter x. 4, 9.   † Chapter v. 26.

were bearded figures, wearing high, pointed miters, and had probably been placed, for some religious purpose, beneath the foundations of the building. Objects somewhat similar, and in the same material, were discovered at Khorsabad, under the pavement slabs, between the great bulls.

Near the southern entrance to the great hall was found, amid a mass of charred wood and charcoal, and beneath a fallen slab, part of a beam in good preservation, apparently of mulberry wood.

It may be inferred that a very long interval intervened between the time of the construction of the N. W. and of the S. W. palaces. A considerable period must have elapsed before a monarch destroyed the monuments of his predecessors to raise out of the materials a new habitation for himself or his divinities. It is highly probable that some great change had taken place before such an event could have happened,—that a new dynasty of kings had ejected the older family ; and that, as conquerors, they had introduced a new element into the nation. There are remarkable differences in the costume of the king, the forms of the chariots, the trappings of the horses, and the arms and armor of the warriors, which further tend to prove that some such change had taken place in Assyria between the destruction of the N. W. palace at Nimroud and the erection of that at Khorsabad. The state of art, as shown in the treatment of the sculptures, in their forms and in their ornaments, differed materially during the two periods, and points to a very great change in manners, the state of civilization, and religion.

The southeast corner of the mound, which was considerably above the level of any other part, appears to have been the principal burying-place of those who occupied the country after the destruction of the Assyrian palaces. Beside the two tombs already described, many others were subsequently discovered there. The sarcophagi were mostly of the same shape, that of a dish-cover ; but there were other tombs constructed of bricks well fitted together and covered by a slab, similar to those about the ruins in the center of the mound. In nearly all were

M

earthen vases, copper and silver ornaments, and small alabaster bottles. The skeletons, as soon as uncovered, crumbled to pieces, although entire when first exposed, and one skull alone has been preserved. Scattered among these tombs were vases of all sizes, lamps, and small objects of pottery, some uninjured, others broken into fragments.*

Removing the tombs I discovered beneath them the remains of a building, and explored seven chambers. No sculptures or inscriptions were found in them; the lower part of the walls being paneled with plain slabs of limestone, three feet seven inches high, and from two to three feet wide, and the upper being of sun-dried bricks, covered by a thick coat of white plaster.

In the rubbish, near the bottom of the chambers, were found several small objects; among them a female head in white ala- baster, now in the British Museum.

It only remains for me to mention a singular discovery on the eastern face of the mound near its northern extremity. A trench having been opened from the outer slope, the workmen came upon a small vaulted chamber, about ten feet high, and the same in width, fifteen feet below the level of the mound, and in the center of a wall of sun-dried bricks, nearly fifty feet thick. The arch was built of baked bricks. The cham- ber was filled with rubbish, the greater part of which was a kind of slag, and the bricks forming the vault and walls were almost vitrified, evidently from exposure to very intense heat. The chamber had thus the appearance of a large furnace for making glass, or fusing metal. I am unable to account for its use, as there was no access to it, as far as I could ascertain from any side.

Much, of course, remained to be explored in the ruins; but with the limited means at my disposal, I was unable to pursue my researches to the extent that I could have wished. If, after carrying a trench to a reasonable depth and distance, no

. * Many of the small objects are in the British Museum.

remains of sculpture or inscription were discovered, I abandoned it, and renewed the experiment elsewhere. I could thus ascertain whether any very extensive edifice was still standing. There were too many tangible objects in view to warrant an outlay in excavations promising no immediate results; and a great part of the mound of Nimroud was left to be explored, when the ruins of Assyria should be further examined.

CHAPTER XI.

EXCAVATIONS AT KALAH SHEBGHAT.—DEPARTURE FOR THE RUINS.—
THE BITUMEN PITS.—ABD'RUBBOU.—MY RECEPTION.—DISCOVERY OF A
SITTING FIGURE.—ARAB ENCAMPMENT.—ARAB LIFE.—EXCAVATIONS
IN THE MOUND.—DISCOVERY OF TOMBS.—RETURN TO NIMROUD.

I HAD long wished to excavate in the mounds of Kalah
Sherghat, which rivaled in extent those of Nimroud and
Kouyunjik. An Arab, from the Shammar Bedouins, would
occasionally spend a night among my workmen, and entertain
them with accounts of idols and sculptured figures of giants,
which had long been the cause of wonder and awe to the wandering tribes, who pitch their tents near the place. On my first
visit I had searched in vain for such remains; but the Arabs,
who are accustomed to seek for pasture during the spring in the
neighborhood, persisted in their assertions, and offered to show
me where these strange statues, carved, it was said, in black
stone, were to be found. Scarcely a ruin in Mesopotamia is
without its wondrous tale of apparitions and Frank idols, and I
concluded that these sculptures only existed in the fertile imagination of the Arabs. As the vicinity of Kalah Sherghet is noto-
riously dangerous, being a place of rendezvous for plundering
parties of the Shammar, Aneyza, and Obeid Bedouins, I had deferred a visit to the spot, until I could remain there for a short
time, under the protection of some powerful tribe. This safe-
guard was also absolutely necessary in the event of my sending
workmen to excavate.

There being no pasture in the neighborhood of Mosul this
year, on account of the want of rain, the three great divisions
of the Jebour Arabs sought the jungles on the banks of the
Tigris. Abd'rubbou with his tribe descended the river, and first
pitching his tents at Senidij, near the confluence of the Tigris

and the Zab, subsequently moved toward Kalah Sherghat. I thought this a favorable time for excavating in the great mound; and the sheikh having promised to supply me with Arabs for the work, and with guards for their defense, I sent Mansour, one of my superintendents, to the spot. I followed some days afterward, accompanied by Mr. Hormuzd Rassam, the bairakdar, and several well-armed men, chosen from among the Jebours who were employed at Nimroud.

We crossed the Tigris on a small raft,—our horses having to swim the river. Striking into the desert by the Wadi Jehainah, we rode through a tract of land, at this time of year usually covered with vegetation; but then, from the drought, a barren waste. During some hours' ride we scarcely saw any human being, except a solitary shepherd in the distance, driving before him his half-famished flocks. We reached at sunset a small encampment of Jebours. The tents were pitched in the midst of a cluster of high reeds on the banks of the Tigris, and nearly opposite to the tomb of Sultan Abd-Allah. They were so well concealed, that it required the experienced eye of a Bedouin to detect them* by the thin smoke rising above the thicket. The cattle and sheep found scanty pasturage in a marsh formed by the river. The Arabs were as poor and miserable as their beasts; they received us, however, with hospitality, and killed a very lean lamb for our entertainment.

Near the encampment was a quadrangle, resembling on a small scale the great inclosures of Nimroud and Kouyunjik, formed by low mounds, and evidently marking the site of an Assyrian town or fort. I searched for some time, but without success, for fragments of pottery or brick inscribed with cunei-form characters.

On the following day we passed the bitumen pits, or the "Kiyara," as they are called by the Arabs. They cover a con-

---

* In the desert, the vicinity of an encampment is generally marked by some sign well known to the members of the tribe. It would otherwise be very difficult to discover the tents, pitched, as they usually are, in some hollow or ravine to conceal them from hostile plundering parties.

siderable extent of ground ; the bitumen bubbling up in springs from crevices in the earth and forming small ponds. The Jebours, and other tribes encamping near the place, carry the bitumen for sale to Mosul, and other parts of the pashawlic. It is extensively used for building purposes, for coating the boats on the river, and particularly for smearing camels, when suffering from certain diseases of the skin to which they are liable. Before leaving the pits, the Arabs, as is their habit, set fire to the bitumen, which sent forth a dense smoke, obscuring the sky, and visible for many miles. We reached the tents of Abd'rubbou early in the afternoon. They were pitched about ten miles to the north of Kalah Sherghat, at the upper end of a long tongue of rich alluvial soil, lying between the river and a range of low hills. The great mound was visible from this spot, rising high above the zor, or jungle, which clothes the banks of the Tigris.

No sheikh could have made a more creditable show of friendship than did Abd'rubbou. He rode out to meet me, and, without delay, ordered sheep enough to be slain to feast half his tribe. I declined, however, to spend the night with him, as he pressed me to do, on the plea that I was anxious to see the result of the excavations at Kalah Sherghat. He volunteered to accompany me to the ruins after we had breakfasted, and declared that if a blade of grass were to be found near the mound, he would move all his tents there immediately for my protection. In the meanwhile, to do me proper honor, he introduced me to his wives, and to his sister, whose beauty I had often heard extolled by the Jebours, and who was not altogether undeserving of her reputation. She was still unmarried. Abd'rubbou himself was one of the handsomest Arabs in Mesopotamia.

We started for the ruins in the afternoon, and rode along the edge of the jungle. Hares, wolves, foxes, jackals, and wild boars continually crossed our path, and game of all kinds seemed to abound. The Arabs gave chase ; but the animals were able to enter the thick brushwood, and conceal themselves before my greyhounds could reach them. Lions are sometimes found near Kalah Sherghat, rarely higher up on the Tigris.* As I floated down to Baghdad a year before, I had heard the roar of a lion not far from this spot: they are, however, seldom seen, and we beat the bushes in vain for such noble game.

As for grass, except in scanty tufts at the foot of the trees in the jungle, there appeared to be none at all. The drought had been felt all over the desert: in the place of the green meadows of last year, covered with flowers, and abounding in natural reservoirs of water, there was a naked yellow waste, in which even the abstemious flocks of the Bedouin could scarcely escape starvation. As we rode along, Abd'rubbou examined every corner and ravine in the hope of finding an encamping place, and a little pasture for his cattle, but his search was not attended with much success.

The workmen on the mound, seeing horsemen approach, made ready for an encounter, under the impression that we were a foraging party from a hostile tribe. As soon, however, as they recognized us, they threw off the few superfluous garments they possessed. Dropping their shirts from their shoulders, and tying them round the waists by the arms, they set up the war-cry, and rushed in and out of the trenches like madmen.

The principal excavations had been made on the western side of the mound. After I had succeeded in obtaining silence, and calming the sudden fit of enthusiasm which had sprung up on my arrival, I descended into the trenches. A sitting figure in black basalt, of the size of life, had been uncovered. It was, however, much mutilated. The head and hands had been destroyed, and other parts of the statue had been injured. The

---

* The lion is frequently met with on the banks of the Tigris below Baghdad, rarely above. On the Euphrates it has been seen, I believe, almost as high as Bir, where the steamers of the first Euphrates expedition, under Colonel Chesney, were lanched. In the Sinjar, and on the banks of the Kabour, they are frequently caught by the Arabs. They abound in Khuzistan, the ancient Susiana: I have frequently seen three or four together, and have hunted them with the chiefs of the tribes inhabiting that province.

square stool, or block, upon which the figure sat, was covered
on three sides with a cuneiform inscription. The first line, containing the name and titles of the king, was almost defaced;
but one or two characters enabled me to restore a name, identical with that on the great bulls in the center of the mound at
Nimroud. On casting my eye down the first column of the
inscription, I found the names of this king's father (the builder
of the most ancient palace of Nimroud), and of his grandfather.
An Arab soon afterward brought me a brick bearing a short
legend, which contained the three names entire. I was thus
enabled to fix the comparative epoch of the newly-discovered
ruins.

Sitting Figure in Basalt, from Kalah Sherghat.

The figure, unlike the sculptures of Nimroud and Khorsabad,
was in full, and not in relief; and probably represented the
king. Part of the beard was still preserved; the hands appear
to have rested on the knees, and a long robe, edged with tassels,
reached to the ankles. The Arabs declared that this statue

had been seen some years before; and it is possible that, at some period of heavy rain, it may have been for a short time exposed to view, and subsequently reburied. It stood on a spur of the mound, and probably in its original position. Mansour had dug trenches at right angles with it on four sides, in the expectation of finding a corresponding figure; but he was disappointed in his search, and no remains of building were discovered near it.*

In other parts of the mound there were ruins of walls, but we found no more sculptures. Several tombs, similar to those above the palaces of Nimroud, had been opened; and Mansour brought me earthen vases and cups taken from them. He had also picked up, among the rubbish, a few fragments of black stone with small figures in relief, and cuneiform characters, and a piece of copper similarly inscribed.

Having made a hasty survey of the trenches, I rode to my tent, which had been pitched in the midst of those of my workmen. The Arabs had chosen for their encampment a secure place in the jungle at the northern foot of the mound, and not far from the Tigris. A ditch, leading from the river, nearly surrounded the tents, which were completely concealed by the trees and shrubs. Abd'rubbou remained with me for the night. While I was examining the ruins, he had been riding to and fro, to find a convenient spot for his tents, and grass for his cattle. Such is the custom of the Arabs. When the grass, within a certain distance of their encampment, has been exhausted, they prepare to seek new pastures. The sheikhs, and the principal men of the tribe, mount their mares, and ride backward and forward over the face of the country, until they find herbage sufficient for the wants of their flocks. Having fixed on a suitable spot, they return to acquaint their followers with their success, and announce their intention of moving thither on the following morning. The sheikh's tent is generally the first

* This statue is now in the British Museum.

M*

struck; and the rest of the tribe, if they feel inclined, follow his example. If any have cause of complaint against their chief and wish to desert him, they seize this occasion; they leave their tents standing until the others are gone, and then wander in another direction.

Abd'rubbou having, at length, found a convenient site on the banks of the river, to the south of the mound, he marked out a place for his tents, and sent a horseman to his tribe, with orders for them to move to Kalah Sherghat on the following morning. These preliminaries having been settled, he adjourned to my tent to supper. It was cold and damp, and the Arabs, collecting brushwood and trunks of trees, made a great fire, which lighted up the recesses of the jungle. As the night advanced, a violent storm broke over us; the wind rose to a hurricane—the rain descended in torrents—the thunder rolled in one long peal—and vivid streams of lightning, almost incessant, showed the surrounding landscape. When the storm had abated, I walked to a short distance from the tents to gaze upon the scene. The huge fire we had kindled threw a lurid glare over the trees around our encampment. The great mound could be distinguished through the gloom, rising like a distant mountain against the dark sky. From all sides came the melancholy wail of the jackals, who had issued from their subterranean dwellings in the ruins, as soon as the last gleam of twilight was fading in the western horizon. The owl, perched on the old masonry, occasionally sent forth its mournful note. The shrill laugh of the Arabs would sometimes rise above the cry of the jackal. Then all earthly noises were buried in the deep roll of the distant thunder. It was desolation such as those alone who have witnessed such scenes, can know—desolation greater than the desolation of the sandy wastes of Africa: for there was the wreck of man, as well as that of nature.

Soon after sunrise, on the following morning, stragglers on horseback from Abd'rubbou's late encampment, began to arrive. They were soon followed by the main body of the tribe. Long lines of camels, sheep, laden donkeys, men, women, and children,

such as I have described in my visit to Sofuk, covered the small
plain, near the banks of the river. A scene of activity and
bustle ensued.   Every one appeared desirous to outdo his
neighbor in vehemence of shouting, and violence of action.
A stranger would have fancied that there was one general
quarrel ; in which, out of several hundred men and women
concerned, no two persons took the same side of the question.
Every one seemed to differ from every one else.   All this confusion, however, was but the result of a friendly debate on the
site of the respective tents ; and when the matter had been
settled to the general satisfaction, without recourse to any more
violent measures than mere yelling, each family commenced
raising their temporary abode.   The camels being made to
kneel down, and the donkeys to stop in the place fixed upon,
their loads were rolled off their backs.   The women next
spread the black goat-hair canvas.   The men rushed about
with wooden mallets to drive in the stakes and pegs ; and in a
few minutes the dwellings, which were to afford them shelter,
until they needed shelter no longer, and under which they had
lived from their birth upward, were complete.   The women
and girls were then sent forth to fetch water, or to collect
brushwood and dry twigs for fire.   The men, leaving all household matters to their wives and daughters, assembled in the tent
of the sheikh ; and crouching in a circle round the entire trunk
of an old tree, which was soon enveloped in flames, they prepared to pass the rest of the day in that desultory small-talk, relating to stolen sheep, stray donkeys, or successful robberies,
which fills up the leisure of an Arab, unless he be better employed in plundering or in war.

Leaving Abd'rubbou and his Arabs to pitch their tents and
settle their domestic matters, I walked to the mound.   The
trenches dug by the workmen around the sitting figure were
almost sufficiently extensive to prove that no other remains of
building existed in its immediate vicinity.   Had not the figure
been in an upright position I should have concluded, at once,
that it had been brought from elsewhere ; as I could not find

traces of pavement, nor any fragments of sculpture or hewn
stone, near it. Removing the workmen, therefore, from this part
of the mound, I divided them into small parties, and employed
them in making experiments in different directions. Wherever
trenches were opened, remains of the Assyrian period were
found, but only in fragments ; such as bits of basalt, with small
figures in relief, portions of slabs bearing cuneiform inscriptions, and bricks similarly inscribed. Many tombs were also discovered. Like those of Nimroud, they belonged to a period long
subsequent to the destruction of the Assyrian edifices, and were
in the rubbish and earth which had accumulated above them.
The sarcophagi resembled those I have already described—large
cases of baked clay, some square, others in the form of a dish-
cover; as at Nimroud, they were all much too small to hold a
human body, unless it had been violently forced in, or the
limbs had been separated. That the bodies had not been
burned, was proved by the bones being found entire. They
may have been exposed, as is the custom among the Parsees,
until the skeleton was made bare by the usual process of de-
composition, or by birds and beasts of prey, and then buried in
these earthen cases. In the sarcophagi were found numerous
small vases, metal ornaments, and a copper cup, resembling in
shape and in the embossed designs one held by the king, in a
bas-relief from the N.W. palace of Nimroud.*

Above these ancient tombs were graves of more recent date ;
some of them, indeed, belonged to the tribes which had, but a
few days before, encamped among the ruins.† The tenant of
one had been removed from his last resting-place by the hungry
hyenas and jackals, who haunt these depositories of the dead.
The rude casing of stones, forming the interior of an Arab

---

* This cup was taken out entire, but was unfortunately broken by the
man who was employed to carry it to Mosul.

† The Arabs generally seek some elevated spot to bury their dead. The
artificial mounds, abounding in Mesopotamia and Assyria, are usually chosen
for the purpose, and there is scarcely one whose summit is not covered with
them. On this account I frequently experienced great difficulty while excavating, and was compelled to leave unexamined one or two ruins.

grave, had been opened; and the bones and skull, still clothed with shreds of flesh, were scattered around.

Although I spent two days at Kalah Sherghat I was unable to reach the platform of sun-dried bricks upon which the edifice, now in ruins, and covered with earth, must originally have been built. Remains of walls were found in abundance; but they were evidently of a more recent period than the Assyrian building, to which the inscribed bricks and the fragments of sculptured stone belonged. The ruins were consequently not thoroughly explored. I saw no remains of the alabaster or Mosul marble so generally employed in the palaces to the north of Kalah Sherghat. Unbaked bricks alone may have been used in the edifice; and if so, the walls built with them could no longer, without very careful examination, be distinguished from the soil in which they are buried.

The Tigris has been gradually encroaching upon the ruins, and is yearly undermining and wearing away the mound. Large masses of earth are continually falling into the stream, leaving exposed to view vases, sarcophagi, and remains of building. Along the banks of the river, several shafts of circular masonry, having the appearance of wells, had been thus uncovered. At the time of my first visit, we observed similar wells, and were at a loss to account for their use. I now opened two or three of them. They were filled with earth, mixed with human bones and fragments of vases and pottery;* which may have been originally deposited there, or may have fallen in from above with the rubbish. It is possible that these wells may have been constructed, at a very early period, for purposes of irrigation, or to supply water to the inhabitants of the city.

The principal ruin at Kalah Sherghat, like those of Nimroud, Khorsabad, and other ancient Assyrian sites, is a large square mound, surmounted by a cone or pyramid, which rises nearly in the center of the north side of the great platform. Imme-

---

* I found similar wells, containing human remains and pottery, among the ruins on the banks of the rivers of Susiana.

diately below it, and forming a facing to the great mound, is a wall of well-hewn stones, carefully fitted together, and beveled. The battlements, which still exist, are cut into gradines, and resemble those of castles and towers in the Nimroud sculptures. The wall is therefore, I think, Assyrian. It is not improbable that much of the masonry, still visible on the summit of the mound, may be the remains of an Arab fort. Long lines of smaller mounds or ramparts form a quadrangle, and are the remains of the walls which once inclosed the town.

The principal ruin of Kalah Sherghat, is one of the largest with which I am acquainted in Assyria. I was unable to measure it accurately during this visit; but when on the spot with Mr. Ainsworth, we carefully paced round it; and the result, according to that gentleman's calculation, gave a circumference of 4685 yards.* A part of it, however, is not artificial. Irregularities in the face of the country, and natural eminences, have been united into one great platform by earth and layers of sundried bricks. It is, nevertheless, a stupendous structure; yielding in extent to no other artificial mound in Assyria. In height it is unequal; to the south it slopes off nearly to the level of the plain, while to the north, where it is most lofty, its sides are perpendicular, in some places rising to nearly one hundred feet.

I will not attempt to connect, without better materials than we now possess, the ruins of Kalah Sherghat with any ancient city whose name occurs in the sacred books, or has been preserved by ancient geographers. That it was one of the oldest cities of Assyria, is proved by the identification of the name of the king found on its monuments and bricks, with that on the center bulls and obelisk of Nimroud; but whether it be Chalah, one of the four primitive cities mentioned in Genesis,† I will not venture to decide.

Having directed Mansour to continue the excavations, I prepared to return to Mosul. Abd'rubbou offered to accompany

* Journal of the Royal Geographical Society, vol. xi. p. 5.
† Chap. x. 11.

me; and as the desert between Kalah Sherghat and Ham-mum Ali was infested by roving parties of the Shammar and Aneyza Arabs, I deemed it prudent to accept his escort. He chose eight horsemen from his tribe, and we started together for the desert.

We slept the first night at the tents of a Seyyid, or descendant of the Prophet, of some repute for sanctity, and for the miraculous cure of diseases, which he effected by merely touching the patient. The Arabs were fully persuaded of the existence of his healing power; but I never saw any one who even pretended to have been cured, although there was certainly no lack of subjects for the Seyyid to practice upon. The old gentleman's daughter, a dark, handsome girl, was claimed by a sheikh of the Jebours, to whom, according to some accounts, she had been betrothed. The greater part of the night was spent in quarreling and wrangling upon this subject. The Seyyid resolutely denied the contract, on the mere plea that one of such holy descent could not be united to a man in whose veins the blood of the Prophet did not flow. Abd'rubbou and his friends, on the other hand, as stoutly contended for the claims of the lover, not treating, I thought, so great a saint with a proper degree of respect. Although my tent was pitched at some distance from the assembly, the discordant voices, all joining at the same time in the most violent discussion, kept me awake until past midnight. Suddenly the disputants appeared to have talked themselves out, and there was a lull. Vainly flattering myself that they had sunk into sleep, I prepared to follow their example. But I had scarcely closed my eyes, when I was roused by a fresh outbreak of noises. An Arab had suddenly arrived from the banks of the Khabour—the old pasture-grounds of the tribe: he was overwhelmed with a thousand questions, and the news he brought of struggles between the Aneyza and the Asai, and the defeat of the former enemies of the Jebours, led to continual bursts of enthusiasm, and to one or two attempts to raise a general shouting of the war-cry. Thus they passed the night to my great discomfort.

On the morrow I started early with Abd'rubboù and his horsemen. We struck directly across the desert, leaving my servants and baggage to follow leisurely along the banks of the river, by a more circuitous but safer road. When we were within four or five miles of that part of the Tigris at which the raft was waiting for me, I requested the sheikh to return, as there appeared to be no further need of an escort. Mr. Hormuzd Rassam and myself galloped over the plain. We disturbed, as we rode along, a few herds of gazelles, and a solitary wolf or jackal; but we saw no human beings. Abd'rubbou and his Arabs, however, had scarcely left us, when they observed a party of horsemen in the distance, whom they mistook for men of their own tribe returning from Mosul. It was not until they drew nigh that they discovered their mistake. The horsemen were plunderers from the Aneyza. The numbers were pretty equal. A fight ensued, in which two men on the side of the enemy, and one of the Jebours, were killed; but the Aneyza were defeated, and Abd'rubbou carried off in triumph a couple of mares.

A few days after my return to Nimroud, the Jebours were compelled, by want of pasturage, to leave the neighborhood of Kalah Sherghat. The whole desert, as well as the jungle on the banks of the river, which generally supplied, even in the driest seasons, a little grass to the flocks, having been completely dried up, Abd'rubbou, with his tribe, moved to the north. A few of his people came to Nimroud to cultivate millet; but the sheikh himself, with the greater part of his followers, left the district of Mosul altogether, migrating to the sources of the Khabour and to the Nisibin branch of that river—the ancient Mygdonius. The desert to the south of the town was now only frequented by wandering parties of plunderers, and the position of my workmen at Kalàh Sherghat became daily more insecure. After they had been once or twice exposed to molestation from the Aneyza and the Obeid, I found it necessary to withdraw them—had I not, they would probably have run away of themselves. I renounced the further examination of these ruins with regret, as they had not been properly explored ; and I have little doubt, from the fragments discovered, that many objects of interest, if not sculptured slabs, exist in the mound.

CHAPTER XII.

ASSYRIA PROPER, like Babylonia, owed its ancient fertility as
much to artificial irrigation, as to the rains which fall during
the winter and early spring. The Tigris and Euphrates, unlike the Nile, do not overflow their banks and deposit a rich
manure on the face of the land. They rise sufficiently at the
time of the melting of the snows in the Armenian hills, to fill
the numerous canals led from them into the adjacent country ;
but these are generally so deep, or their banks so high, that
when the stream returns to its usual level, water can only be
raised by artificial means.

The great canals dug in the most prosperous period of the
Assyrian Empire, and used for many centuries by the inhabitants of the country—even after the Arab invasion—have
long since been choked up and are now useless. When the
waters of the rivers are high, it is still only by the labor of
man that they can be led into the fields. I have already described the rude wheels constructed for the purpose along the
banks of the Tigris. Even these are scarce. The government, or rather the local authorities, levy a considerable tax
upon machines for irrigation, and the simple buckets of the
Arabs become in many cases the source of exaction and oppression. Few being, consequently, bold enough to make use of
them, the land near the rivers, as well as the interior of the
country, is entirely dependent for its fertility upon the winter
rains, which are amply sufficient to insure the most plentiful

crops; such being the richness of the soil, that even a few heavy showers in the course of the year, at the time of sowing the seed, and when the corn is about a foot above the ground, are sufficient to insure a good harvest.

Herodotus* describes the extreme fertility of Assyria, and its abundant harvests of corn, the seed producing two and three hundred-fold. The blades of wheat and barley, he declares grew to full four fingers in breadth; and such was the general richness of Babylonia, that it supplied the Persian king and his vast army with subsistence for four months in the year, while the rest of the Persian dominions furnished provisions for the other eight. But in his day the Assyrians depended as much upon artificial irrigation, as upon the winter rains. They were skillful in constructing machines for raising water, and their system of canals was as remarkable for its ingenuity as for the knowledge of hydraulics it displayed. In the hills, the vine, olive, and fig tree were cultivated anciently as they are now; and Rabshakeh, to tempt the Jews, describes Assyria as " a land of corn and wine, a land of bread and vineyards, a land of olive-oil and of honey."†

It sometimes happens that the season passes without rain. Such was the case this year. During the winter and spring no water fell. The inhabitants of the villages, who had been in-duced to return by the improved administration and conciliatory measures of the late pashaw, had put their whole stock of wheat and barley into the ground. They now looked in despair upon the cloudless sky. I watched the young grass as it struggled to break through the parched earth; but it was burnt up almost at its birth. Sometimes a distant cloud hanging over the soli-tary hill of Arbela, or rising from the desert in the far west, led to hopes, and a few drops of rain gave rise to general rejoicings. The Arabs would then form a dance, and raise

---

* Lib. i. c. 192 and 193.
† 2 Kings xviii. 32. On a black stone in the possession of Lord Aber-deen, a plow is represented, nearly resembling that now in use in the country.

songs and shouts, the women joining with the shrill *tahlehl*.
But disappointment always ensued. The clouds passed over,
and the same pure blue sky was above us. To me the total
absence of verdure in spring was very painful. For months
my eye had not rested upon a green thing ; and that unchang-
ing yellow, barren waste, has a depressing effect upon the
spirits. The jaif, which the year before had been a flower
garden and had teemed with life, was now as naked and bare as
a desert in the midst of summer. I had been looking forward
to the return of the grass to encamp outside the village, and
had meditated many excursions to ancient ruins in the desert
and the mountains ; but I was doomed to disappointment like
the rest.

The pashaw issued orders that Christians, as well as Mussulmans, should join in a general fast and in prayers. Supplications were offered up in the churches and mosques. The
Mohammedans held a kind of three days' Ramazan, starving
themselves during the day, and feasting during the night. The
Christians abstained from meat during the same length of time.
If a cloud were seen on the horizon, the inhabitants of the
villages, headed by their mullahs, would immediately walk into
the open country to chant prayers and verses from the Koran.
Sheikhs—crazy ascetics who wandered over the country, either
half clothed in the skins of lions or gazelles, or stark naked—
burnt themselves with hot irons, and ran shouting about the
streets of Mosul. Even a kind of necromancy was not neglected,
and the cadi and the Turkish authorities had recourse to all
manner of mysterious incantations, which were pronounced to
have been successful in other parts of the sultan's dominions
on similar occasions.

Still there was no rain, and a famine appeared to be in-
evitable. It was known, however, that there were abundant
supplies of corn in the granaries of the principal families of
Mosul ; and the fact having been brought to the notice of the
pashaw, he at once ordered the stores to be opened, and their
contents to be offered for sale in the market at moderate prices,

As usual, the orders were given to the very persons who were speculating upon the miseries of the poor and needy—to the cadi, the mufti, and the head people of the town. They proceeded to obey them with great zeal and punctuality, but somehow or another overlooked their own stores and those of their friends, and ransacked the houses of the rest of the inhabitants. In a few days, consequently, those who had saved up a little grain for their own immediate wants, were added to the number of the starving; and the necessities and misery of the town were increased.

The Bedouins, who are dependent upon the village for supplies, now also began to feel the effects of the failure of the crops, and were preparing to make up for their sufferings by plundering the caravans of merchants, and the peaceable inhabitants of the districts within reach of the desert. Although the spring had already commenced, the Shammar and other formidable tribes had not yet encamped in the vicinity of Mosul; still casual plundering parties had made their appearance among the villages, and it was predicted that as soon as their tents were pitched nearer the town, the country without the walls would be not only very unsafe, but almost uninhabitable.

These circumstances induced me to undertake the removal of the larger sculptures as early as possible. I determined to embark them for Busrah in the month of March or April, foreseeing that as soon as the Bedouins had moved northward from Babylonia, and had commenced their plundering expeditions in the vicinity of Mosul, I should be compelled to leave Nimroud.

The Trustees of the British Museum had not contemplated the removal of either a winged bull or lion, and I had at first believed that, with the means at my disposal, it would have been useless to attempt it. I was directed to leave them, where discovered, until some favorable opportunity of moving them entire might occur; and to heap earth over them, after the excavations had been brought to an end. Being loth, however,

to abandon all these fine specimens of Assyrian sculpture, I
resolved upon attempting the removal and embarkation of two
of the smallest and best preserved, and fixed upon a lion and
a bull from the great central hall.   Thirteen pairs of these
gigantic sculptures, and several fragments of others, had been
discovered; but many of them were too much injured to be
worth sending to England.   I had wished to secure the lions
forming the great entrance to the principal chamber of the
N. W. palace; the finest specimens of Assyrian sculpture discovered in the ruins.   But after some deliberation I determined to leave them for the present; as, from their size, the
expense attending their conveyance to the river would have
been very considerable.

I formed various plans for lowering the lion and bull,
dragging them to the river, and placing them upon rafts.   Each
step had its difficulties, and a variety of original suggestions
were made by my workmen, and by the good people of Mosul.
At last I resolved upon constructing a cart sufficiently strong
to bear the sculptures.   As no wood but poplar could be procured in the town, a carpenter was sent to the mountains with
directions to fell the largest mulberry-tree, or any tree of
equally compact grain, he could find; and to bring back with
him beams of it, and thick slices from the trunk.

By the month of March this wood was ready.   I purchased
from the dragoman of the French consulate a pair of strong
iron axles, formerly used by M. Botta in moving sculptures
from Khorsabad.   Each wheel was formed of three solid pieces,
nearly a foot thick, bound together by iron hoops.   Across the
axles were laid three beams, and above them several cross-
beams.   A pole was fixed to one axle, to which were also
attached iron rings for ropes, to enable men, as well as buffaloes,
to draw the cart.   The wheels were provided with movable
hooks for the same purpose.

Simple as this cart was, it became an object of wonder in the
town.   Crowds came to look at it, as it stood in the yard of the
vice-consul's khan; and the pashaw's topjis, or artillery-men,

who, from their acquaintance with the mysteries of gun carriages, were looked up to as authorities on such matters, daily declaimed on the properties and use of this vehicle, and of carts in general, to a large circle of curious and attentive listeners. As long as the cart was in Mosul, it was examined by every stranger who visited the town. But when the news spread that it was about to leave the gates, and to be drawn over the bridge, the business of the place was completely suspended. The secretaries and scribes from the palace left their divans; the guards their posts; the bazars were deserted; and half the population assembled on the banks of the river to witness the manœuvers of the cart, which was forced over the rotten bridge of boats by a pair of buffaloes, and a crowd of Chaldeans and shouting Arabs.*

To lessen the weight of the lion and bull, without in any way interfering with the sculpture, I reduced the thickness and considerably diminished the bulk of the slabs, by cutting away as much as possible from the back, which, being placed against the wall of sun-dried bricks, was never meant to be seen. As, in order to move these figures at all, I had to choose between this plan and that of sawing them into several pieces, I did not hesitate to adopt it.

To enable me to move the bull from the ruins, and to place it on the cart in the plain below, a trench or road nearly two hundred feet long, about fifteen feet wide, and, in some places, twenty feet deep, was cut from the entrance, in which stood the bull, to the edge of the mound. As I had not sufficient mechanical power at command to raise the sculpture out of the trenches, like the smaller-bas-reliefs, this road was necessary. It was a tedious undertaking, as a very large accumulation of

---

* The bridge of Mosul consists of a number of rude boats bound together by iron chains. Planks are laid from boat to boat, and the whole is covered with earth. During the spring floods this frail bridge would be unable to resist the force of the stream; the chains holding it on one side of the river are then loosened, and it swings round. All communication between the two banks of the river is thus cut off, and a ferry is established until the waters subside, and the bridge can be replaced.

Assyrian Warriors hunting a Lion.   (N. W. Palace, Nimroud.)

earth had to be removed.   About fifty Arabs and Nestorians were employed in the work.

On digging this trench it was found that a chamber had once existed to the west of the great hall.   The sculptured slabs had been destroyed or carried away ; but part of the walls of unbaked bricks could still be traced.   The only bas-relief discovered was lying flat on the pavement, where it had evidently been left when the adjoining slabs were removed.   It was the small relief of the lion-hunt now in the British Museum, and remarkable for its finish, the elegance of the ornaments, and the spirit of the design.   It resembles, in the general treatment, the battle-scene first discovered in the S. W. palace, and I am inclined to believe that they both belonged to this ruined chamber ; in which, perhaps, the sculptures were more elaborate and more highly finished than in any other part of the building.   The work of different artists may be plainly traced in the Assyrian edifices.   Frequently when the outline is spirited and correct, and the ornaments designed with considerable taste, the execution is defective or coarse ; evidently showing, that while the subject was drawn by a master, the carving of the stone had been intrusted to an inferior workman.   In many bas-reliefs some parts are more highly finished than others, as if they had been retouched by an experienced sculptor.   The figures of the enemy are generally rudely executed and left unfinished, to show probably that, being those of the conquered or captive race, they were unworthy the care of the artist.   It is rare to find an entire bas-relief equally well executed in all its parts.   The most perfect hitherto discovered in Assyria, are probably, the lion-hunt from the principal chamber, the lion-hunt just described, and the large group of the king sitting on his throne, in the midst of his attendants and winged figures, all now placed in the British Museum.

While making this trench, I also discovered, about three feet beneath the pavement, a drain, which appeared to communicate with others previously opened in different parts of the

N

building. It was probably the main sewer, through which all the minor water-courses were discharged. It was built of baked bricks, and covered in with large slabs and tiles.

As the bull was to be lowered on its back, the unsculptured side of the slab having to be placed on rollers, I removed the walls behind it to form a clear space large enough to receive the sculpture when prostrate, and to leave room for the workmen to pass on all sides of it. The principal difficulty was of course to lower the mass: when once on the ground, or on rollers, it could be dragged forward by the united force of a number of men; but, during its descent, it could only be sustained by ropes. If these ropes, not strong enough to bear the weight, chanced to give way, the sculpture would be precipitated to the ground, and would, probably, be broken in the fall. The few ropes I possessed had been sent to me, across the desert, from Aleppo; but they were small and weak. From Baghdad I had obtained a thick hawser, made of the fibers of the palm. In addition I had been furnished with two pairs of blocks, and a pair of jack-screws belonging to the steamers of the Euphrates expedition. These were all the means at my command for moving the bull and lion. The sculptures were wrapped in mats and felts, to preserve them, as far as possible, from injury in case of a fall, and to prevent the ropes chipping or rubbing the alabaster.

The bull was ready to be moved by the 18th of March. The earth had been taken from under it, and it was now only supported by beams resting against the opposite wall. With the wood obtained from the mountains were several thick rollers. These were placed upon sleepers or half-beams, formed out of the trunks of poplar-trees, well greased and laid on the ground parallel to the sculpture. The bull was to be lowered upon these rollers. A deep trench had been cut behind the second bull, completely across the wall, and, consequently, extending from chamber to chamber. A bundle of ropes coiled round this isolated mass of earth served to hold two blocks, two others being attached to ropes wound round the bull to be moved. The ropes, by which the sculpture was to be lowered, were passed through these blocks; the ends, or falls of the tackle, as they are technically called, being led from the blocks above the second bull, and held by the Arabs. The cable which was first passed through the trench, and then round the sculpture, was held by two bodies of men. Several of the strongest Chaldeans placed thick beams against the back of the bull, and were directed to withdraw them gradually, supporting the weight of the slab, and checking it in its descent.

My own people were reinforced by a large number of the Abou-Salman. I had invited Sheikh Abd-ur-rahman to be present, and he came attended by a body of horsemen. The inhabitants of Naifa and Nimroud, having volunteered to assist on the occasion, were placed among my Arabs. The workmen, except the Chaldeans who supported the beams, were divided into four parties, two of which were stationed in front of the bull, and held the ropes passed through the blocks, while the rest clung to the ends of the cable, and were directed to slack off gradually as the sculpture descended.

The men being ready, and all my preparations complete, I stationed myself on the top of the high bank of earth over the second bull, and ordered the wedges to be struck out from under the sculpture to be moved. Still, however, it remained firmly in its place. A rope having been passed round it, six or seven men easily tilted it over. The thick, ill-made cable stretched with the strain, and almost buried itself in the earth round which it was coiled. The ropes held well. The mass descended gradually, the Chaldeans propping it up with the beams. It was a moment of great anxiety. The drums and shrill pipes of the Kurdish musicians increased the din and confusion caused by the war-cry of the Arabs, who were half frantic with excitement. They had thrown off nearly all their garments; their long hair floated in the wind; and they indulged in the wildest postures and gesticulations as they clung to the ropes. The women had congregated on the sides of the trenches, and by their incessant screams, and by the ear-

piercing *tahlehl*, added to the enthusiasm of the men. The bull
once in motion, it was no longer possible to obtain a hearing.
The loudest cries I could produce were lost in the crash of discordant sounds. Neither the hippopotamus-hide whips of the
cawasses, nor the bricks and clods of earth with which I
endeavored to draw attention from some of the most noisy of
the group, were of any avail. Away went the bull, steady
enough as long as supported by the props behind; but as it
came nearer to the rollers, the beams could no longer be used.
The cable and ropes stretched more and more. Dry from the
climate, as they felt the strain, they creaked and threw out
dust. Water was thrown over them, but in vain, for they all
broke together when the sculpture was within four or five feet
of the rollers. The bull was precipitated to the ground. Those
who held the ropes, thus suddenly released, followed its example,
and were rolling one over the other, in the dust. A sudden
silence succeeded to the clamor. I rushed into the trenches,
prepared to find the bull in many pieces. It would be difficult
to describe my satisfaction, when I saw it lying precisely where
I had wished to place it, and uninjured! The Arabs no sooner
got on their legs again, than, seeing the result of the accident,
they darted out of the trenches, and, seizing by the hands the
women who were looking on, formed a large circle, and, yelling
their war-cry with redoubled energy, commenced a most mad
dance. The musicians exerted themselves to the utmost; but
their music was drowned by the cries of the dancers. Even
Abd-ur-rahman shared in the excitement, and, throwing his cloak
to one of his attendants, insisted upon leading off the *debké*.
It would have been useless to endeavor to put any check upon
these proceedings. I preferred allowing the men to wear themselves out,—a result which, considering the amount of exertion
and energy displayed by limbs and throat, was not long in taking
place.

I now prepared, with the aid of Behnan, the bairakdar, and
the Tiyari, to move the bull into the long trench which led to
the edge of the mound. The rollers were in good order; and

as soon as the excitement of the Arabs had sufficiently abated to enable them to resume work, the sculpture was dragged out of its place by ropes.

Sleepers were laid to the end of the trench, and fresh rollers were placed under the bull as it was pulled forward by cables, to which were fixed the tackles held by logs buried in the earth, on the edge of the mound. The sun was going down as these preparations were completed. I deferred any further labor to the morrow. The Arabs dressed themselves; and, placing the musicians at their head, marched toward the village, singing their war-songs, occasionally raising a wild yell, throwing their lances into the air, and flourishing their swords and shields over their heads.

I rode back with Abd-ur-rahman. Schloss and his horsemen galloped round us, playing the jerrid, and bringing the ends of their lances into a proximity with my head and body which was far from comfortable; for it was evident enough that had the mares refused to fall almost instantaneously back on their haunches, or had they stumbled, I should have been transfixed on the spot. As the exhibition, however, was meant as a compliment, and enabled the young warriors to exhibit their prowess, and the admirable training of their horses, I declared myself highly delighted, and bestowed equal commendations on all parties.

The Arab sheikh, his enthusiasm once cooled down, gave way to moral reflections. "Wonderful! Wonderful! There is surely no God but God, and Mohammed is his prophet," exclaimed he, after a long pause. "In the name of the Most High, tell me, O Bey, what you are going to do with those stones. So many thousands of purses spent upon such things! Can it be, as you say, that your people learn wisdom from them; or is it, as his reverence the cadi declares, that they are to go to the palace of your Queen, who, with the rest of the unbelievers, worships these idols? As for wisdom, these figures will not teach you to make any better knives, or scissors, or chintzes; and it is in the making of those things that the

English show their wisdom. But God is great! God is great! Here are stones which have been buried ever since the time of the holy Noah,—peace be with him! Perhaps they were under ground before the deluge. I have lived on these lands for years. My father, and the father of my father, pitched their tents here before me; but they never heard of these figures. For twelve hundred years have the true believers (and, praise be to God! all true wisdom is with them alone) been settled in this country, and none of them ever heard of a palace under ground. Neither did they who went before them. But lo! here comes a Frank from many days' journey off, and he walks up to the very place, and he takes a stick (illustrating the description at the same time with the point of his spear), and makes a line here, and makes a line there. Here, says he, is the palace; there, says he, is the gate; and he shows us what has been all our lives beneath our feet, without our having known any thing about it. Wonderful! Wonderful! Is it by books, is it by magic, is it by your prophets, that you have learned these things? Speak, O Bey; tell me the secret of wisdom."

The wonder of Abd-ur-rahman was certainly not without cause, and his reflections were natural enough. While riding by his side I had been indulging in a reverie, not unlike his own, which he suddenly interrupted by these exclamations. Such thoughts crowded upon me day by day, as I looked upon every newly discovered sculpture. A stranger laying open monuments buried for more than twenty centuries, and thus proving to those who dwelt around them, that much of the civilization and knowledge of which we now boast, existed among their forefathers when our "ancestors were yet unborn," was, in a manner, an acknowledgment of the debt which the West owes to the East. It is, indeed, no small matter of wonder, that far distant, and comparatively new, nations should have preserved the only records of a people once ruling over nearly half the globe; and should now be able to teach the descendants of that people, or those who have taken their place, where their cities and monuments once stood. There was more than enough to excite the astonishment of Abd-ur-rahman, and I seized this opportunity to give him a short lecture upon the advantages of civilization and of knowledge, I will not pledge myself, however, that my endeavors were attended with as much success as those of some may be who boast of their missions to the East.   All I could accomplish was, to give the Arab shiekh an exalted idea of the wisdom and power of the Franks ; which was so far useful to me, that through his means the impression was spread about the country, and was not one of the least effective guarantees for the safety of my property and person.

This night was, of course, looked upon as one of rejoicing. Abd-ur-rahman and his brother dined with me ; although, had it not been for the honor and distinction conferred by the privilege of using knives and forks, they would rather have exercised their fingers with the crowds gathered round the wooden platters in the court-yard. Sheep were as usual killed, and boiled or roasted whole ;—they formed the essence of all entertainments and public festivities. They had scarcely been devoured before dancing was commenced. There were fortunately relays of musicians ; for no human lungs could have furnished the requisite amount of breath. When some were nearly falling from exhaustion, the ranks were recruited by others. And so the Arabs went on until dawn. It was useless to preach moderation, or to entreat for quiet. Advice and remonstrances were received with deafening shouts of the war-cry, and outrageous antics as proofs of gratitude for the entertainment and of ability to resist fatigue.

After passing the night in this fashion, these extraordinary beings, still singing and capering, started for the mound. Every thing had been prepared on the previous day for moving the bull, and the men had now only to haul on the ropes. As the sculpture advanced, the rollers left behind were removed to the front, and thus in a short time it reached the end of the trench. There was little difficulty in dragging it down the precipitous side of the mound. When it was within three or four feet of the bottom, sufficient earth was removed from beneath it to admit the cart, upon which the bull itself was then lowered by still further digging away the soil. It was soon ready to be dragged to the river. Buffaloes were first harnessed to the yoke ; but, although the men pulled with ropes fastened to the rings attached to the wheels, and to other parts of the cart, the animals, feeling the weight behind them, refused to move. We were compelled, therefore, to take them out ; and the Tiyari, in parties of eight, lifted the pole by turns, while the Arabs, assisted by the people of Naifa and Nimroud, dragged the cart. The procession was thus formed. I rode first, with the bairakdar, to point out the road. Then came the musicians, with their drums and fifes, drumming and fifing with might and main. The cart followed, dragged by about three hundred men, all screeching at the top of their voices, and urged on by the cawasses and superintendents. The procession was closed by the women, who kept up the enthusiasm of the Arabs by their shrill cries. Abdur-rahman's horsemen performed divers feats round the group, dashing backward and forward, and charging with their spears.

We advanced well enough, although the ground was very heavy, until we reach the ruins of the former village of Nimroud.* The villagers of Assyria dig deep pits to store their corn, barley, and straw for the autumn and winter. These pits generally surround the villages. Being only covered by a light framework of boughs and stakes, plastered over with mud, they become, particularly when half empty, a snare, and a trap to the horseman, who, unless guided by some one acquainted with the localities, is pretty certain to find the hind legs of his horse on a level with its ears, and himself suddenly sprawling i front. The corn-pits around Nimroud had long since been emptied of their stores, and had been concealed by the light

---

* The village was moved to its present site after the river had gradually receded to the westward, as the inhabitants had been left at a very inconvenient distance from water.

PROCESSION OF THE BULL BENEATH THE MOUND OF NIMROUD

sand and dust, which, blown over the plain during summer, soon
fill up every hole and crevice.   Although I had carefully examined the ground before starting, one of these holes had escaped
my notice, and into it two wheels of the cart completely sank.
The Arabs pulled and yelled in vain.   The ropes broke, but the
wheels refused to move.   We tried every means to release them,
but unsuccessfully.   After working until dusk, we were obliged
to give up the attempt.   I left a party of Arabs to guard the
cart and its contents, suspecting that some adventurous Bedouins, attracted by the ropes, and by the mats and felts, with
which the sculpture was enveloped, might turn their steps toward the spot during the night.   My suspicions did not prove
unfounded ; for I had scarcely got into bed before the whole
village was thrown into commotion by the reports of fire-arms
and the war-cry of the Jebours.   Hastening to the scene of action, I found that a party of Arabs had fallen upon my workmen.
They were beaten off, leaving behind them, however, their
mark ; for a ball struck and indented the side of the bull.   I
was anxious to learn who the authors of this wanton attack
were, and had organized a scheme for taking summary vengeance.   But they were discovered too late ; for, anticipating
punishment, they had struck their tents, and had moved off into
the desert.

Next morning we succeeded in clearing away the earth, and
in placing thick planks beneath the buried wheels.   After a
few efforts the cart moved forward amid the shouts of the
Arabs ; who, as was invariably their custom on such occasions,
indulged, while pulling at the ropes, in the most outrageous
antics.   The procession was formed as on the previous day, and
we dragged the bull triumphantly down to within a few hundred yards of the river.   Here the wheels buried themselves in
the sand, and it was night before we contrived, with the aid of
planks and by increased exertions, to place the sculpture on
the platform prepared to receive it, and from which it was to
slide down on the raft.   The tents of the Arabs, who encamped
near the river, were pitched round the bull, until its com-

N*

panion, the lion, should be brought down ; and the two embarked together for Baghdad. The night was passed in renewed re-joicings, to celebrate the successful termination of our labors. On the following morning I rode to Mosul, to enjoy a few days' rest after my exertions.

The bull having thus been successfully transported to the banks of the river, preparations were made, on my return to Nimroud, for the removal of the second sculpture ; and I ordered the trench, already opened for the passage of the bull to be con-tinued to the entrance formed by the lions, or about eighty feet to the north.

My arrangements were completed by the middle of April. I determined to lower the lion at once on the cart, and not to drag it out of the mound over the rollers. This sculpture, during its descent, was supported in the same manner as the bull had been ; but, to avoid a second accident, I doubled the number of ropes and the coils of the cable. Enough earth was removed to bring the top of the cart to a level with the bottom of the lion. While clearing away the wall of unbaked bricks, I discovered two ala-baster tablets, similar to those already described.* They bore the standard inscription, and had evidently been placed in the foundations of the palace : probably, as coins and similar tablets are now buried under edifices, to commemorate the period and object of their erection.

As the lion was cracked in more than one place, considerable care was required in lowering, and moving it. Both, however, were effected without accident. The Arabs assembled as they had done at the removal of the bull. Abd-ur-rahman and his horsemen rode over to the mound. We had the same shouting and the same festivities. The lion descended into the place I had prepared for it on the cart, and was easily dragged out of the ruins. It was two days in reaching the river, as the wheels sank more than once into the loose soil, and were with difficulty extricated. It was, however, at length placed by the side of

* Page 76.

the bull, on the banks of the Tigris, ready to proceed to Busrah, as soon as I could make the necessary arrangements for
their embarkation.

The sculptures, which I had hitherto sent to Busrah, had
been floated down the river on rafts, as far only as Baghdad,
where they had been transferred to boats built by the natives
for the lower part of the Tigris and Euphrates. These vessels
were much too small and weak to carry either the lion or the
bull ; and, indeed, had they been large enough, it would have
been difficult, if not impossible, in the absence of proper machinery, to lift such heavy masses into them. I resolved,
therefore, to attempt the navigation of the lower, as well as of
the upper, part of the river with rafts ; and to embark the lion
and bull at once for Busrah. The raftmen of Mosul, who are
accustomed to descend the Tigris to Baghdad, but never venture further, declared the scheme to be impracticable, and refused to attempt it. Even my friends at Baghdad doubted of
my success ; principally, however, on the ground that the prejudices and customs of the natives were against me,—and
every one knows how difficult it is to prevail upon Easterns to
undertake any thing in opposition to their established habits.
Such has been their nature for ages. As their fathers have
done, so have they done after them, forgetting or omitting many
things, but never adding or improving. As rafts meet with no
insurmountable difficulties in descending, even from the mountainous districts of Diarbekir, to Baghdad, there was no good
reason why they should not continue their voyage to Busrah.
Obstructions might occur in the upper part of the river, which
abounds in rapids, rocks, and shallows ; but not in the lower,
where there is depth of water, and nothing to impede the passage of large boats. The stream below Baghdad is sluggish,
and the tide ascends nearly sixty miles above Busrah : these
were the only objections, and they merely affected the time to
be employed in the descent, and not its practicability.

It was impossible by the most convincing arguments, even
though supported by the exhibition of a heap of coins, to pre-

vail upon the raftmen of Mosul to construct such rafts as
I required, or to undertake the voyage. I applied, therefore, to
Mr. Hector, and through him found a man at Baghdad, who
declared himself willing to make the great sacrifice generally
believed to be involved in the attempt. He was indebted in
a considerable sum of money, and being the owner of a large
number of skins, now lying useless, he preferred a desperate
undertaking to the prospect of a debtor's prison.

Mullah Ali—for such was the name of my raft-contractor
—at length made his appearance at Nimroud. He was followed by a dirty half-naked Arab, his assistant in the construction of rafts; and, like those who carried on his trade
some two thousand years before, by a couple of donkeys laden
with skins ready for use. Like a genuine native of Baghdad, he
had exhausted his ingenuity in the choice of materials for the
composition of his garments. There could not have been a
more dextrous mixture of colors than that displayed by his
antari, cloak, and voluminous turban. He began, of course,
with a long speech, protesting, by the Prophet, that he would
undertake for no one else in the world what he was going to
do for me ; that he was my slave and my sacrifice, and that the
man who was not was worse than an infidel. I cut him short
in this complimentary discourse. He then, as is usual in such
transactions, began to make excuses, to increase his demands,
and throw difficulties in the way. On these points I declined
all discussion, directing Ibrahim Agha to give him an insight
into my way of doing business, to recommend him to resign
himself to his fate, as the contract had been signed, and to
hint that he was now in the power of an authority from which
there was no appeal.

Mullah Ali made many vain efforts to amend his condition,
and to induce on my part a fuller appreciation of his merits.
He expected that these endeavors might, at least, lead to an
additional amount of bakshish. At last he resigned himself to
his fate, and slowly worked, with his assistant, at the binding
together of beams and logs of wood with willow twigs to form a

framework of a raft. There were still some difficulties and obstacles to be surmounted. The man of Baghdad had his own opinions on the building of rafts in general, founded upon immemorial customs, and the traditions of the country. I had my theories, which could not be supported by equally substantial arguments. Consequently, he, who had all the proof on his side, may not have been wrong in declaring against any method, in favor of which I could produce no better evidence than my own will. But, like many other injured men, he fell a victim to the "droit du plus fort," and had to sacrifice at once prejudice and habit.

I did not doubt that the skins, once blown up, would support the sculptures without difficulty as far as Baghdad, a voyage of eight or ten days, under favorable circumstances. But there they would require to be opened and refilled, or they would scarcely sustain so heavy a weight during the longer voyage to Busrah. However carefully the skins are filled, the air gradually escapes, and rafts, bearing merchandise, are generally detained several times during their descent, to enable the raftmen to examine and refill the skins.

It may interest the reader to know how these rafts, which have probably been for ages the only means of traffic on the upper parts of the rivers of Mesopotamia, are constructed. The skins of full-grown sheep and goats, taken off with as few incisions as possible, are dried and prepared, one aperture being left, through which the air is forced by the lungs. A framework of poplar beams, branches of trees, and reeds, having been constructed of the size of the intended raft, the inflated skins are tied to it by osier twigs. The raft is then complete, and is moved to the water and lanched. Care is taken to place the skins with their mouths upward, that, in case any should burst or require refilling, they can be easily reached. Upon the framework of wood are piled bales of goods, and property belonging to merchants and travelers. When persons of rank or wealth descend the river, small huts are constructed for them on the raft by covering a common wooden *takht*, or bedstead of the country, with a hood formed of reeds and lined with felt. The poorer passengers seek shade or warmth by burying themselves among the bales and other cargo, and sit patiently, almost in one position, until they reach their destination. They carry with them an earthen *mangal* or chafing-dish, containing a charcoal fire, which serves to light their pipes, and to cook their coffee and food. The only real danger to be apprehended on the river is from the Arabs; who, when the country is in a disturbed state, invariably attack and pillage the rafts.

The raftmen impel and guide these rude vessels by long poles, to the ends of which are fastened a few pieces of split cane. They skillfully avoid the rapids; and, seated on the bales, row continually, even in the hottest sun. They will seldom travel after dark before reaching Tekrit, on account of the rocks and shoals, which occur in the upper part of the river; but when they have passed that place, they resign themselves, night and day, to the sluggish stream. During the floods in the spring, or after heavy rains, small rafts may float from Mosul to Baghdad in about eighty-four hours; but the larger are generally six or seven days in performing the voyage. In summer, and when the river is low, they are frequently nearly a month in reaching their destination. When they have been unloaded, they are broken up, and the beams, wood, and twigs, sold at a considerable profit. The skins are washed, and afterward rubbed with a preparation of pounded pomegranate skins, to keep them from cracking and rotting. They are then brought back, either upon the shoulders of the raftmen or upon donkeys, to Mosul and Tekrit, where the men engaged in the navigation of the Tigris usually reside.

On the 20th of April, there being fortunately a slight rise in the river, and my arrangements being complete, I determined to attempt the embarkation of the lion and bull. The two sculptures had been so placed on beams of poplar wood that, by withdrawing wedges from under them, they would slide nearly into the center of the rafts. The high bank of the river had

been cut away into a rapid slope to the water's edge. The beams
having first been well greased, a raft of six hundred skins
was brought opposite the bull, which, on the wedges being
removed, immediately descended into its place. To prevent
its moving too rapidly, and bursting the skins by the sudden
pressure, the Arabs checked it by ropes, and it was placed
without accident. The lion was then embarked, with equal
success, upon a second raft of the same size; in a few hours
the two sculptures, with several large bas-reliefs from the same
ruins, were properly secured, and before night they were
ready to float down the river to Busrah.

After the labors of the day were over, sheep were slaughtered for the entertainment of Abd-ur-rahman's Arabs, who had
assisted on the occasion, and for the workmen. The Abou-
Salman returned to their tents after dark. Abd-ur-rahman
took leave of me, and we did not meet again : the next day he
moved toward the district of Jezirah in search of pasture. I
heard of him on my journey to Constantinople ; the Kurds by
the road complaining, that his tribe were making up the number of their flocks, by appropriating the stray sheep of their
neighbors. I had seen much of the sheikh during my residence at Nimroud ; and although, like all Arabs, he was not
averse to ask for what he thought there might be a remote
chance of getting by a little importunity, he was, on the whole,
a very friendly and useful ally.

On the morning of the 22d, the rafts being ready, I gave two
sheep to the raftmen to be slain on the banks of the river, as a
sacrifice to insure the success of their voyage. The carcasses
were distributed, as is proper on such occasions, among the
poor. A third sheep was reserved for a propitiatory offering,
to be immolated at the tomb of Sultan Abd-Allah,—a saint
who appears to interfere considerably with the navigation of
the Tigris, and who closed the further ascent of the river
against the infidel crew of the Frank steamer the " Euphrates,"
because they had neglected to make the customary sacrifice.
All ceremonies having been duly performed, Mullah Ali kissed

my hand, placed himself on one of the rafts, and slowly floated, with the cargo under his charge, down the stream.*

As I watched the rafts, until they disappeared behind a projecting bank forming a distant reach of the river, I could not forbear musing upon the strange destiny of their burdens; which, after adorning the palaces of the Assyrian kings, the objects of the wonder, and may be the worship of thousands, had been buried unknown for centuries beneath a soil trodden by Persians under Cyrus, by Greeks under Alexander, and by Arabs under the first successors of their prophet. They were now to visit India, to cross the most distant seas of the southern hemisphere, and to be finally placed in a British Museum. Who can venture to foretell how their strange career will end?

After the departure of the Abou-Salman, the plain of Nimroud was a complete desert. The visits of armed parties of Arabs became daily more frequent, and we often watched them from the mound, as they rode toward the hills in search of pillage, or returned from their expeditions driving the plundered flocks and cattle before them. We were still too strong to fear the Bedouins; but I was compelled to put my house into a complete state of defense, and to keep patrols round my premises during the night to avoid surprise. The Jebours

---

* It is not improbable that the great obelisk which, according to Diodorus Siculus (lib. ii. c. 1), was brought to Babylon from Armenia by Semiramis, was floated down on rafts supported by skins, in the same way that I transported the sculptures of Nineveh to Busrah. It was 130 feet in height, and 25 feet square at the base; and being cut out of the solid rock, if the account be not a little exaggerated, must have been of prodigious weight. The principal difficulty might probably appear to have been to place it on the raft; but this could have been accomplished by a simple method—by putting the beams forming the framework of wood, and fastening the skins under the obelisk, in some dry place, which would be overflowed during the periodical floods. When the water began to rise, by gradually removing the earth from beneath the skins, they could easily be filled with air; and when the stream had reached the raft they would lift up the obelisk, which could then be floated into the center of the river. I should have adopted this method of moving the larger lions and bulls, had I been required to send them to Busrah without being provided with any mechanical contrivance sufficiently powerful to embark such large weights by a simpler process.

were exposed to constant losses, in the way of donkeys or tent furniture, as the country was infested by petty thieves, who issued from their hiding-places, and wandered to and fro, like jackals, after dark. Nothing was too small or worthless to escape their notice. I was roused almost nightly by shoutings and the discharge of fire-arms, when the whole encampment was thrown into commotion at the disappearance of a copper pot or an old grain sack. I was fortunate enough to escape their depredations.

The fears of my Jebours increased with the number of the plundering parties, and at last, when a small Arab settlement, within sight of Nimroud, was attacked by a band of Aneyza horsemen, who murdered several of the inhabitants, and drove away the sheep and cattle, the workmen protested in a body against any further residence in so dangerous a vicinity. I found that it would not be much longer possible to keep them together, and I determined, therefore, to bring the excavations to an end.

I therefore commenced covering with earth those parts of the ruins which still remained exposed, according to the instructions I had received from the Trustees of the British Museum. Had the numerous sculptures been left, without any precaution having been taken to preserve them, they would have suffered, not only from the effects of the atmosphere, but from the spears and clubs of the Arabs, who are always ready to knock out the eyes, and to otherwise disfigure, the idols of the unbelievers. The rubbish and earth removed on opening the building, was accordingly brought back in baskets, thrown into the chambers, and heaped over the slabs until the whole was again covered over.

But before leaving Nimroud and reburying its palaces, I would wish to lead the reader once more through the ruins of the principal edifice, and to convey as distinct an idea as I am able of the excavated halls and chambers. Let us imagine ourselves issuing from my tent near the village in the plain.

On approaching the mound, not a trace of building can be perceived, except a small mud-hut covered with reeds, erected for the accommodation of my Chaldean workmen. We ascend this artificial hill, but still see no ruins, not a stone protruding from the soil. There is only a broad level platform before us, perhaps covered with a luxuriant crop of barley, or may be yellow and parched, without a blade of vegetation, except a scanty tuft of camel-thorn. Low black heaps, surrounded by brushwood and dried grass, a thin column of smoke rising from the midst of them, are scattered here and there. These are the tents of the Arabs; and a few miserable old women are groping about them, picking up camel's-dung or dry twigs. One or two girls, with firm step and erect carriage, are just reaching the top of the mound, with the water-jar on their shoulders, or a bundle of brushwood on their heads. On all sides of us, issuing from underground, are long lines of wild-looking beings, with disheveled hair, their limbs only half concealed by a short loose shirt, some jumping and capering, and all hurrying to and fro shouting like madmen. Each one carries a basket, and as he reaches the edge of the mound, or some convenient spot near, empties its contents, raising a cloud of dust. He then returns at the top of his speed, dancing and yelling as before, and flourishing his basket over his head; again he suddenly disappears in the bowels of the earth, from whence he emerged. These are the workmen employed in removing the rubbish from the ruins.

We will descend into the principal trench, by a flight of steps rudely cut in the earth, near the western face of the mound. As we approach it, we find a party of Arabs bending on their knees, and intently gazing at something beneath them. Each holds his long spear, tufted with ostrich feathers, in one hand; and in the other the halter of his mare, which stands patiently behind him. The party consists of a Bedouin sheikh from the desert, and his followers; who, having heard strange reports of the wonders of Nimroud, have made several days' journey to remove their doubts and satisfy their curiosity. He rises as he hears us approach, and if we wish to escape the embrace of a very dirty stranger we had better at once hurry into the trenches.

We descend about twenty feet, and suddenly find ourselves between a pair of colossal lions, winged and human-headed, forming a portal. I have already described my feelings when gazing for the first time on these majestic figures. Those of the reader would probably be the same, particularly if caused by the reflection, that before those wonderful forms Ezekiel, Jonah, and others of the prophets stood, and Sennacherib bowed ; that even the patriarch Abraham himself may possibly have looked upon them.

In the subterraneous labyrinth which we have reached, all is bustle and confusion. Arabs are running to and fro ; some bearing baskets filled with earth, others carrying water-jars to their companions. The Chaldeans or Tiyari, in their striped dresses and conical felt caps, are digging with picks into the tenacious earth, raising a dense cloud of fine dust at every stroke. The wild strains of Kurdish music may be occasionally heard issuing from some distant part of the ruins, and if they are caught by the parties at work, the Arabs join their voices in chorus, raise the war-cry, and labor with renewed energy. Leaving behind us a small chamber, in which the sculptures are distinguished by a want of finish in the execution, and considerable rudeness in the design of the ornaments, we issue from between the winged lions, and enter the remains of the principal hall. On both sides of us are colossal winged figures : some with the heads of eagles, others entirely human, and carrying mysterious symbols in their hands. To the left is another portal, also formed by winged lions. One of them has, however, fallen across the entrance, and there is just room to creep beneath it. Beyond this portal is a winged figure, and two slabs with bas-reliefs ; but they have been so much injured that we can scarcely trace the subject upon them. Further on there are no traces of wall, although a deep trench has been opened. The opposite side of the hall has also dis-

appeared, and we only see a high wall of earth. On examining
it attentively, we can detect the marks of masonry; and we
soon find that it is a solid structure built of bricks of unbaked
clay, now of the same color as the surrounding soil, and scarcely to be distinguished from it.

The slabs of alabaster, fallen from their original position,
have, however, been raised; and we tread in 'the midst of a
maze of small bas-reliefs, representing chariots, horsemen,
battles, and sieges. Perhaps the workmen are about to raise
a slab for the first time; and we watch, with eager curiosity,
what new event of Assyrian history, or what unknown custom
or religious ceremony, may be illustrated by the sculpture
beneath.

Having walked about one hundred feet among these scattered
monuments of ancient history and art, we reach another doorway, formed by colossal winged bulls in yellow limestone. One
is still entire; but its companion has fallen, and is broken into
several pieces—the great human head is at our feet.

We pass on without turning into the part of the building to
which this portal leads. Beyond it we see another winged
figure, holding a graceful flower in its hand, and apparently
presenting it as an offering to the winged bull. Adjoining
this sculpture we find a perfect series of highly-finished bas-
reliefs. There is the king, slaying the lion and wild bull, engaged in battles and in sieges, and receiving as captives the
chiefs of the conquered people. We have now reached the
end of the hall, and find before us an elaborate and beautiful
sculpture, representing two kings, standing beneath the emblem
of the supreme deity, and attended by winged figures. Between
them is the sacred tree. In front of this bas-relief is the great
stone platform, upon which, in days of old, may have been placed
the throne of the Assyrian monarch, when he received his captive enemies, or his courtiers.

As we gaze upon these singular sculptures the description of
Ezekiel is brought vividly to our minds. The prophet, in
typifying the corruptions which had crept into the religious

system of the Jews, and the idolatrous practices they had borrowed from the strange nations with which they had been brought into contact, thus illustrates the influence of the Assyrians. "She saw men portrayed upon the wall, the images of the Chaldeans portrayed with vermilion, girded with girdles upon their loins, exceeding in dyed attire upon their heads, all of them princes to look to, after the manner of the Babylonians of Chaldea, the land of their nativity."* The prophet is prophesying on the banks of the Chebar, or Khabour, in the immediate vicinity of Nineveh, previous to the destruction of the Assyrian capital, an event which he most probably witnessed. He points out the rich and highly ornamented head-dress of the sculptured kings, and evidently alludes to the prevalence of that red color, remains of which are so frequent in the ruins of Nimroud and Khorsabad. Nor can the resemblance between the symbolical figures pictured on the walls and those seen by Ezekiel in his vision fail to strike us. As the prophet had beheld the Assyrian palaces, with their mysterious images and gorgeous decorations, it is highly probable that, when seeking to typify certain divine attributes, and to describe the divine glory, he chose forms that were not only familiar to him, but to the people whom he addressed, captives like himself in the land of Assyria. He chose the four living creatures, with four faces, *four wings, and the hands of a man under their wings on the four sides*, the faces being those of a man, a lion, an ox, and an eagle,—the four creatures continually introduced on the sculptured walls,—and by them was a wheel, the appearance of which "was as a wheel in the middle of a wheel."† May not this wheel have been the winged circle, or globe, which, hovering above the

---

* Ch. xxiii. 14, 15. The literal translation of this remarkable passage is, "she saw men of sculptured (or painted) *workmanship* upon the wall, likenesses of the Chaldeans, pictured (or sculptured) in shashar (red ochre·or vermilion) ; girded with girdles on their loins, with colored flowing *head-dresses* upon their heads, *with the* aspect of princes all of them, *the* likeness of the sons of Babel-Chaldea, the land of their nativity."

† Ezekiel i. 16.

head of the kings, typifies the Supreme Deity of the Assyrian nation?

Emblem of the Deity.   (N. W. Palace, Nimroud.)

To the left of the great bas-relief at the eastern end of the hall is a fourth outlet formed by another pair of lions. We pass between them, and find ourselves on the edge of a deep ravine, to the north of which rises, high above us, the lofty pyramid. Figures of captives bearing objects of tribute,—ear-rings, bracelets, and monkeys,—are sculptured on the walls ; and two enormous bulls, with two winged figures above fourteen feet high, are lying prostrate on the ground.

As the ravine bounds the ruins on this side, we must return to the yellow bulls. The entrance formed by them, leads us into a large chamber surrounded by eagle-headed figures : at one end of it is a doorway guarded by two priests or divinities, and in the center another portal with winged bulls. Whichever way we turn, we find ourselves in the midst of a nest of rooms ; and without an acquaintance with the intricacies of the place, we should soon lose ourselves in this labyrinth. The accumulated rubbish being generally left in the center of the chambers, the whole excavation consists of a number of narrow passages, paneled on one side with slabs of alabaster ; and shut in on the other by a high wall of earth, half buried in which may here and there be seen a broken vase, or a brick painted with brilliant colors. We may wander through these galleries for an hour or two, examining the marvelous sculptures, or the numerous inscriptions that surround us.

Here we meet long rows of kings, attended by their eunuchs and priests,—there lines of winged figures, carrying fir-cones and religious emblems, and seemingly in adoration before the mystic tree.   Other entrances formed by winged lions and bulls, lead us into new chambers.   In every one of them are fresh objects of curiosity and surprise.   At length, wearied, we issue from the buried edifice by a passage on the side opposite to that by which we entered, and find ourselves again upon the naked platform.   We look around in vain for any traces of the wonderful remains we have just seen, and are half inclined to believe that we have dreamed a dream, or have been listening to some tale of Eastern romance.

Some, who may hereafter tread on the spot when the grass again grows over the ruins of the Assyrian palaces, may indeed suspect that I have been relating a vision.

CHAPTER XIII.

THE chambers at Nimroud had been filled up with earth, and
the sculptures once more concealed from the eye of man.   The
surrounding country became daily more dangerous from the in-
cursions of the Arabs of the desert, who now began to encamp
even on the east bank of the Tigris.   It was time, therefore, to
leave the village.   As a small sum of money still remained at
my disposal, I resolved to devote it to an examination of the
ruins opposite Mosul; particularly of the great mound of
Kouyunjik.   Although excavations on a small scale had already
been made there, I had not hitherto had time to superintend
them myself, and in such researches the natives of the country
can not be trusted.   It is well known that almost since the fall
of the Assyrian empire, a city of some extent, representing the
ancient Nineveh, although no longer the seat of government,
nor a place of great importance, has stood on the banks of the
Tigris in this part of its course.   The modern city may not
have been built above the ruins of the ancient; but it certainly
rose in their immediate vicinity, either to the east of the river,
or to the west, as the modern Mosul.   The slabs, which had
once lined the walls of the old palaces, and still remained concealed within mounds of earth, had been frequently exposed by
accident or by design.   Those who were settling in the neighborhood soon found that the ruins were an inexhaustible
mine of building materials.   The alabaster was dug out to be
either used in the construction of houses, or to be burnt for
lime.   A few years before, a bas-relief had been discovered in
one part of the ruins, during a search after stones for the repair

of a bridge. The removal of slabs, and the destruction of sculptures, for similar purposes, may have been going on for centuries. There was, therefore, some reason to doubt whether any edifice, except in a very imperfect state, still existed in Kouyunjik. I knew that under the village, containing the tomb of the prophet Jonah, there were remains of considerable importance, probably as entire as those at Nimroud. They owe their preservation to the existence, from a very remote period, of the tomb and village above them. Portions of sculpture, and inscriptions, had frequently been found, when the inhabitants of the place had made the foundations of their dwellings; and when Ali Pashaw of Baghdad caused a well to be dug for the benefit of the mosque, a pair of winged bulls had been discovered at a considerable depth beneath the surface. But the prejudices of the people of Mosul forbade any attempt to explore a spot so venerated for its sanctity.

The palaces of Nimroud being far distant from any large town, when once buried were not disturbed. It does not appear that after the fall of the empire any place of importance rose near them, except Selamiyah. This village is three miles from the ruins, and there are no remains near it to show that, at any time since the Assyrian period, it was any thing more than a small market-town. It may, consequently, be inferred that the great mound of Nimroud has never been opened, and its contents carried away for building purposes, since the destruction of the latest palace; except, as it has already been mentioned, when a pashaw of Mosul endeavored to remove one or two slabs to repair the tomb of a Mussulman saint.

There can, I think, be little doubt that the edifices of which the remains exist at Nimroud, Kouyunjik, and Khorsabad, at one time formed part of the same great city. Each of these palace-temples (for such they appear to have been) was probably the center of a separate quarter, built at a different period, and having a different name. Thus on the inscribed bricks we find distinct names applying to the localities from which they are derived; and this will explain the names of Mespila and

O

Larissa assigned by Xenophon, respectively, to the ruins at Kouyunjik and Nimroud, and that of Evorita given to the palace in which Saracus, the last of the Assyrian kings, is said to have destroyed himself. Each quarter being, at one time, a royal residence, was surrounded by a wall and fortifications, and probably contained rather hunting-grounds and gardens than fixed habitations. They resembled, in fact, the paradises or parks of the later Persian kings. The space between these quarters was occupied by private houses standing in the midst of gardens, orchards, and corn-land. I know no other way of reconciling the unanimous statements of ancient historians, as well as of the inspired writers, as to the extent of Nineveh, nor of explaining the fact that each of the great edifices explored, owed their foundation to different kings, and that there are no remains, either at Kouyunjik or Khorsabad, of the same early period as those at Nimroud. The dimensions of the city given by Diodorus Siculus were 150 stadia for the two longest sides of the quadrangle, and 90 for the shortest, the square being 480 stadia or about 60 miles. Jonah calls it " an exceeding great city of three days' journey," the number of inhabitants, who did not know their right hand from their left being six score thousand.* It is certainly remarkable that the three days' journey of Jonah should correspond exactly with the sixty miles of the geographer, and that a square formed by the great ruins on the east bank of the Tigris, taking Nimroud, Kouyunjik, Khorsabad, and Karamless as the four corners, should give very nearly the same result.† These fortified

---

* Various meanings have been assigned to this statement. Some suppose that young children are intended, who would form about one fifth of the population, which would then have been about six hundred thousand. Others contend that this is a mere allusion to the general ignorance of the inhabitants.

† The distance from Kouyunjik to Nimroud is about eighteen miles; that from Nimroud to Karamless about twelve, the opposite sides of the square the same; these measurements correspond accurately with the elongated quadrangle of Diodorus. Twenty miles is a day's journey in the East, and we have, therefore, exactly three days' journey for the circumference of the city. These coincidences are, at least, very remarkable. Within this space was fought the great battle between Heraclius and

quarters were not all inclosed within one wall : it is probable that in the event of a siege, the population of the intermediate spaces and suburbs took refuge within the different fortifications.

It would appear from existing monuments that the city was originally founded on the spot now occupied by the ruins of Nimroud. No better position could be chosen than the Delta formed by the junction of two large rivers, the Tigris and the Zab. The N. W. palace was the first built ; successive monarchs added the center palace, and other edifices which rose by its side. As the population increased, and conquered nations were brought, like the people of Samaria, from distant lands and settled around the Assyrian capital, the dimensions of the city increased also. A king founding a new dynasty, or anxious to perpetuate his fame, and to record his conquests, chose a new site for the erection of a palace. The city, gradually spreading, at length embraced all these buildings. Thus Nimroud represents the original site of Nineveh. The son of the builder of the oldest palace founded a new edifice at Baashiekhah. At a much later period subsequent monarchs erected their temple-palaces at Khorsabad and Kouyunjik. Their descendants returned to Nimroud, the principal buildings of which had been allowed to fall to decay, and were probably already concealed by a mass of ruins and rubbish. The city had now attained the dimensions assigned to it by the Greek geographers, and by the sacred writings. The numerous royal residences, surrounded by gardens and parks, and inclosed by fortified walls, each being a distinct quarter known by a different name, formed together the great city of Nineveh.

It is not difficult to account for the total disappearance of the dwelling-places which occupied the space between the palaces. They were probably little superior to the huts of the present inhabitants of the country, and, like them, constructed entirely

Rhazates (A.D. 627). " The city, and even the ruins of the city, had long since disappeared ; the vacant space afforded a spacious field for the operations of the two armies."—Gibbon's Decline and Fall, ch. xlvi.

of sun-dried bricks. As soon as they were allowed to fall to
decay, the materials of which they were built became again
mingled with the soil, and after a lapse of the very few years
scarcely a trace of them would exist. Thus a modern village
of Assyria, when once deserted, is rapidly replaced by a mere
inequality in the plain. There is, however, still sufficient to
indicate that buildings were once spread over the space I have
described ; for scarcely a husbandman drives his plow over the
soil without turning up the vestiges of former habitations. The
larger and more important monuments are fully represented
by the numerous mounds which are scattered over the plain.
It must be remembered that even the palaces would have
remained undiscovered had not slabs of alabaster marked the
walls.

We can not identify in any other way than that I have
suggested, all the ruins described with the site of Nineveh ;
unless, indeed, we suppose that there were more than one city
of that name, the later rebuilt on a new site after the destruction of the earlier. In this case Nimroud and Kouyunjik
may each represent the Nineveh of a different epoch. The
size, which I have assigned to the city at the time of its greatest
prosperity, can not, I think, be deemed extravagant when the
nature of Eastern cities is taken into consideration. They do
not bear the same proportion to their populations as those of
Europe. A place as extensive as London or Paris would not
contain one third of the inhabitants of either. The custom,
prevalent from the earliest period in the East, of secluding
women in apartments removed from those of the men, renders
a separate house for each family almost indispensable.* It was
probably as rare, in the time of the Assyrian monarchy, to
find more than one family residing under one roof, unless com-

---

* We learn from the book of Esther that such was the custom among
the early Persians, although the intercourse between the sexes was at that
time much less circumscribed than after the spread of Mohammedanism.
Ladies were even admitted to public banquets, and received strangers in
their own apartments, while they resided habitually in dwellings separate
from the men.

posed of persons very intimately related, such as father and
son, as it is at present in an Arab or Turkish city. Moreover,
that gardens and arable land were inclosed by the houses, we
learn from Diodorus Siculus and Quintus Curtius, who state
that there was space enough, even within the precincts of
Babylon, to cultivate corn for the sustenance of the whole
population in case of siege, besides orchards and gardens.*
From the expression of Jonah that there was much cattle
within the city,† it may be inferred that there was also pasture
for them; and we learn from the sculptures that a large portion of the population even resided in tents within the walls,—
a custom still prevailing in Baghdad, Mosul, and the neighboring towns; and a far larger space must have been required for
such encampments than for huts or cottages. The cities of
Isfahan and Damascus, with their gardens and suburbs, must,
during the time of their greatest prosperity, have been little
inferior in size to Nineveh.

A House.‡   (Kouyunjik.)   The Interior of a Tent.   (Kouyunjik.)

Existing ruins show that Nineveh had acquired its greatest
extent and prosperity in the time of the kings of the second

---

* Diod. Sic. lib. ii. c. 9. Quint. Curt. v. cap. 1.   † Ch. iv. 11.
‡ This house appears to resemble the model of an Egyptian dwelling in
the British Museum. (See also Sir Gardner Wilkinson's Ancient Egyptians, vol. ii., woodcuts 98 and 99.) From a bas-relief discovered in the
center of the mound at Nimroud, it would appear that the upper part was
sometimes of canvas.

dynasty, that is to say, of the kings mentioned in the Scriptures. It was then that Jonah visited it, and that reports of its size and magnificence were carried to the west, and gave rise to those traditions from which the Greeks mainly derived the information handed down to us. It was then, too, that the wealth, luxury, and power of its inhabitants called forth the indignant protests of the prophets, and led to those vices and that effeminacy which ultimately brought about the destruction of the city and the fall of the empire.

By the middle of May, I had finished my work at Nimroud. My house was dismantled. The windows and doors, which had been temporarily fitted up, were taken out; and, with the little furniture that had been collected together, were placed on the backs of donkeys and camels to be carried to the town. The Arabs struck their tents and commenced their march. I remained behind until every one had left, and then turned my back upon the deserted village. We were the last to quit the plains of Nimroud; and, indeed, nearly the whole country to the south of Mosul, as far as the Zab, became, after our departure, a wilderness.

Half-way between Mosul and Nimroud the road crosses a low hill. From its crest, both the town and the ruins are visible. On one side, in the distance, rises the pyramid, in the midst of the broad plain of the Jaif, and on the other may be faintly distinguished the great artificial mound of Kouyunjik, and the surrounding remains. The leaning minaret of the old mosque of Mosul may also be seen springing above the dark patch which marks the site of the town. The river can be traced for many miles, winding in the midst of the plain, suddenly losing itself among low hills, and again emerging into the level country. The whole space over which the eye ranges from this spot, was probably once covered with the buildings and gardens of the Assyrian capital—that great city of three days' journey. At an earlier period, that distant pyramid directed the traveler from afar to Nineveh, when the limits of the city were small. It was then one of those primitive settlements which, for the first time, had been formed by the congregated habitations of men. To me the long dark line of mounds in the distance were objects of deep interest. I reined up my horse to look upon them for the last time—for from no other part of the road are they visible—and then galloped on toward Mosul.

In excavating at Kouyunjik, I pursued the plan adopted at Nimroud. I resided in the town. The Arabs pitched their tents on the summit of the mound, at the entrances to the trenches. The Tiyari encamped at its foot, on the banks of the Khausser, the small stream which flows through the ruins. The nearness of the ruins to Mosul, enabled the inhabitants of the town to gratify their curiosity by a constant inspection of my proceedings; and a crowd of gaping Mussulmans and Christians was continually gathered round the trenches. I rode to the mound early every morning, and remained there during the day.

The French consul had carried on his excavations for some time at Kouyunjik, without finding any traces of building. He was satisfied with digging pits or wells, a few feet deep, and then renouncing the attempt, if no sculptures or inscriptions were uncovered. By excavating in this desultory manner, if any remains of building existed underground, their discovery would be a mere chance. An acquaintance with the nature and position of the ancient edifices of Assyria, will at once suggest the proper method of examining the mounds which inclose them. The Assyrians, when about to build a palace or temple, appear to have first constructed a platform of sun-dried bricks and earth, about thirty or forty feet above the level of the plain. Upon it they raised the monument. When the building was destroyed, its ruins, already half-buried by the falling in of the upper walls and roof, were in process of time completely covered by the dust and sand, carried about by the hot winds of summer. Consequently, in digging for remains, the first step is to reach the platform of sun-dried bricks. When this is discovered, the trenches must be opened to the level of it, and not deeper; they should then be continued in opposite directions, care being always taken to keep along the platform. By these means, if there be any ruins, they must necessarily be discovered, supposing the trenches to be long enough; for the chambers of the Assyrian edifices are generally narrow, and their walls, or the slabs which cased them if fallen, must sooner or later be reached.

At Kouyunjik, the accumulation of rubbish and earth was very considerable, and to reach the platform of unbaked bricks, trenches were dug to the depth of twenty and even thirty feet. Before beginning the excavations, I carefully examined all parts of the mound, to ascertain where remains of buildings might most probably exist; and at length decided upon continuing my researches where I had commenced them last summer, near the S. W. corner.

The workmen had been digging for several days without finding any other remains than fragments of calcined alabaster, sufficient, however, to encourage me to persevere in the examination of this part of the ruins. One morning as I was in Mosul, two Arab women came to me, and announced that sculptures had been discovered. They had hurried from the mounds as soon as the first slab had been exposed to view; and blowing up the skins, which they always carry with them, had crossed the river upon them. They had scarcely received the present claimed in the East by the bearers of good tidings, and the expectation of which had led to the display of so much eagerness, than one of my overseers, who was generally known from his corpulence as Toma Shishman, or fat Toma, made his appearance, breathless from his exertions. He had hurried as fast as his legs could carry him over the bridge, to obtain the reward carried off, in this instance, by the women.

I rode immediately to the ruins; and, on entering the trenches, found that the workmen had reached a wall, and the remains of an entrance. The only slab as yet uncovered had been almost completely destroyed by fire. It stood on the edge of a deep ravine which ran far into the southern side of the mound.

As the excavations at Kouyunjik were carried on in precisely the same manner as those at Nimroud, I need not trouble the reader with any detailed account of my proceedings. The wall first discovered proved to be the side of a chamber. By following it we reached an entrance formed by winged bulls, leading into a second hall. In a month nine chambers had been explored.

The palace had been destroyed by fire. The alabaster slabs were almost reduced to lime, and many of them fell to pieces as soon as uncovered. The places, which others had occupied, could only be traced by a thin white deposit, like a coat of plaster, left by the burnt alabaster upon the wall of sun-dried bricks.

In its architecture, the newly discovered edifice resembled the palaces of Nimroud and Khorsabad. The chambers were long and narrow; the walls of unbaked brick, with a paneling of sculptured slabs. The bas-reliefs were, however, much larger in their dimensions than those generally found at Nimroud, being about ten feet high, and from eight to nine feet wide. The winged human-headed bulls, forming the entrances, were from fourteen to sixteen feet square. The slabs, unlike those I had hitherto discovered, were not divided in the center by bands of inscription, but were completely covered with figures. The bas-reliefs were greatly inferior in general design, and in the beauty of the details, to those of the earliest palace of Nimroud ; but in many parts they were very carefully and minutely finished : in this respect Kouyunjik yields to no other known monument in Assyria. The winged bulls resembled those of Khorsabad in their head-dress and high cap, surmounted by a crest of feathers and richly ornamented with rosettes, like that of the winged monsters of Persepolis. Some of the bulls had four legs, others five, as at Nimroud.* In the costumes of

---

* It has already been mentioned that the winged lions of the N. W. palace at Nimroud were furnished with five legs, that the spectator, in whatever position he stood, might have a perfect front and side view of the animal.

the warriors, and in the trappings and caparisons of the horses, the sculptures resembled those of Khorsabad.

Head of Winged Bull. (Khorsabad and Kouyunjik.)   Head of Winged Monster. (Persepolis.)

Inscriptions were not numerous. They occurred between the legs of the winged bulls, above the head of the king, on bas-reliefs representing the siege or sack of a city, and on the backs of slabs; but they were all more or less injured. Those on the bulls were long, the same inscription being continued on the two sides of an entrance. As four pairs of these colossal figures were discovered, each pair bearing nearly the same inscription, the whole may be restored from the fragments.*

The king, whose name is on the sculptures and bricks from Kouyunjik, was the father of the builder of the S. W. palace at Nimroud, and the son of the Khorsabad king. Long before the discovery of the ruins, I had conjectured, from a hasty examination of a few fragments of sculpture and inscription picked up on the mound, that the building which once stood

---

* A restored inscription is included in the collection printed for the Trustees of the British Museum.

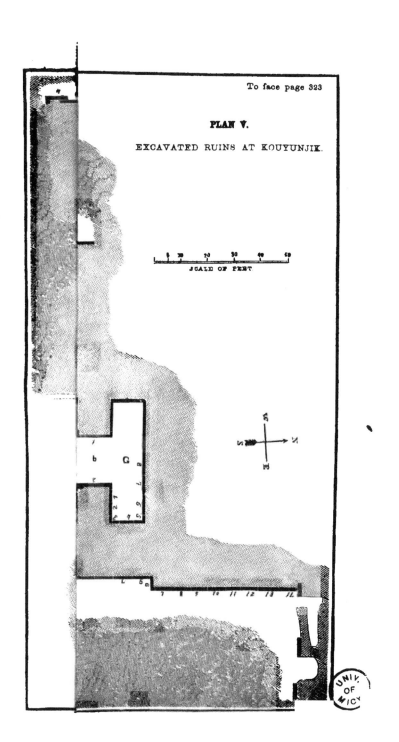

PLAN V.

EXCAVATED RUINS AT KOUYUNJIK.

SCALE OF FEET.

there must be referred to the time of the Khorsabad king, or of his immediate predecessors or successors.

A few vases and fragments of pottery were discovered in the earth, above the ruins; but no sarcophagi, or tombs with human remains, like those of Nimroud and Kalah Sherghat. The foundations of buildings, of roughly hewn stone, were also found above the Assyrian edifice. One or two small glass bottles, many fragments of glass, several inscribed tablets in clay, and one or two detached slabs covered with inscriptions, were taken out of the rubbish.*

The slabs forming the entrance to the first chamber† in the excavations had been almost destroyed. The colossal figures which had been sculptured upon them were probably those of mythic deities such as had been found at Nimroud. The extremities of these figures were alone preserved. They were those of an eagle or vulture: to them were united, it would appear from subsequent discoveries, the body of a man and the head of a lion. The walls of the chamber had suffered no less than the doorway. Upon them could be traced processions of warriors, and captives passing through a thickly wooded, mountainous country; the mountains being represented, as in the bas-reliefs of Nimroud, by a network of lines. On the fragment of a slab was an eunuch carrying a utensil resembling a censer, and standing before an altar, near which were vessels of various shapes.

The southern extremity of the great hall,‡ into which the chamber just described opened, had been completely destroyed. Its width was about forty-five feet, and the length of the western wall from the entrance of the small chamber (to the south of which it could not be traced), was nearly one hundred and sixty feet. The first bas-relief on entering represented the burning

---

* The greater part of these small objects are in the British Museum.
† Ch. A, plan 5.
‡ Ch. B, plan 5.

and sacking of a city, and was divided into several compartments by parallel lines. In the upper, which occupied about
half the sculpture, were represented houses, some two and three
stories high ; they had been fired by the enemy, and flames were
issuing from the windows and doors. Beneath were three rows
of warriors, marching in regiments, each distinguished by different helmets, arms, and shields. Some wore the pointed helmet peculiar to the Assyrians in the Nim-
roud sculptures, but with the addition of
lappets falling over the ears. They bore
concave oval shields, large enough to cover
the greater part of the person—probably
of metal, the center and margin being ornamented with bosses. The conquerors
were carrying away the spoil, consisting
of furniture, vases, chariots and horses.
Beneath the figures were vines bearing
grapes. The captured city stood upon a
mountain. Above it was a short inscription, unfortunately almost illegible, containing its name, and a record of the event
represented in the bas-relief.

Warrior with Shield.
(Kouyunjik.)

On an adjoining slab was a mountain
clothed with forests. Among the trees
were warriors, some descending in mili-
tary array, and leading prisoners toward a castle ; others ascending the steep rocks with the aid of their spears, or resting,
seated under the trees. The same subject had evidently been
continued on the next slab, which had been destroyed.

After these bas-reliefs came an entrance formed by two winged
bulls, nearly sixteen feet and a half square, and sculptured out of
one slab. The human heads of these colossal animals had been
entirely destroyed. Of the inscription which once covered the
parts of the slabs not sculptured, there remained only a few lines.
Notwithstanding the size of the bulls, this entrance scarcely

exceeded six feet in width, thus differing from those at Nimroud. The pavement was formed by one slab, elaborately ornamented with flowers resembling the lotus. Behind the sculptures was a short inscription containing the names and titles of the king.

Beyond this entrance, to the distance of nearly sixty feet, only two slabs were preserved. On one was the interior of a castle, the walls and towers represented, as at Nimroud, by a kind of ground plan. The city had been taken by the Assyrians, and the king, seated on his throne, placed within the walls, was receiving the prisoners and spoil brought to him by his vizier. His dress differed in many respects from that of the monarch in the earlier sculptures at Nimroud.

His tiara was higher, more pointed, made up of several bands, and richly ornamented. The ornaments on his robes consisted of rosettes and fringes, elaborate groups of men and animals not being introduced as in the more ancient sculptures. He was seated on a chair with a high back, and his feet rested on an elegant footstool. Behind the throne stood two eunuchs holding fans over the head of the monarch. The arms of the prisoners were fastened in front by fetters, probably of metal.* Within the

Head Dress of the King. (Kouyunjik.)

* "To bind their kings with chains, and their nobles with fetters of iron." (Psalm cxlix. 8.) "They put out the eyes of Zedekiah, and bound him with fetters of brass, and took him to Babylon." (2 Kings xxv. 7.)

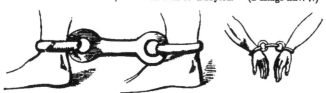

Manacles for the Feet.   Manacles for the Hands.
(Khorsabad and Kouyunjik.)

Samson was bound with fetters of brass. (Judges xvi. 21.) In a bas-relief at Khorsabad, were represented captives as led before the king by rings of

walls of the city, as in the bas-reliefs discovered at Nimroud,
were houses and tents, in which were men engaged in a variety
of domestic occupations, and articles of furniture, such as tables,
couches, and chairs. Suspended to the tent-poles were vases,
probably, as is still the custom in the East, to cool water. Above
the head of the king was one line of inscription containing his
name and titles. The castle was built on a mountain, and was
surrounded by trees.

On the other slab was represented the invasion of a mountainous country. The enemy defended the summit of a wooded
hill against Assyrian warriors, who were scaling the rocks,
supporting themselves with their spears and with poles, or
drawing themselves up by the branches of trees. Others,
returning from the combat, were descending the mountains
driving captives before them, or carrying away the heads of the
slain.

A spacious entrance at the upper, or northern end of the hall
opened into a small chamber, which will be hereafter described.*
The bulls forming this portal were in better preservation than
those previously discovered. Their human heads, with the
high and elaborately adorned tiara of the later Assyrian period,
although greatly injured, could still be distinguished. The
greater part of the inscription was also entire.

Upon the two slabs beyond this entrance was a bas-relief of
considerable interest. Vessels filled with warriors, and females,
were seen leaving a castle, built on the sea-shore at the foot
of a mountain. At a gate opening upon the water stood a man
placing in the open arms of a woman, who had already
embarked in one of the ships, a young child. The sea was
indicated by wavy lines, covering the slab from top to bottom,
among which were fish, crabs, and turtles. The vessels were
of two kinds. The larger had one mast, to the top of which

---

iron passed through the nose and lips, to which was attached a cord ; thus
illustrating the passage, " I will put my hook in thy nose, and my bridle in
thy lips."

* Ch. G. plan 5.

was attached a long yard, held in its place by ropes. The sail was furled. It had two, or perhaps three decks, as there were double tiers of rowers. On the upper deck, which was high out of the water when compared with the depth of the keel, were warriors armed with spears, and women wearing high turbans or caps, to the back of which long vails were attached. The fore-part of the vessel rose perpendicularly from a low sharp prow, resembling a plowshare, which may have been of metal, as in the Roman galleys, to disable and sink the enemy's ships. The stern was curved from the keel, and ended in a high point rising above the upper deck. The vessel appears to have been steered by two long oars. Eight rowers were represented on a side, but the number was probably conventional. The lower tier was concealed by the sides of the vessel, the oars issuing

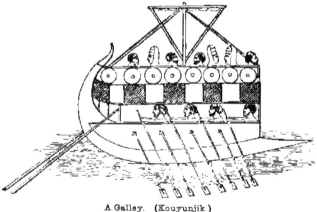

A Galley. (Kouyunjik.)

from small port-holes. The smaller vessel had no mast, and the head and stern were alike ; it was furnished with a double deck, and had the same number of rowers as the larger. Shields were suspended around the upper decks of both.*

* In the Khorsabad sculptures the ships are of different form to those described in the text. That they did not belong to the Assyrians, but to

A Galley. (Kouyunjik.)

some allied or conquered nation, appears to be indicated by the peculiar costume of the figures in them. They are in the shape of a sea-monster,

A Galley. (Khorsabad.)

the head of a horse forming the prow, and the tail of a fish the stern. The mast is supported by ropes, and is surmounted by a kind of stand, or what a seaman would call a crow's-nest, which in the Egyptian sculptures holds an archer.

The larger vessel closely resembles in form the galleys represented on coins of a very early date, which were probably struck by Phœnician colonies during the Persian supremacy, the reverse bearing the effigy of the Persian king in his chariot, as found on Darics and cylinders of the same period.   The galleys

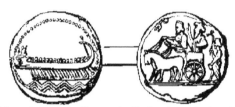

Coin probably of a City on the Syrian Coast during the
Persian Occupation.

on these coins and in the bas-reliefs are further identified with those of the Syrian coast by the coins of Sidon of a later period, which bear on one side a vessel of similar shape, and on the other the head of an Assyrian goddess.   It is highly probable, therefore, that the sculptures described represent the siege and capture of Tyre, Sidon, or some other city on the Mediterranean, and the flight of the conquered people.   History has recorded the wars of Shalmaneser with the Tyrians, under their king Elulæus, and the subjection of the whole of Phœnicia by the Assyrian monarch;* and, according to Eusebius, who quotes from Abydenus, Sennacherib defeated the Greek fleet on the Cilician coast.   It is to one of these two kings that I would attribute the foundation of the great palace of which the ruins opposite Mosul are the remains; and it is remarkable that the rock-tablets at the mouth of the Nahr-el-Kelb river near Beyrout in Syria were erected by the Kouyunjik

* Josephus, lib. ix. c. 14.   The Tyrians having revolted, Shalmaneser attacked them with 60 vessels and 800 rowers, furnished by the inhabitants of other maritime cities.   The Tyrians, however, defeated this large fleet and took 500 men prisoners.   The Assyrians then invested the city for five years, cutting off the inhabitants from the rivers and wells which furnished them with fresh water.

king, and bear his name. Records of the Khorsabad king, his
father, have been discovered in Cyprus.*

Materials derived from distant countries, and of the most
costly description, were employed in the construction of the,
Tyrian vessels. The "ship-boards were of the fir-trees of
Senir," the masts of the cedars of Lebanon, the oars of the oaks
of Bashan, and the benches of ivory brought from the isles
of Chittim, and carved by the Ashurites, probably the Assyrians, of whose skill we have full proof in the beautiful
ivories from Nimroud. " Fine linen, with broidered work from
Egypt," was used for sails, and the ornaments were of "blue
and purple, from the Isles of Elishah." The men of Zidon and
Arvad were employed as mariners, and the management and
sailing of the vessel were confided to the pilots of Tyre, who,
by long experience, were well versed in the art of navigation,
and were consequently looked upon as "the wise men" in a
city of sailors and merchants.† In these vessels the Phœnicians
coasted along the shores of the Mediterranean and entered the
ocean, carrying on an active commerce with the most distant

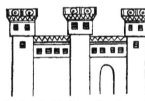

nations, establishing their colonies, and diffusing far and wide
their civilization, their arts, and
their language.

The castles of the people
who are taking refuge in the
ships, are distinguished by the

Castle of a Maritime People, prob-
. ably the Tyrians. (Kouyunjik.)

shields hung round the walls, a
peculiarity which appears to il-
lustrate a passage in Ezekiel ‡ concerning Tyre : " The men

---

* The inscriptions recently brought by me from Kouyunjik completely
confirm my conjectures as to the period of the Kouyunjik palace, and as
to its probable founder, who appears to have been Sennacherib. Colonel
Rawlinson communicated the contents of one of these inscriptions to the
Athenæum of August 23. 1851.

† The 27th chapter of Ezekiel contains a complete description of the
vessels and trade of the Tyrians, and is a most important and interesting
record of the commercial intercourse of the nations of antiquity.

‡ Chap. xxvii. 11.

of Arvad, with thine army, were upon thy walls round about, and the Gammadims were in thy towers : *they hanged their shields upon thy walls round about.*"

On the two slabs adjoining the sea-piece was represented the besieging army. The upper part of both had been destroyed ; on the lower were still preserved a few Assyrian warriors, protected by the high wicker shield, and discharging arrows in the direction of the castle, and rows of prisoners, with their hands bound, led away by the conquerors.

On the eastern side of the hall was a third entrance, also formed by human-headed bulls. Adjoining were bas-reliefs representing a battle in a hilly country, wooded with pines or fir-trees.

Beyond this entrance the slabs, although in some places entire, had been so much injured by fire that only one bas-relief was preserved. It represented a battle and the sack of a city, and was divided into six compartments. Warriors were dragging chariots, and driving horses and cattle out of the castle gates, others were combating with horsemen and footmen, and in the two lower compartments were lines of chariots, each holding three warriors. The chariots differed in many respects from those of the earlier sculptures of Nimroud, and appear to resemble more closely the chariot of the Persepolitan bas-reliefs, and of the Mosaic in the museum at Naples, supposed to be that of Darius. They were much more roomy and higher, the wheels being almost the height of a man. The ornamented frame-work stretching from the fore-part to the end of the pole of the ancient chariots, was replaced by a thin rod, or by a rope or leather thong, knotted in the center. The harness of the horses also differed. The upper part of the chariot was square and not rounded, and a projection in front, instead of the quivers suspended at the sides, held the arrows of the archer. The panels were carved and adorned with rosettes ; the wheels had eight, and not six spokes, the felloes being bound and strengthened by four metal bands.*

* See woodcut, facing p. 334.

An Archer. (Kouyunjik.)   A Spearman. (Kouyunjik.)

The western entrance led into a second hall,* the four sides

of which, although the bas-reliefs had
unfortunately suffered greatly from fire,
were almost entire.

The slabs to the left appear to have
been divided into three compartments,
each occupied by rows of warriors differently armed and accoutered, probably
denoting the allies of the Assyrians.
In the first were archers distinguished
by their short tunics richly embroidered
and by their head-dress, consisting of a
simple fillet confining their long hair ;
in the second, were slingers wearing

A Slinger. (Kouyunjik.) the pointed helmet, and in the third
spearmen with a circular shield and a
crested casque. The slingers held a second stone in the left hand,

* Hall C, plan 5.

and in front of them was a pile of stones ready for use. Their slings appear to have been formed by a double rope or leather thong.* They were attired in armor and greaves. The spearmen wore a short linen tunic, confined round the waist by a belt, probably of metal. A kind of cross-belt passed over their shoulders and was ornamented in front with a circular disk. They also wore greaves.

On the following slabs was one subject—the taking by assault of a city or castle, built near a river in a mountainous country and surrounded by trees. Warriors armed with spears were scaling the rocks, slaying the besieged on the house-tops, and leading off the captives.

Scribes writing down the Number of the Slain.   (Kouyunjik.)

On the adjoining corner-stone were two scribes, one an eunuch, writing down on rolls of leather or some flexible material, the number of heads of the slaughtered enemy laid

* Xenophon frequently alludes to the expertness of the slingers of Assyria (see particularly Anab. lib. iii. c. 3). They used very large stones, and could annoy the enemy, while out of reach of their darts and arrows.

at their feet by the Assyrian warriors. Thus were the heads of the seventy sons of Ahab brought in baskets to Jezreel and laid " in two heaps at the entering in of the gate ;"* and such is still the mode of reckoning the loss of an enemy in the East.

The remainder of the wall from this slab to an entrance formed by human-headed bulls, had been greatly injured by fire. The bas-reliefs appear to have represented the conquest of a mountainous and wooded country. The king in his chariot was receiving the prisoners and the spoil.

Beyond the entrance, as far as the bas-reliefs could be traced, the same subject appears to have been continued. The king was again represented standing in his chariot, holding a bow in his left hand, and raising his right in token of triumph. He was accompanied by a charioteer, and by an attendant bearing an open umbrella, from which fell a long curtain as a complete screen from the sun. The chariot was drawn by two horses, and was preceded by spearmen and archers. Above the king there had originally been a short inscription, probably containing his name and titles, but it had been entirely defaced. Horsemen, crossing well-wooded mountains, were separated from the group just described, by a river abounding in fish.

The remaining bas-reliefs in this chamber appear to have recorded similar events,—the conquests of the Assyrians, and the triumphs of their king. Only four of them had been preserved; the rest were almost completely destroyed. On two of them was portrayed, with great spirit, the taking by assault of a city. Warriors, armed with spears, were mounting ladders, placed against the walls; those who manned the battlements and towers being held in check and assailed by archers who discharged their arrows from below. The enemy defended themselves with spears and bows, and carried small oblong shields. Above the castle a short inscription recorded the name of the captured city. Under the walls were captives, driven off by the conquerors; and above and below were

* 2 Kings, x. 8.

To face page 334.

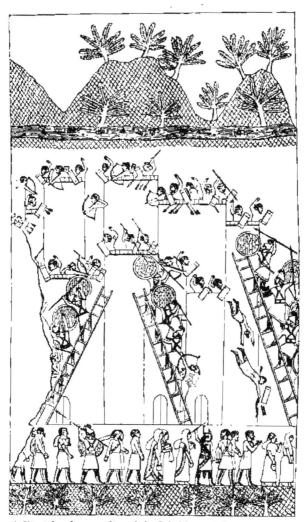

A City taken by Assault, and the Inhabitants led away Captive.
(Kouyunjik.)

mountains, trees, and a river, to indicate the nature of the country.

The west entrance of this hall* led into a further chamber, a part only of which I was able to explore. On two slabs was a mountainous country, with a river running through the midst of it. The higher parts of the mountains were clothed with a forest of pines or firs, the middle region by vineyards, and the lower by trees resembling those sculptured on other slabs, probably the dwarf oak of the country. As the king was represented in his chariot, accompanied by many horsemen in the midst of the forest, it may be presumed that the Assyrians had opened roads through the mountainous districts of their empire.

Warriors forming a Phalanx before the Walls of a besieged City.
(Kouyunjik.)

The remaining slabs were covered from top to bottom with rows of warriors, spearsmen, and archers, in their respective costumes, and in martial array. Each slab must have contained several hundred minute figures, which probably represented regularly disciplined troops; for like the Egyptians, the

* Entrance *b*, chamber C, plan 5.

Assyrians were evidently acquainted with military tactics, and possessed organized armies. In several bas-reliefs, troops were represented, drawn up to form a kind of phalanx, or the more modern military square.

The three small chambers to the west of the hall last described* had been so much injured by fire that few slabs retained traces of sculpture. Among the bas-reliefs remaining, were the siege and capture of a city standing on the banks of a river in the midst of forests and mountains, with warriors cutting down trees, to form an approach to the castle, and carrying away the idols of the conquered people ; a fisherman fishing with a hook and line in a pond ;† and warriors receiving long lines of captives, among whom were women and children riding mules.

The wide portal, formed by the winged bulls at the upper end of the great hall first discovered, opened into a small chamber, which had no other entrance.‡ One side of it had been completely destroyed. The remaining bas-reliefs represented the siege and sack of a city between two rivers, in the midst of the groves of palm-trees, and consequently, it may be conjectured, in some part of Mesopotamia. There was, fortunately an inscription above the captured city, which probably contains its name. The king was represented, several times, in his chariot, superintending the operations of the siege. The besiegers were cutting down the palms to open and clear the approaches to the walls.

A part only of the chamber to the east of the great hall§ was uncovered. Many of the sculptures had been intentionally destroyed with some sharp instrument, and all had suffered, more or less, from fire. On some could be traced warriors urging their horses at full speed ; and others discharging their arrows backward. Beneath the horsemen were rows of chariots

---

* Chambers D, E, and F, plan 5.   † In the British Museum.
‡ Chamber G, plan 5.   § Chamber H, plan 5

A HORSEMAN PURSUED BY ASSYRIAN WARRIORS. (Kouyunjik.)

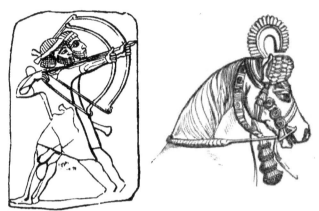

Enemies of the Assyrians discharging their   Head-dress of a Riding
      Arrows behind them. (Kouyunjik.)   Horse. (Kouyunjik.)

and led horses. In their trappings and harness the Kouyunjik horses differed completely from those represented in the bas-

Groom leading Horses. (Khorsabad.)

reliefs of Nimroud. Their heads were generally surmounted
by an arched crest, and bells or tassels were hung round their
necks ; or, as at Khorsabad, high plumes, generally three in
number, rose between their ears. After my departure from
Mosul, Mr. Ross continued the excavations in this chamber,
and found several other slabs, and an entrance formed by four
sphinxes. The bas-reliefs appear to have been part of the
series previously uncovered, and represented chariots, horsemen,
archers, and warriors in mail. The country in which the
events recorded took place, was indicated by a river and palm-
trees. In front of these bas-reliefs, he discovered an immense
square slab, which he conjectures to have been a dais or
altar, resembling that in the great hall of the N. W. palace at
Nimroud.

This was the extent of my discoveries at Kouyunjik. From
the dimensions of some of the halls, it is evident that the ruins
are those of a building of great extent and magnificence. The
mound upon which it stood was once washed by the river.
Then also the edifice, now covered by the village of Nebbi
Yunus, rose above the stream, and the two palaces were inclosed
in one vast square by lofty walls cased with stone—their towers
adorned with sculptured alabaster, and their gateways formed
by colossal bulls.

As I have described the ruins as they were discovered
during the excavations, it may not be here out of place to add a
few words on the subject of the architecture of the Assyrians,
and restore, as far as the remains will permit, the fallen
palaces.

The architecture of a people must naturally depend upon the
materials afforded by the country, and upon the object of their
buildings. The descriptions, already given in the course of
this work of the ruined edifices of ancient Assyria, are sufficient to show that they differed, in many respects, from those
of any other nation with which we are acquainted. Had the
Assyrians, so fertile in invention, so skillful in the arts, and

so ambitious of great works, dwelt in a country as rich in stone and costly granites and marbles as Egypt or India, it can scarcely be doubted that they would have equaled, if not excelled, the inhabitants of those countries in the magnitude of their pyramids, and in the magnificence of their rock temples and palaces. But their principal settlements were in the alluvial plains watered by the Tigris and Euphrates. On the banks of those great rivers, which spread fertility through the land, and afford the means of easy and expeditious intercourse between distant provinces, they founded their first cities. On all sides they had vast plains, unbroken by a single eminence until they approached the foot of the Armenian hills.

The earliest habitations, constructed when little progress had been made in the art of building, were probably but one story in height. In this respect the dwelling of the ruler scarcely differed from the meanest hut. It soon became necessary, however, that the temples of the gods, and the palaces of the kings, depositories at the same time of the national records, should be rendered more conspicuous than the humble edifices by which they were surrounded. The nature of the country also required that the castle, the place of refuge in times of danger, or the permanent residence of the garrison, should be raised above the city so as to afford the best means of resistance to an enemy. As there were no natural eminences in the country, the inhabitants were compelled to construct artificial mounds. Hence the origin of those vast, solid structures which have defied the hand of time ; and, with their grass-covered summits and furrowed sides, rise like natural hills in the Assyrian plains.

Let us picture to ourselves the migration of one of the primitive families of the human race, seeking for some spot favorable to a permanent settlement, where water abounded, and where the land, already productive without cultivation, promised an ample return to the labor of the husbandman. They may have followed him who went out of the land of Shinar, to found new

habitations in the north ;* or they may have descended from the
mountains of Armenia; whence came, according to the Chaldean historian, the builders of the cities of Assyria.† It was not
until they reached the banks of the great rivers, if they came
from the high lands, or only while they followed their course, if
they journeyed from the south, that they could find a supply of
water adequate to the permanent wants of a large community.
The plain, bounded to the west and south by the Tigris and Zab,
from its fertility, and from the ready means of irrigation afforded
by two noble streams, may have been first chosen as a resting-
place ; and there were laid the foundations of a city, destined to
be the capital of the eastern world.

The materials for building were at hand, and in their preparation required neither much labor nor ingenuity. The soil,
an alluvial deposit, was rich and tenacious. The builders moistened it with water, and, adding a little chopped straw that it
might be more firmly bound together, they formed it into squares,
which, when dried by the heat of the sun, served them as
bricks. In that climate the process required but two or three
days. Such were the earliest building materials ; and they are
used to this day almost exclusively in the same country. In
Egypt, too, they were employed at the remotest period ; and the
Egyptians, to harass their Jewish captives, withheld the straw
without which their bricks could not preserve their form and
consistency.

Huts for the people were speedily raised, and roofed with the
branches and boughs of trees from the banks of the river.

The inhabitants of the new settlement now sought to build a
place of refuge in case of attack, or a dwelling-place for their
leader, or a temple to their gods. In order to raise the edifice
above the plain, and to render it conspicuous among the surrounding habitations, it was erected on an artificial mound

---

* Genesis x. 11.
† Xithurus and his followers: Berosus, apud Euseb. The similarity
between the history of this Chaldean hero, and that of the Noah of Scripture is very singular.

constructed for the purpose of earth and rubbish, or of sun-dried bricks.*

The palaces and temples appear to have been at the same time public monuments, in which were preserved the records or archives of the nation, carved on stone. In them were represented in sculpture the exploits of the kings, and the forms of the divinities; while the history of the people, and invocations to their gods, were inscribed in written characters upon the walls. It was necessary, therefore, to use in the building, some material upon which figures and inscriptions could be carved. The plains of Mesopotamia, as well as the low lands between the Tigris and the hill-country, abound in a kind of coarse alabaster or gypsum. Large masses of it everywhere protrude in low ridges from the alluvial soil, or are exposed in the gullies formed by winter torrents. It yields readily to the chisel, and its color and transparent appearance are agreeable to the eye. Thus while offering few difficulties to the sculptor, it was an ornament to the edifice in which it was placed. This alabaster cut into slabs, from eight to ten feet high, four to six wide, and about one foot thick, served as a kind of paneling to the walls of sun-dried bricks. On the back of all the slabs, was carved an inscription recording the name, title, and genealogy of the royal founder of the edifice, and they were kept in their places and held together by iron, copper, or wooden cramps in the form of double dovetails, fitting into corresponding grooves in two adjoining slabs. The corners of the chambers were generally formed by one angular stone; and all the walls were either at right angles, or parallel to each

---

* Such is the custom still existing among the inhabitants of Assyria. When some families of a nomad tribe wish to settle in a village, they choose an ancient mound; it being no longer necessary to form a new platform, for the old abound in the plains. On its summit they erect a rude castle, and the huts are built at the foot. The same plan appears to have been followed since the Arab invasion, and perhaps long previous during the Persian occupation. There are few ancient mounds containing Assyrian ruins upon which castles, cities, or villages have not at some period been built. Such are Arbela, Tel Afer, Nebbi Yunus, &c. &c.

other.   Upon the slabs were sculptured the bas-reliefs and
inscriptions.

At the principal entrances to the chambers were placed
gigantic winged bulls and lions with human heads.   The smaller
doorways were guarded by colossal figures of divinities, or
priests.   There were no remains of doors or gates ; but metal
hinges have been discovered, and holes for bolts exist in many
of the slabs.   The priests of Babylon " made fast their temples
with doors, with locks and bars, lest their gods be spoiled by
robbers,"* and the gates of brass of Babylon are continually
mentioned by ancient authors.   On all the slabs forming entrances, in the oldest palace of Nimroud, were marks of a black
fluid, resembling blood, which appeared to have been daubed on
the stone.   I have not been able to ascertain the nature of this
fluid ; but its appearance can not fail to call to mind the Jewish ceremony, of placing the blood of the sacrifice on the lintel
of the doorway.   Under the pavement slabs, at the entrances,
were deposited small figures of the gods, probably as a protection to the building.†   Sometimes, as in the N.W. palace at
Nimroud, tablets on which were inscribed the name and title of
the king, with a short notice of his principal conquests, as a
record of the time of the erection of the building, were embedded
in the walls.

The upper part of the walls of the chambers, above the alabaster slabs, was built either of baked bricks, richly colored, or
of sun-dried bricks covered by a thin coat of plaster, on which
were painted figures and ornamental friezes.   It is to these
upper walls that the complete covering up of the building, and
the consequent preservation of the bas-reliefs, may be attributed ;
for when once the edifice had been deserted they fell in, and
the unbaked bricks, again becoming earth, encased the sculp-

---

* Epistle of Jeremy, Baruch, vi. 18.
† It has already been mentioned, that these small figures in unbaked
clay, were found beneath the pavement in all the entrances at Khorsabad.
They were only discovered at Nimroud under the most recent palace, in
the S. W. corner of the mound.

tured slabs. Many chambers at Nimroud were entirely constructed of sun-dried bricks, the walls having been painted with
figures and ornaments.

The mode of roofing the palaces and lighting the chambers,
many of which were in the very center of the building with no
other inlet for light but the door, is one of the most difficult
questions in Assyrian architecture. I am inclined, on the whole,
to concur with Mr. Fergusson in thinking that light was admitted through galleries or open rows of low pilasters above the
alabaster slabs, and that wooden columns were sometimes used
to support the roof in the larger halls.* It is, however, remarkable that no remains whatever of columns have been discovered,
nor are there any traces of them. Unless they were employed,
the chambers exceeding a certain width must have been left
open to the sky. There is no proof whatever of any of the
rooms having been vaulted, although the Assyrians were well
acquainted with the principle of the arch.

The chambers were paved with alabaster slabs, covered with
inscriptions recording the name and genealogy of the king, and
the chief events of his reign, or with baked bricks, or rather
tiles, each also bearing a short inscription. The alabaster slabs
were laid upon bitumen. The bricks or tiles were generally
in two layers, one above the other, with sand between and beneath them probably to exclude damp. Between the lions and
bulls forming the entrances, was usually one large inscribed or
ornamented slab.

The drains discovered beneath almost every chamber in the
older palace of Nimroud joined a large drain, probably running
from under the great hall into the river, which originally flowed
at the foot of the mound.

The interior of the Assyrian palaces must have been as magnificent as imposing. I have led the reader through their ruins,
and he may judge of the impression their halls were calculated to

---

* The subject is very fully treated and very ably illustrated in his work
entitled "the Palaces of Nineveh and Persepolis restored," which contains,
at the same time, many valuable suggestions on the arts and architecture
of the Assyrians.

P*

make upon one who, in the days of old, entered for the first time the abode of the Assyrian kings. Passing through a portal guarded by colossal lions or bulls, he found himself surrounded by the sculptured records of the empire. Battles, sieges, triumphs, the exploits of the chase, and the ceremonies of religion, were portrayed on the walls,—sculptured in alabaster, and painted in gorgeous colors. Above the sculptures were painted other events—the king, attended by his eunuchs and warriors, receiving his prisoners, entering into alliances with distant monarchs, or performing holy rites. These pictures were inclosed in colored borders or friezes of elaborate and elegant design, in which were introduced the emblematic tree, winged bulls, and monstrous animals. At the upper end of the hall was the colossal figure of the king in adoration before the supreme deity, or receiving from his attendants the sacred cup. He was attended by warriors bearing his arms, and ministered to by winged priests or presiding divinities. His robes, and those of his followers, were adorned with groups of human figures, animals, and flowers.

The ceiling above him was gorgeously painted, or inlaid with ivory and precious woods. The beams were of cedar, and gold leaf and plates of gold and silver were probably used with profusion in the decorations.*

These edifices, as it has been shown, were great national monuments, upon the walls of which were represented in sculpture, or recorded by inscriptions, the chronicles of the empire.

---

* Sun-dried bricks, with remains of gilding, were discovered at Nimroud. Herodotus states that the battlements of the innermost walls of the royal palace of Ecbatana, the ornaments of which were most probably imitated from the edifices of Assyria, were plated with silver and gold (lib. i. c. 98). The precious metals appear to have been generally used in decorating the palaces of the East. Even the roofs of the palace at Ecbatana are said to have been covered with silver tiles. The gold, silver, ivory, and precious woods in the ceilings of the palaces of Babylon, attributed to Semiramis, are frequently mentioned by ancient writers. Zephaniah (ii. 14) alludes to the "cedar work" of the roof; and in Jeremiah (xxii. 14) chambers "ceiled with cedar and painted with vermilion" are mentioned. Sometimes the walls and ceilings were paneled or wainscoted with this precious wood. (1 Kings vi. 15, vii. 3.)

He who entered them might thus read the history, and learn the glory and triumphs of the nation. They served, at the same time, to bring continually to the remembrance of those who assembled within them on festive occasions, or for the celebration of religious ceremonies, the deeds of their ancestors, and the power and majesty of their gods.

The exterior walls of these palaces were either cased with sculptured slabs or painted. On the outside of the principal palace of Babylon, assigned by tradition to Semiramis, were portrayed men and animals, and on the towers hunting scenes, in which were represented Semiramis herself on horseback, throwing a javelin at a panther, and Ninus slaying a lion with his lance.* The walls of Ecbatana, according to Herodotus,† were each painted of a different color; the outer (there were seven round the city) being white, the next black, the third purple, the fourth blue, the fifth orange, and the two inner having their battlements plated, one with silver and the other with gold.‡ Walls thus sculptured and painted must, in the clear atmosphere and brilliant sunshine of Assyria, have been peculiarly pleasing to the eye, and have had a beautiful appearance even from afar.

Were these magnificent mansions palaces or temples? or, while the king combined the character of a temporal ruler with that of a high-priest or type of the religion of the people, did his residence unite the palace, the temple, and a national monument raised to perpetuate the triumphs and conquests of the nation? These are questions which can not yet be satisfactorily answered. We can only judge by analogy. A very superficial examination of the sculptures will prove the sacred character of the king. The priests or presiding deities (whichever the winged figures so frequently found on the Assyrian monuments may be) are represented as waiting upon, or min-

* Diodorus Siculus, lib. ii.
† Lib. i. c. 98.
‡ Herod. lib. 1. c. 98. These colors, with the number seven of the walls, have evidently allusion to the heavenly bodies, and their courses.

istering to, him; above his head are the emblem of the
supreme deity, the winged figure within the circle, and the
sun, moon, and planets. As in Egypt, he may have been regarded as the representative, on earth, of the deity, receiving his
power directly from the gods, and being the organ of communication between them and his subjects.* The intimate connection between the public and private life of the Assyrians and
their religion, is abundantly proved by the bas-reliefs. As
among most Eastern nations, not only public and social duties
appear to have been more or less influenced by religion, or to
have been looked upon as typical, but all the acts of the king,
whether in peace or war, were evidently connected with the
national faith, and were believed to be under the special protection and superintendence of the deity. Hence the emblem
of the supreme God is represented above his head in battle,
during his triumphs, and when he celebrates the sacred ceremonies. The embroideries upon his robes, and the ornaments
upon his weapons, have likewise mythic meanings. His contests
with the lion and other wild animals denote not only his prowess
and skill, but his superior strength and wisdom. The archi-
tectural decorations have the same religious and typical sig-
nification. All the edifices hitherto discovered in Assyria have
precisely the same character; so that we have most probably
the palace and temple combined; for in them the deeds of the
king, and of the nation, are united with religious symbols, and
with the statues of the gods.

We have no means of ascertaining the nature of the private
dwellings of the Assyrians, nor of learning any particulars concerning their internal economy and arrangement. No such
houses have been preserved either in Assyria Proper or Babylonia, their complete disappearance being attributable to the
perishable materials of which they were constructed; for although the palace-temples were of such extraordinary magnificence, the bulk of the people appear to have lodged, as in

* Diodorus Siculus, lib. i. c. 90; and Wilkinson's Ancient Egyptians,
vol. i. p. 245, and vol. ii. p. 67.

Egypt, and indeed in Greece and Rome, in very small and miserable dwellings, which, when once abandoned, soon fell to dust, leaving no trace behind.

Of the walls of the city, or rather of its principal quarters (for the entire city was not, I am convinced, surrounded by one consecutive wall), nothing now remains but the long lines of mounds inclosing the ruins of Nimroud, Khorsabad, and Kouyunjik. In some places the earth still conceals the basement of hewn stones, upon which rose the lofty structure of sun-dried brick, the wonder and admiration of the ancients.* The dimensions of the walls of Nineveh and Babylon, as given by Herodotus, Xenophon, and Diodorus Siculus, may fairly be considered fabulous; those of Nineveh being 100 feet high, wide enough for three chariots to pass abreast, and furnished with 1500 towers, each 200 feet in height, and those of Babylon nearly 300 feet high and 75 thick.

In the edifices of Assyria reeds and bitumen were not employed, as at Babylon, to cement the layers of bricks, although both materials are found in abundance in the country.† A tenacious clay, moistened and mixed with a little chopped straw, was used, as it still is in the neighborhood of Mosul, for mortar. With it were united the sun-dried bricks, baked bricks being rarely used in Assyria, and no such masses of them existing among the ruins of Nineveh as at Babylon. These simple materials have successfully resisted the ravages of time, and still mark the stupendous nature of the Assyrian edifices.

Although there is but little difference in the architecture of the various buildings explored in Assyria, the change which had taken place in the manners, religion, and dress of the inhabitants of the country between the foundation of the N. W. palace at Nimroud, and of the edifices at Khorsabad and

* Such, according to Xenophon, were the walls of Larissa and Mespila, the plinth or lower part of the wall of which was 50 feet high, and the upper 100. The stone was full of shells. (Anab. lib. 3.) His description agrees pretty accurately with the actual remains.

† Bitumen was, however, sometimes used to unite stones, and even burnt bricks.

Kouyunjik must be evident on a most cursory examination of the sculptures from those buildings. The difference, indeed, is so considerable and so radical that even several centuries must have elapsed between the erection of the palaces, or some fundamental change must have taken place in the people. The first appears to me the most probable conjecture. The fact of the S. W. palace at Nimroud being built of materials taken from the N. W. proves that the interval between their erection must have been very great. As in Egypt the more ancient monuments show the purest taste and the highest knowledge of art, and we have that phenomenon which is to be remarked in the history of all nations, ancient or modern, of a gradual decline of art, after a state of comparative perfection. In the later monuments of Nineveh, moreover, particularly in the ornaments, and in the small objects discovered, we find an Egyptian taste, unknown in the earlier remains. This would indicate a foreign influence which may have been the principal source of the change I have pointed out, and which may be traced either to conquest or to intimate family alliances.

By the middle of the month of June my labors in Assyria had drawn to a close. The funds assigned to the Trustees of the British Museum for the excavations had been expended, and further researches were not, for the present at least, contemplated. I prepared, therefore, to turn my steps homeward, after an absence of some years. The ruins of Nimroud had been again covered up, and its palaces were once more hidden from the eye. The sculptures taken from them had been safely removed to Busrah, and were awaiting their final transport to England. The inscriptions, which promise to instruct us in the history and civilization of one of the most ancient and illustrious nations of the earth, had been carefully copied. On looking back upon the few months that I had passed in Assyria, I could not but feel some satisfaction at the result of my labors. Scarcely a year before, with the exception of the ruins of Khorsabad, not one Assyrian monument was known. Almost sufficient materials had now been obtained to enable us to restore much of

the lost history of the country, and to confirm the vague traditions of the learning and civilization of its people. It had often
occurred to me during my labors, that the time of the discovery
of these remains was so opportune, that it might be looked upon
as something more than accidental. Had these palaces been
by chance exposed to view some years before, no European
could have protected them from complete destruction, or could
have preserved a record of their existence. Had they been
discovered a little later, it is highly probable that there would
have been insurmountable objections to the removal of even
any part of their contents. It was consequently just at the right
moment that they were disinterred ; and we have been fortunate
enough to acquire the most convincing and lasting evidence of
that magnificence, and power, which made Nineveh the wonder
of the ancient world, and her fall the theme of the prophets, as
the most signal instance of divine vengeance. Without the
evidence that these monuments afford, we might almost have
doubted that the great Nineveh ever existed, so completely " has
she become a desolation and a waste."

Before my departure I was desirous of giving a last entertainment to my workmen, and to those who had kindly aided
me in my labors. On the western side of Kouyunjik there is a
small village, belonging, with the mound, to a former slave of a
pashaw of the Abd-el-Jeleel family, who had received his liberty,
and the land containing the ruins, as a reward for long and
faithful services. This village was chosen for the festivities,
and tents for the accommodation of my guests were pitched
around it. Large platters filled with boiled rice, and divers
inexplicable messes, only appreciated by Arabs, and those who
have lived with them,—the chief components being garlic and
sour milk—were placed before the various groups of men and
women, who squatted in circles on the ground. Dances were
then commenced, and were carried on through the greater part
of the night, the Tiyari and the Arabs joining in them, or
relieving each other by turns. The dancers were happy and
enthusiastic, and kept up a constant shouting. The quiet

Christian ladies of Mosul, who had scarcely before this occasion ventured beyond the walls of the town, gazed with wonder and delight on the scene; lamenting, no doubt, that the domestic arrangements of their husbands did not permit more frequent indulgence in such gayeties.

At the conclusion of the entertainment I spoke a few words to the workmen, inviting any who had been wronged, or ill-used, to come forward and receive such redress as it was in my power to afford, and expressing my satisfaction at the success-ful termination of our labors without a single accident. One Sheikh Khalaf, a very worthy man, who was usually the spokes-man on such occasions, answered for his companions. They had lived, he said, under my shadow, and, God be praised, no one had cause to complain. Now that I was leaving, they should leave also, and seek the distant banks of the Khabour, where at least they would be far from the Turks, and be able to enjoy the little they had saved. All they wanted was each man a teskerè, or note, to certify that he had been in my service. This would not only be some protection to them, but they would show my writing to their children, and would tell them of the days they had passed at Nimroud. Please God, I should return to the Jebours, and live in tents with them on their old pasture-grounds, where there were as many ruins as at Nimroud, plenty of plunder within reach, and gazelles, wild boars, and lions for the chase. After Sheikh Khalaf had con-cluded, the women advanced in a body and made a similar address. I gave a few presents to the principal workmen and their wives, and all were highly satisfied with their treatment.

A few days afterward, the preparations for my departure were complete. I paid my last visit to Essad Pashaw, called upon the principal people of the town, bid adieu to my friends, and on the 24th of June was ready to leave Mosul.

I was accompanied on my journey to Constantinople by Mr. Hormuzd Rassam, Ibrahim Agha, and the bairakdar, and by several members of the household of the late pashaw; who were ready, in return for their own food and that of their horses, to

serve me on the road.   We were joined by many other travelers,
who had been waiting for an opportunity to travel to the north
in company with a sufficiently strong party.   The country was
at this time very insecure.   The Turkish troops had marched
against Beder Khan Bey, who had openly declared his independence, and defied the authority of the sultan.   The
failure of the crops had brought parties of Arabs abroad, and
scarcely a day passed without the plunder of a caravan and the
murder of travelers.   The pashaw sent a body of irregular horse
to accompany me as far as the Turkish camp, which I wished
to visit on my way.   With this escort, and with my own party,
all well armed and prepared to defend themselves, I had no cause
to apprehend any accident.

   Mr. and Mrs. Rassam, all the European residents, and many
of the principal Christian gentlemen of Mosul, rode out with
me to some distance from the town.   On the opposite side of
the river, at the foot of the bridge, were the ladies who had
assembled to bid me farewell.   Beyond them were the wives
and daughters of my workmen, who clung to my horse, many
of them shedding tears as they kissed my hand.   The greater
part of the Arabs insisted upon walking as far as Tel Kef with
me.   In this village supper had been prepared for the party.
Old Gouriel, the kiayah, still rejoicing in his drunken leer,
was there to receive us.   We sat on the house-top till midnight.   The horses were then loaded and saddled.   I bid a last
farewell to my Arabs, and started on the first stage of our long
journey to Constantinople.

INDEX.

THE END.

www.ingramcontent.com/pod-product-compliance
Lightning Source LLC
LaVergne TN
LVHW012206040326
832903LV00003B/154